THE GEOGRAPHY OF HOME

HEYDAY BOOKS (through its imprint, The Roundhouse Press)
and *Poetry Flash* have formed an exciting new publishing effort, the
CALIFORNIA POETRY SERIES.

This groundbreaking series of books, published quarterly, features poets
and poetry with strong ties to California.

For more information, please contact The Roundhouse Press,
Box 9145, Berkeley, CA 94709, tel. 510/549-3564
email: roundhouse@heydaybooks.com

·

HEYDAY BOOKS publishes high quality and accessible books on
California literature, history, natural history, and culture. For a free cata-
log, please contact us at Box 9145, Berkeley, CA 94709, tel. 510/549-3564
email: heyday@heydaybooks.com

THE GEOGRAPHY OF HOME
CALIFORNIA'S POETRY OF PLACE

Selected and Edited by
Christopher Buckley and Gary Young

HEYDAY BOOKS in conjunction with
THE CLAPPERSTICK INSTITUTE
BERKELEY, CA

Library of Congress Cataloging-in-Publication Data
    The geography of home : California's poetry of place / selected and edited by Christopher Buckley and Gary Young.
        p.   cm .
    ISBN 1-890771-19-8 (pbk.)
    1. American poetry—California. 2. California—Poetry. I. Buckley, Christopher, 1948– . II. Young, Gary, 1951– .
    PS571.C2G46 1999
    811'.5408032794—dc21   99-19043

Cover design: David Bullen Design
Interior design: Amy Evans McClure
Cover photo: Roman Loranc
Title page art: "California Series #4," Gary Young
Printing and Binding: Publishers Press, Salt Lake City

Orders, inquiries, and correspondence should be addressed to:

HEYDAY BOOKS
P.O. Box 9145
Berkeley, CA 94709
510/549-3564; Fax 510/549-1889
heyday@heydaybooks.com

Printed in the United States of America

10 9 8 7 6 5 4 3 2 1

CONTENTS

ACKNOWLEDGMENTS

The editors would like to thank the University of California Academic Senate for a research grant that helped with the production of this book. Thanks to Cheryl Michelle (Mitsy) Andrews for her many hours of valuable editorial assistance on this project. We would also like to thank the poets who participated, and especially their many publishers whose generosity made this book possible.

INTRODUCTION

Language is a country, and the heart is a country, and at their shared borders we encounter the geography of home. Born, raised, and educated in California, having come to writing here, it did not take us long to recognize that one of California's greatest riches both in quality and quantity was its poets. It also did not take long to realize that California the *place*—the mountains, rivers, deserts, ocean, even the light—was the source and inspiration for much of the poetry we loved best.

This is a collection of contemporary poets who have made or are making their writing lives out of the raw materials and experiences of California today. A historical approach, one going back to Ivor Winters, Robinson Jeffers, and others would be welcome, but for practical and aesthetic reasons that is rightly the focus of another book.

Many of the poets in this anthology offer an informed moral consciousness that rises out of their unique situation at the western edge of the continent. Humility and a modest transcendence in the face of the state's natural splendor is a recurring theme, but readers will also find poems of social conscience and political outrage as well. The failures of society, the effects of corporate greed, and the loss of so many natural wonders are a compelling part of the poetic response to this state. Whether for good or ill, the influence of the unique California habitats these poets call home to a great extent defines their poetry.

We set out to gather the best poems we could find that celebrate and witness California and its people, poems we had known and admired for many years. We tried to collect poems that take their secular and spiritual sustenance from a sense of place rooted in California. There was much from which to choose, and it soon became obvious that other editors could make a second anthology with the same number of poets and never repeat our efforts. Many of the poets represented here are native Californians, but the poems of those who arrived here from someplace else, or who grew up here and left, are all marked with the land-scape and salient imagery that could only be California. We have included the work of many well-known poets, poets in mid-career, and quite a few newer voices as well.

It is the nature of anthologies that you cannot include everyone; some reader's favorite poets or poems are sure to be missing. A few of our own favorite California poets are not included because they did not have poems that focused on place. Some poets we simply overlooked, and of course, there is only so much space. But we believe this anthology presents a cross-section of the many voices speaking out of the various cultures and experiences that define this state. We also offer a diversity of styles—free and formal verse, narrative, lyric, imagistic, long poems and short—another reflection of the state's diversity.

Most of the poets presented here offer a prose complement to their poems—not an explication of their work, but a statement to reinforce and to amplify the individual lives behind the voices in their poems. We would not be the first to suggest that the history of a place is its people, but we might be the first to suggest that the history of a people is to be found in a place. Here are seventy-six of the best poets we know saying what it means to write from California, to make meaning from this place, to sing in the light of home.

When we first took up this project in 1993, William Everson and Larry Levis were still with us, and were both committed to the anthology. We lost these two great California poets—and major American poets—before the book could see publication. Interestingly, though they were quite different poets from different generations, they were both sons of Selma in the San Joaquin Valley. This book is dedicated to them, to their lives that were committed to poetry, to their high art and achievement, to the profound humanity of their voices and visions.

Christopher Buckley
Gary Young

KIM ADDONIZIO

Kim Addonizio has two poetry collections from BOA Editions. A third, *Tell Me,* is forthcoming. She is co-author with Dorianne Laux of *The Poet's Companion: A Guide to the Pleasures of Writing Poetry* (W.W. Norton). Her awards include two NEA Fellowships and a Pushcart Prize.

© Jeanne C. Finley

"I came to San Francisco from Washington, D.C., in the late seventies and never looked back. This is where I found my vocation as a poet, and where I've been able to create a life for myself in which writing plays a central part. Here I found a community of aspiring writers—both at S.F. State and in the thriving open-mic café scene, where week after week I stood up on a stage, read appallingly bad poetry, and was encouraged to go on. The Bay Area was, and continues to be, a place where poetry is not only possible, but supported by a highly literate audience.

"I'm an urban poet, and it's the landscape of the city that has most informed my work. My second book, *Jimmy & Rita,* is set in some of the meaner streets of San Francisco. That this city, despite a steeply escalating cost of living, is still home to an astonishing mix of people; that it has a rich literary legacy; that it's forty-nine square miles perched on the western edge of the continent—these are some of the things that make it an exciting place for writers of all stripes."

Conversation in Woodside

Joe insisted that life is extreme,
but Nadja and I argued for dailiness:
the stove's small flame under the kettle,
the lover who, turning over in bed,

reaches for an absence
that still holds your warmth, recoverable.

We were sitting after dinner, the wine finished,
our plates not yet cleared away,

and Joe, full of grief and memory,
said *My friends are dying every day.*
I thought of all the evidence
against us, against the pink poppies

opening in a glass vase, the fragrant candles,
the living room where the others were dancing
while we kept on, talking about loss,
and our childhoods, and whether evil

enters us from somewhere
or only lies dormant, waiting to bloom;
suddenly the dark outside the big windows,
rising from the fences and fields, seemed

to be listening, as though it needed
something from us, not permission exactly,
but something only we could give it.
And I felt we were safe, as long

as we stayed around the cluttered table,
safe, even, for the few days we'd spend working here,
and Joe tipped back on two legs
of his chair, balancing there.

China Camp, California

Here's the long trough, covered by a screen,
where they cleaned shrimp.
Easier to imagine their catch
than to glimpse the ghosts of the fishermen
who lived here in these few wood buildings,
some now in need of repair, tin-roofed,
boarded windows whose gaps we peer through
to see shadowed dirt, a rusted wheelbarrow.
Of their boats, only a lone hull remains,
hauled to the sand and half-sunk there,
surrounded by chain link.

Yet everything is the same: the bay,
tamed by the curve of land that makes the cove,
still curls in
easily as hands turning over
to close, and close again, a book whose pages
ceaselessly open. Shards of their dishes
and rice bowls wash back
with the frail skeletons of crabs, glass
dulled and polished, indecipherable bits
of broken shells, jade-green kelp.
It's said they were driven out by hatred,
or concern that they'd leave nothing
for the next boats, but no one recorded
where they went. This was the home they made,
miles from China: brief shore,
a sky brushed with clouds,
gulls following them in each sunset,
the women stirring soup
with buried spoons, lost silk
of their sashes, black hair unpinned
and carried out with the tide,
tangling in the empty nets and sinking
to the coldest dark water.

At Moss Beach

At night along this coast the boats
slipped to shore with their illegal cargo.
The long cars waited, lights hushed,
for the liquor to be hauled up the cliff.
We've stopped at the edge of it this morning,
held by the lush purple spread of iceplant
in the hollows below. Whoever was here then
could not have imagined our lives, just as I
can't imagine the face of some new lover
after we're over. But the past opens so easily:
the stars sink, the prow cleaves dense fog,
the sleek unseen shapes of the limousines are humming
somewhere ahead, and behind the boat

the white froth of the wake travels
over the churning water. Packed in roped crates
are the bottles, in each one the rattle
of dice thrown down, a man loosened from
his money, a woman in a blue dress leaning
against him, the thrilling surf of her laughter.
Gliding through the dark, can the crew hear
our voices? You pull one vivid flower from its home
in the earth. I tell you it will always
make me think of you, this startling
brush stroke that repeats itself for miles
along the shore, this particular water
that today holds a lone freighter heading out,
a black crow arrowing after it.

FRANCISCO X. ALARCÓN

Francisco X. Alarcón, Chicano poet and educator, was born in Wilmington, California, in 1954. As a child, he lived in Guadalajara, Mexico, and ever since he was eighteen years old he has lived in California. He is the author of ten volumes of poetry, including *Body in Flames/Cuerpo en llamas, De amor oscuro/Of Dark Love, Snake Poems: An Aztec Invocation* and *No Golden Gate for Us.* His book of bilingual poetry for children, titled *Laughing Tomatoes and Other Spring Poems/Los jitomates risueños y otros poemas de primavera,* was awarded the 1997 Pura Belpré Honor Award by the American Library Association. His most recent book is another collection of bilingual poetry for children, *From the Bellybutton of the Moon and Other Summer Poems/Del ombligo de la luna y otros poemas de verano.*

© Francisco Domínguez

"My family first came to California in 1919 as a result of the Mexican Revolution when 10 percent of Mexico's population moved to *El Norte.* My great-grandmother never went back to Mexico, but neither did she learn one word of English. Since then my family has crossed the border many times in both directions. In 1931 my grandfather Adolfo took his family to his home-town of Atoyac, in the western state of Jalisco in Mexico. But my uncles and my mother returned to the U.S. in the 1940s to join the war efforts. My mother later married my father in Mexico and came back to California to work in the fish canneries in the 1950s.

"I myself spent the first six years of my life in the Mexican barrio of Wilmington, the dirty port of Los Angeles, but later was raised in Guadalajara, Mexico. Thus, in my own lifetime I have lived in many differ-ent life and time zones: among traditional peasants in the small town of Atoyac, in many working-class barrios in Los Angeles and San Francisco, and even in elitist Stanford University, where I did my graduate studies.

"For me, California is both a mirage and a nightmare, a physical landscape and a state of mind. My life journey has taken me through the pre-AIDS Eden of San Francisco and the euphoria of Santa Cruz to the unbearable summers and desolate winters of the Central Valley, where I presently live in utopian Davis, surrounded by fields where migrant farmworkers from Mexico are not only exploited but even blamed by many for *El Niño.* And in spite of all the English-only and anti-bilingual education propositions,

California continues to sound to me as Spanish as ever. That's why I write my Californian poems both in English and Spanish. My poetry only reflects my home, from where I can see and dream in two tongues of the magnificent Sierra Nevada of California."

Blues del SIDA

casi todos
nuestros amigos
de San Francisco
ya se han ido

no más postales
no más llamadas
no más lágrimas
no más risas

silencio y nieblina
ahora oscurecen
nuestro antes asoleado
Distrito de la Misión

dondequiera
que ahora vamos
sólo somos un par
de extraños

AIDS Blues

almost all
our friends
in San Francisco
nowadays are gone

no more cards
no more calls
no more tears
no more laughs

silence and fog
now darken
our once sunny
Mission District

everywhere
we now go
we're just a pair
of strangers

Viernes Santo

al dar
el reloj
las tres

calvario es
California
otra vez

por todo
el Valle
Central

Good Friday

at three
o'clock in
the afternoon

once again
California is
a calvary

throughout
the Central
Valley

se oye
un gemido
general

nos clava
con su luz
el sol

la tierra
tiembla
de dolor

las penas
nos alivia
María

Judas
nos echa
la policía

familias
morenas
en cruz

y
la voz
de Jesús:

"¡perdónalos
Dios
mío!

¡que
no saben
lo que hacen!"

a general
wail
is heard

the Sun
nails us
with its light

the Earth
trembles
out of grief

Mary
eases
our sorrow

Judas calls
the police
on us

brown
families
on a cross

and
the voice
of Jesus:

"forgive
them
Lord!

for they
know not
what they do!"

Los árboles son poetas
Sacramento, Califas

los árboles
aquí son
poetas
en otoño

Trees Are Poets
Sacramento, Califas

around here
trees are
poets
in fall

les da	they turn
melancolía	heavyhearted
tristes	sad
cambian	they change
de color	colors
dramáticos	acting up
se deshacen	they let go
de sus hojas	their leaves
por meses	for months
parecen	they seem
clamar:	to cry:
"¡estamos	"we're
muertos	dead
de frío! "	cold!"
un día	some day
como	they awake
si nada.	oblivious
despiertan	and start
y les	coming
salen	up
versos	with
verdes	green verses
otra vez	once again

Las calles lloran

¡ay!

en esta
esquina
lo mataron

¡ay!

por
la espalda
lo balearon

Streets Are Crying

ay!

here
in this corner
they killed him

ay!

from
behind
they shot him

¡ay!

lloran
las calles
del barrio

¡ay!

¡qué roja
es la sangre
a los 16 años

ay!

the streets
of the barrio
are crying

ay!

how red
is the blood
of a 16-year old!

Frontera

ninguna
frontera
podrá
separarnos

Border

no
border
can ever
separate us

ABIGAIL ALBRECHT

Abigail Albrecht is a native California. She was born in Los Angeles and has lived in the beachside city of Carpinteria on California's central coast for twenty years. A publicist and community event organizer as well as a noted regional poet, she has developed and implemented readings and poetry festival events, judged contests, and edited poetry journals. She is co-founder of the Santa Barbara Poetry Festival, which has hosted such distinguished American poets as Galway Kinnell, Philip Levine, Diane di Prima, and the late

William Stafford. Albrecht has been teaching poetry for many years through the Carpinteria Poetry Workshop. Her work has appeared in numerous journals and anthologies, including *Café Solo; Crosswinds; Art/Life; Spectrum; Verve; Talus and Scree;* and *Red Tiles, Blue Skies: More Tales of Santa Barbara.*

"I began my life on a dead-end street in West L.A. In my memory, the sky is clear and bright. At the cul-de-sac, Ballona Creek ran through an open meadow—my favorite place to roam. Corn and cucumber farms surrounded the neighborhood. Those fields are now thick with clustered apartments, the stucco houses along the street have all received face-lifts. The creek is a channel of cement. As a child, our street felt safe and inviting. I investigated every detail of the foliage that grew on our block—tearing live flowers apart, stripping leaves and thorns from their stems. I experimented with various mashed flower petals, using them like crayons, like lipstick, writing geranium graffiti on the curb. I do not remember an awareness of seasons in my childhood. It all seemed random and incredibly surprising: floods, earthquakes, heat waves, hailstones—and swarms of ladybugs in the fields.

"I was eight when the ocean entered my landscape, when we moved to a hill by the shore. I have lived near the coastline ever since. I can still taste the brine of my earliest memories, when I was washed out to sea in a riptide at Playa del Rey. Yet this didn't dissuade me from reveling at the beach: bodysurfing, examining life in the tide pools, gathering driftwood, rare shells, and rusted pennies after storms. California's sensuousness and subtle seasons permeate every impression from which I write. As often as I drive up or down the coast, I open my window and smell the musty salt air. Every night I slide into bed and listen closely, barely hearing the waves as I fall sleep."

Passing Piedras Blancas

The highway is narrow, the curves dangerous.
Even more dangerous is the scenery,
which tears my eyes from the road.

A lone black bull guards his pasture by the sea.
He looks ironclad, mighty and mythic in his stance
as he stares the horizon down.
Piedras Blancas Lighthouse stands beside him, blinking
through thick afternoon strands of fog.
The oceanward pasture looks so remote
I think the bull must swim away.

I drive on through low meadows, ragged cliffs:
fog streamers rise into low, light haze,
sea and sky dance and whirl in each other's blue.
Gold pampas grass banners hail me from every ridge.

My mind brings new music up from the shore—
lonely oboe answers a low-pitched bassoon—
the lowing lighthouse and the roaring voice of the bull,
as they help one another watch over their kingdom,
this coast of broken white stones.

Below White Cliffs

Air shrill with life
thick with death
sunbakes amidst the beached mess
of rubbery kelp
steaming beneath clouds
of tiny flies

The reeling sky
an explorer's dream:
birds whirl
thick as galaxies
pinwheeling wings
gulls terns pelicans
fill every space

plunge down green seas
pull up beakful after beakful
of slithering shimmering fish

Rippling beneath the waves
torrents of baitfish
rivers of anchovies
churn and swirl the surf
like silver tides

We slip stagger
risk ankles and kneecaps
to treacherous stairsteps
of saltscarred rock
hungrily inhaling the seething fume
of wet sand fresh brine
blood plankton roe
in our urge to be closer
to the beginning

Elkhorn Slough:
View from the Southbound Train
for W. B.

Out from tight railway seams along Highway 101,
we emerge through fields and cattle land
into another landscape of tracks.
Beyond my rattling west-facing window,
marsh and waterways reach indefinitely.
No sign of the nearby Monterey coast,
though it feeds its brine through this sieve.

Shallow channels meander through wetlands,
watery surface glazed cerulean blue and white
from the passing day and its clouds.
The dark cut banks shine with slick black earth.
Above the banks, upon marshy mud flats—
ochre, chartreuse, drab gold, moss green—
low-growing plants flourish in tidal mire.

Sudden appearance: tall stick-legged birds.

Blue heron poised beside lithe white egret.
My startled eye becomes a wing,
lifting them gracefully,
unfolding my own longing, this wild duet.
High and spiraling seaward, I send them,
beyond this labyrinth, this inverted winter sky.

Anacapa

Hard to image—
   because you live far from the coast—
      the way the islands drift in winter,
            floating fragments lining the horizon,
   breaking the skyline into mirage
upon an unseen fog.

     I'm sure your eyes would disbelieve
this vision of islands caught in suspense,
   hanging in mid-light above the sea,
    slowly separating,   gently expanding
until they splinter
      and float apart.

     I want to take you sailing there,
across the channel to phantom shores,
where the hard-packed soil feels
     just like homeland, dusty and solid
    despite the illusion,
          waiting like a dream.

B. H. BOSTON

B. H. Boston and his wife, Marsha, have lived in San Diego—where they both teach—since Nixon fled the White House. Boston's work has appeared in numerous magazines over the years, and he has published a chapbook of his poems entitled *Only the Living* (Helix Press).

"Thirty years ago we moved south of the Tehachapis and settled eventually in what used to be San Diego. More and more the poems seem to come from a kind of tension between my earliest images of California and the pain of witnessing the relentless assault of commerce against the state's beauty, the methodical mutilation of the body of this world. Here the pursuit of California's golden promise has rendered it permanently beyond reach, blotted out by the smoke of the bulldozers, displaced by the stuccoed bunkers of industrial parks, eclipsed by the gun metal facades of the twenty story banks extruded overnight from the wounds hacked out of the mesas. What remains is a pervading sense of dislocation, of anxiety bred of the violation of place, of irretrievable loss. Southern California has become a kind of ground zero where memory and the future are gleefully obliterated, where we level the terrain and befoul the beaches, where we annihilate home and habitat, where we engineer the systematic excavation of the soul. Perhaps what California needs most resides now in the landscape of memory and dream, in poems, in the shadow play of ghosts, in the mad hope that reverence and mindfulness might somehow still prevail in those few surviving sacred places we have failed to keep secret."

Apiary

I'm so out of it I can't remember
what *surname* means.
Like the geode, the single bead of turquoise,
like the flint knives lined up on the sill,
like the oncoming sleep,
we've had ideas,

we've made a few plans.
We've dug wells, set out smudge pots
in Orosi between orange rows and lemon rows.

We've unhinged our own daughters.

•

In a backyard in Fresno,
near the barbecue black with fat
and the hives,
my mother trims my father's hair—
unhurried, frugal, precision without words.

In Fresno, *surname* means Sunburn,
Mane Roach, my father swarmed
and stung to a blister,
the emergency room throbbing
until his eyes swell shut. . .

And all morning the cabbage roses
invaded by the worker bees.

•

Howard Boston wins the Wheeling,
West Virginia, Fiddler's Contest.
It's 1942.
He's a conscientious objector.

Now both dreams are mine.

•

In June the mornings never make it here past dawn,
all day the gray sky, then dusk and the starless dark.
In California south past Catalina
the air picks up its somber baggage
and unpacks all month above the steak house
and the shell shop.
Here it's the Chamber of Commerce,
the private school, the Autohaus,
the plates that read *More 4 Me.*

Here what we name is all we have to lose.

By All Lights: 1959

for Larry Levis—Hermano, Hermano...

Across from the tract of cinderblock houses
in Colusa County, California, each summer comes on
like a seizure. The skies blanch sulphur

above the locked gray Lutheran church. Next door,
old man Westcott mows the tall mustard forever,
the earth's sharp breath stalling in air around him,

Sutter's iron buttes racked in heat above the stunned river.
Not himself again, he raises his one fist,
horsing the John Deere with the other.

Soon, my mother lets me skid the black Pontiac on
gravel past the strange new safflower crop
where the town's only cop waves us over.

She's beautiful getting out of a ticket that Thursday.
This afternoon, under the almonds smudged with magpies
and Lucchesi, incorrigible, sprawled

on the culvert's dry bank, I ditch my bike on a dare
and cut unseen across the disced field,
slide wheezing in clod and stubble

before the old father who revs the green tractor along the rows,
closing in on what faint imprint my hips
and shoulders leave in that soil,

plowing under whatever it is, that thirteenth August,
dust blind and shuddering in furrows,
I refuse to become there.

The Savage, Our Fathers

for Levine

plateaus
the trunks of enormous
trees in the sun
the dark obsidian body

the shrug behind stones
the insistent clatter of the fields

in breechcloth
in feathers lit
with Jesuit blood
the plotting of
horizons
their commitment to memory

•

there is no place
to go and not be
in hiding

the mountains are ragged
the mountains do not follow one another
beneath the pale sky
helicopters dare the canyons
into war

for a moment
the blades flicker across
her forehead
my feet
covered and trembling in the dust

CHRISTOPHER BUCKLEY

Christopher Buckley is Chair of the Creative Writing Department at the University of California, Riverside. His ninth book of poems, *Fall From Grace,* was published in 1998 by Bk Mk Press/ University of Missouri, Kansas City. For his poetry he has received a NEA grant, a Fulbright Award to Yugoslavia, four Pushcart Prizes, and he twice received the Gertrude B. Claytor Award from the Poetry Society of America. He is the editor of *On the Poetry of Philip Levine: Stranger to Nothing* (University of Michigan Press, "Under Discussion" series, 1991), and has published a nonfiction book, *Cruising State: Growing Up in Southern California* (University of Nevada Press, 1994). With Christopher Merrill, he edited *What Will Suffice: Contemporary American Poets on the Art of Poetry* (Peregrine Smith Books, 1995). He lives in Lompoc with his wife, the artist Nadya Brown.

"I was born in Arcata, California, but all I remember of it is in a photograph taken of me at nine months. I'm sitting, balanced on the hood of my parents' new white Pontiac, Humboldt Bay distant in the background, and my arms are spread out in a stance I'd use many years later, surfing the beaches of Santa Barbara.

"We moved to Santa Barbara when I was four, and not long after into the woodsy suburb of Montecito at a time when almost any working person could afford to do so. My father was a disc jockey and my mother worked as a secretary for the city schools; they bought an acre, cleared it, and built a house. I went to parochial school and remember writing quatrains in fifth grade about the birds and light, though I was mainly interested in playing baseball, and in clouds, lying around in the fields thinking God knows what as I stared up after the white, unknowable caravans. When I wasn't in school, I was loose in the foothills, and often with friends, would follow the creeks down to the beach. It's hard to imagine a better childhood environment— days spent in the tide pools, climbing oak or avocado trees, the boulders in the hills, building dams across creeks. We were happy, healthy, and free as light.

"Then the seventies—real estate, time certificates, and among other places, America discovered Santa Barbara. I was thinking of going to graduate school, and though I knew next to nothing about contemporary poetry, I knew that I needed to leave town if I was going to write—life was too comfortable, too many friends to sit with admiring the evening light in the eucalyptus. I lived in San Diego, Irvine, and Fresno before coming back to Santa Barbara and teaching at the university in one of those lecturer positions with double the work and half the pay. When I wrote, I responded most often to my immediate surroundings; yet, with the difficulty of finding a job with tenure, benefits, retirement—I was coming up on forty—I moved east, taking the first position I was offered. It quickly became clear to me that what I truly valued and wanted to write about was Home. Though I took up an interest in science and cosmology, though I wrote about places I was lucky enough to travel to overseas, the compelling subject became my home, that almost Edenic environment that built my vision of and desire for the world. After a time, I escaped exile in the east and returned to California where every day I am happy to praise the light, the birds, the jacarandas, eucalyptus, and pittosporum, the acanthus and agave, bougainvillea and bottle brush, clouds and surf—if there is transcendence, I catch a glimpse of it here, and try to get it into lines."

Father, 1952

He must be 30 or 31,
and the brown autumn light is dying
in the tops of jacarandas lining Anacapa Street.
He's just picked me up from school
on the big hill in back of town, and,
riding in our station wagon's wide front seat,
the whole windshield is a field of blue
filled with sea, and a sky bending to meet it
where the earth curves miles out in air…
I'm looking up after unlacing my school shoes
and pulling on cowboy boots, black ones
with white and gold lilies blossoming at the tops—
this is not that long ago…
                    Forty years,
and it all comes back the day I bend down
to try on a pair of wingtips, and there he is
in his camel hair sport coat and green knit tie…
His black and wavy hair blows again in the wind
from the open window of the car—again,
we're taking the curves above the Mission,
the limestone walls and pepper trees aflame

along the road, and in that last blindness of sun,
the mackerel clouds, the clusters of pepper pods
burn red as the bell-tower domes.…
I'm staring into the light spread thick as sawdust
across the windshield. With his college ring
he's tapping out a tune on the steering wheel,
stubbing a Philip Morris. Now he's whistling,
it's 4:30, and the daylight behind us is going
violet on the mountain range. I'm content
in my boots, standing on the green vinyl seat
to see above the dash—below, a harbor mist
rolls in beneath the yellow nettle of stars,
the Xs of seagulls' wings marking their places
as they drift slowly before the dark. I'm looking left,
into the purple sky—we're coasting down
a last silent hill. Nothing, I think, has happened
in our lives—he's happy—this is not that long ago.…

Sycamore Canyon Nocturne

But home is the form of the dream, & not the dream.
Larry Levis

Home again in dreams, I'm walking that foothill road
as the last morning star slips away over canyon walls—
red-gold riprap of creek rock, ferns splayed in the blue
shade of oaks, the high yellow sycamores, oat straw catching
sun at my feet. Wind-switch, then the chalk-thick stillness
saying *angels,* who come down here to dip their wings
and give the water its color.

                        Yet even when I'm allowed back
along the weedy path of sleep to this green and singing space,
I know someday air will be set between my shoulder blades
and arms and all my bones, and, little more than clouds,
the clouds will be my final lesson until I'm taken off
into some clearer imagining.…

                        In exile, it is hard to love God.
What then, must I renounce? The Psalter of evergreens
ringing along Sheffield drive? The loquat and acacia
burning through ocean fog? Can I speak of love

almost a life ago, syllables repeating the skin's sweet salts
and oils like lemon blossoms riding the August heat?

I love the life slowly taken from me, so obviously spun out
flower-like, and for my own use, it seems, against some future
sky—the world, just a small glory of dust above a field
one autumn afternoon—the resinous pines and a back road
full of birds inside you.
                    What more could wishes be,
who would live there again, sent back among the breathing
acanthus to lift unconsciously with morning and with mist?
I would.
                 Moonlight or dreamlight, this is the world, giving
and taking away with the same unseen hand, desires winding
around the soul like fleshy rings on a tree. Where this canyon
levels out, I'd eat the wild sun-red plums, the sweet light
of the juice carrying through me my only hymn.

I know God, old flame wearing through the damp sponge
of the heart, that candle I cannot put out coming back
each time it seems extinguished. And so I must bless everything,
take anything given me—these words, their polish or pity,
the absences they bear like winter trees ascending
the ridge, so many starving angels in the early dusk,
and then the dark, and the broken order of prayer....

I know you are listening. Like the sky. And the birds
going over, aren't they always full of light? But to shine
like these trees again, that air hovering on the canyon walls—
sometimes, all I want to be is the dreaming world.

20 Years of Grant Applications & State College Jobs

> "Why, without theory there is no meaning."
> *former colleague at a committee meeting*

All I want now is a small dirt patio beneath two or three pines,
maybe one palm glittering with dates, one lemon sapling in a terra-cotta pot
standing for hope. A place where I can return to my scholarship of the sky,
re-establish a franchise with the sun. A place—I swear—where I will leave

most of the talking to the trees and purple finches, where I am at last
    renowned
among sparrows for my philosophy of crumbs.
                                                A place where I walk out
each day at 8:00 or 9:00 to appraise the likelihood of daylight advancing
beyond the cool green efforts of the boughs, where I set my coffee
and unread newspaper down on the metal table—a round one, the size
of a trash can lid, just big enough for wine and glasses, a basket of bread—
one painted that thick civic green like those in the sidewalk cafes
and parks in Paris—my last concession to a sentimental education.

I won't mind that the paint's chipped or that salt air eats away the legs;
I will praise the fog, its long beggar's coat dragging in from Point
    Conception
like some lost uncle in an Ingmar Bergman film. I will praise the tiny ranch-
style house the color of fog, my luck to end up in Lompoc, the last place
on the California coast almost no one wanted. I will refold the paper,
my notes scrawled in the margins where I've tried again to locate
the trace elements of God.
                                        To feel industrious, I'll get to my feet
about 11:00 and spray the hose around to keep down the dust—
a bit extra for the lantana lining the flagstones to the door,
a bit more for the aloe vera, the pomegranate, their blossoms aflame.
Every so often, I'll rake the patches of pine needles into a pile,
but before I decide where to move them next, a gust rearranges them
with an abstract but even hand.
                                        What will I care,
sitting in my rain bleached chair, one leg tapping the shade, the other
going to sleep in the sun, content to stare at my hot-pink hibiscus
slowly ascending the stucco wall? After 20 years, what can it matter
how long it takes to burn its way up the glistening air?
Even the stars are wearing down without a thought for us,
unattainable all this time. That should have been a lesson long ago....

I hereby resign all pretenses to the astronomy of New York—
appointments, invitations, awards, the genius grants.
Whenever the phone doesn't ring, it's them.
I'll settle for this wooden gate, a gravel drive announcing friends
who arrive for walks, for the Zinfandel and dish of Spanish olives;
friends who remember the sea, how good it was 20 years ago,
loose as driftwood in our lives, to have nothing and happily

drink that green, hard Chablis each evening by the Pacific
thinking we would have that light.
                              Now, I love the grey
and ragtag gulls whose hoots and aggravation betray their finds—
all that chance deserves. So after our walk, we're satisfied
just sitting outside, a Pavarotti aria holding off death,
drifting out the kitchen window onto the ambered light.

And what can we make of the Maya now? Their lost tongue,
their psalms of stone? They disappeared in the middle
of setting it all down and no one missed them for centuries.
And what was behind the anonymous workers of the Nazca Plains,
scraping off the desert's scrofulous skin for images of animals
and some politico's son, lines so long they only make sense from the sky—
and none of us birds?
                              Whose administrative mission was that?
100 years and the job will still be there. How good now to say Good-bye
to that arrogance which asks if there can be meaning
without first arranging the padded folding chairs of theory.

I'd like to apply for my life. I want the Guggenheim
to give me back my good will, the ease—no, the joy—
I once carried around with me, going down the street
in uncertainty, not enough gas in the tank to get out of town.
But I'll settle for this unpopular valley of fog, cholla flats and sand,
the occasional breeze thumbing my book, humming a blue line.
I'll take a small patio of unglamorous old dirt, a few pines
speaking simply in the resinous language of the only world
there is, immediate and meaningful as your next breath.
I'll praise the uneventful afternoon, and accept the wind
applauding in the silver dollar eucalyptus as my reward.

for Gary Soto, Jon Veinberg, & Gary Young

Concerning Paradise

A little interrogation of the sky
and a thousand starlings break
from the trees—dark river of souls
working their way into the wind. And I

will never satisfy myself with the ambiguous
origins of clouds, above me all my life—
blank invoices which will one day
come due as we await revelation
of a sea-scrolled exegesis of light.

Who is there any more who doubts
our speck on the galaxy's bent rim will burn
out long before another breathing dot
on the pinwheel wonders where, for that moment,
in the stellar backwash, we ever were?
I haven't, by any means, finished with the earth,
though it seems I have no more ambition now
than the sparrows reasoning cheerfully
among the weeds.
        Here, by the pittosporum,
by the plumeria, and bird of paradise's sun-brazed spikes,
by the jade plant jeweled with water drops,
it's clear that whatever is infinite will not be
approached by all the dull admonishments
of grief, thick as sea mist on the fan palms
along the cliff.
        But there's no changing the course
of the blood as it confronts the moon—bright boat
without a country. Who would simply be
the apostle to evening's blue and cloud-shaped trees,
the insubordinate skies? I don't want to write
one more poignant poem about death, about the fissures
of a cosmos beyond my breath.
        The empty road goes with me,
some last thing listening in the manzanita,
in the pause and distance of moonlight there
where the arroyo ends—space enough for St. Francis
to feed his heart again on the rocks,
for his calm colloquy to rise in hosannas
of atoms like the fragrance of sage
peppered across the night.
        This will have to serve
as knowledge, suffice as prayer, one orbit
of somnambulant faith, one stop for the traveler

whose bones ache with the dead fires of creation,
whose soul—in its onion skin, its dust—
would just as soon drift toward that high snowy peak
beyond the thousand embers floating back up
from the lake.

                 I'm still trying to do something here,
all this way from where I started. And though
the world is never going to be anything
more than the world—and the angels of dust
write our names across the backs of clouds—
I will not stop at nothing. So it matters
how the grass turns brown, how its yellow tips
burn, provisional as the stars.

MARILYN CHIN

Marilyn Chin's books of poems include *The Phoenix Gone, The Terrace Empty,* and *Dwarf Bamboo.* Recently, she was included in Bill Moyer's PBS series "The Language of Life." She teaches in the M.F.A. program at San Diego State University.

"I consider myself a Californian poet with a Pacific Rim imagination. I believe that my muse carries a duty-free passport—she may roam from landscape to landscape…from Hong Kong, the place of my birth, to Portland, Oregon, where I was raised, to Hawaii; she may even wish to transcend time and return to a Tang Dynasty Chinese landscape, but she always returns to California, where I presently live and work. I have been a Californian since 1982. I lived in San Francisco for seven years, then, I moved to San Diego in 1989 for a teaching job at San Diego State University. However, someday, I believe that I will cry squatter's rights and return to San Francisco where Chinese culture is not only visible but prevalent, and where my muse could have access to the music of a variety of Chinese dialects.

"California is my home, and I don't believe that I can live anywhere else. We live in the multicultural experiment, which soon will be the blueprint for the rest of the nation. My people, Chinese-Americans, have helped build this state. Our ghosts sing out from the walls of Angel Island, from the gold country, from the railroads, from hundreds of Chinese restaurants and laundromats, from agricultural groves and high tech buildings…My muse is an immigrant's muse, filled with vitality and thwarted dreams, eager to forge a new identity in the promised land."

Leaving San Francisco

for Weldon Kees

The coldest winter's day I remember
was a summer's night in San Francisco.
An old hoary sage-poet said something like that.

But if you live here you must don a new layer
and let the consequences take over.

No, this is not Xian, where the peasants sold you
Ch'in's tomb for a dollar. No, this is not Kaifeng
where the poets ate cinnabar to become immortals.
The connubial geese have stopped migrating;
they've settled on a stagnant tarn near Anza Terrace.

The Bay swells with winter and waits for a reprieve.
This spring the sun will heal the wound on your head
and you'll be famous for a moment. Alone in the motel room
you recite to an audience of one. The crack clambering
the wall deserves a villanelle if not a sestina.

But the Goddess of Mercy is weary; she averts her eyes,
as the demon's dark hand grips us, dragging our regrets
deep into the bay with the bottomfish.
If I float a poem over the Golden Gate Bridge,
Master Weldon, will you answer?

The Year Passes in My Morning Teacup

1984, East Bay

And while stirring I saw
my year's constellation in the dross:
my cousin's dead face auguring
a fruitless autumn, and winter—
too bleak a vision—
a black tree on a white canvas
and a black, black crow.
And before my eyes could unblear
the roads will deliquesce into rivers
to flood all of California;
and we, driving our compact cars
up toward the Golden Crane Pavillion,
must either swim or sink. And now,
a forboding in the shape of Mara:
once again, nobody escapes Oakland,
once again, another thwarted Spring.

How I Got That Name

an essay on assimilation

I am Marilyn Mei Ling Chin.
Oh, how I love the resoluteness
of that first person singular
followed by that stalwart indicative
of "be," without the uncertain i-n-g
of "becoming." Of course,
the name had been changed
somewhere between Angel Island and the sea,
when my father the paperson
in the late 1950s
obsessed with a bombshell blonde
transliterated "Mei Ling" to "Marilyn."
And nobody dared question
his initial impulse—for we all know
lust drove men to greatness,
not goodness, not decency.
And there I was, a wayward pink baby,
named after some tragic white woman
swollen with gin and Nembutal.
My mother couldn't pronounce the "r."
She dubbed me, "Numba one female offshoot"
for brevity: henceforth, she will live and die
in sublime ignorance, flanked
by loving children and the "kitchen deity."
While my father dithers,
a tomcat in Hong Kong trash—
a gambler, a petty thug,
who bought a chain of chopsuey joints
in Piss River, Oregon,
with bootlegged Gucci cash.
Nobody dared question his integrity given
his nice, devout daughters
and his bright, industrious sons
as if filial piety were the standard
by which all earthly men were measured.

•

Oh, how trustworthy our daughters,

how thrifty our sons!
How we've managed to fool the experts
in education, statistics and demography—
We're not very creative but not adverse to rote-learning.
Indeed, they can *use* us.
But the "Model Minority" is a tease.
We know you are watching now,
so we refuse to give you any!
Oh, bamboo shoots, bamboo shoots!
The further west we go, we'll hit east;
the deeper down we dig, we'll find China.
History has turned its stomach
on a black polluted beach—
where life doesn't hinge
on that red, red wheelbarrow,
but whether or not our new lover
in the final episode of "Santa Barbara"
will lean over a scented candle
and call us a "bitch."
Oh God, where have we gone wrong?
We have no inner resources!

•

Then, one redolent spring morning
the Great Patriarch Chin
peered down from his kiosk in heaven
and saw that his descendants were ugly.
One had a squarish head and a nose without a bridge.
Another's profile—long and knobbed as a gourd.
A third, the sad, brutish one
may never, never marry,
And I, his least favorite—
"not quite boiled, not quite cooked,"
a plump pomfret simmering in my juices—
too listless to fight for my people's destiny.
"To kill without resistance is not slaughter"
says the proverb. So, I wait for imminent death.
The fact that this death is also metaphorical
is testament to my lethargy.

•

So here lies Marilyn Mei Ling Chin,
married once, twice to so-and-so, a Lee and a Wong,
granddaughter of Jack "the patriarch"
and the brooding Suilin Fong,
daughter of the virtuous Yuet Kuen Wong
and G. G. Chin the infamous,
sister of a dozen, cousin of a million,
survived by everybody and forgotten by all.
She was neither black nor white,
neither cherished nor vanquished,
just another squatter in her own bamboo grove
minding her poetry—
when one day heaven was unmerciful,
and a chasm opened where she stood.
Like the jowls of a mighty white whale,
or the jaws of a metaphysical Godzilla,
it swallowed her whole.
She did not flinch nor writhe,
nor fret about the afterlife,
but stayed! Solid as wood, happily
a little gnawed, tattered, mesmerized
by all that was lavished upon her
and all that was taken away!

KILLARNEY CLARY

Killarney Clary is the author of two books of poetry, *Who Whispered Near Me* (Farrar, Straus & Giroux, 1989) and *By Common Salt* (Oberlin College Press, 1996), and of a chapbook, *By Me, by Any, Can and Can't be Done* (Greenhouse Review Press, 1980). The recipient of a fellowship from the Lannan Foundation, she lives in Los Angeles.

"Is it fair to say: I haven't lived anywhere else. I haven't lived with any other fingerprints but these. How can I say how my blood affects me?"

© Kathleen Delano

ANOTHER HOT AFTERNOON upstairs after school. I was half asleep. To cool themselves, small birds opened their beaks. They held their wings out for air, feeling dizzy in it. Small, white-hot birds, arguing about how small, how white, how hot they were. It was their way to begin making noise. They got used to it, grew stronger. The sound worked with the light into my nerves. I couldn't close my eyes because staring was part of the throbbing and the endless screen of trees full of silent, white flowers. The argument was inside, in places where I was thinnest. Back there, I could pull it to a hum and lie quiet till dinner.

Only talking. Only moving. On the terrace of the hotel, my mother ordered coffee. She read the paper, in front of Angel Island, in front of San Francisco. I was only doing one thing at a time. Watching her, watching the city, listening to her read about the deer. What we avoided—it's just noise, the way things go on.

Helen and I were cleaning the beach house. We were working each other, starting to shout. I could hear both of us shouting at once and I could feel my heart as it spread itself throughout me and into what I saw of her—larger, smaller. Then there was nothing but Helen's laughter and sand blowing across the porch. As I stood waiting to leave, I was losing, finding out. In my unsteady hands, in listening to the whole sound. Bare nerve. I'd wanted to last with it.

IN THIS WIND, THE SHARP BLUE CUT of the San Gabriels flattens against the neon east; eucalyptus want to break loose but hold, thrashing, to what is. Just air, all air, all tossed and secured at once; and when I see I am in a dry room, listen to the flyer as it's banded to the outer doorknob, I say, "here." But I am all pull.

I am walking in the arroyo. I am in love. I am scared. Everyone is still alive. The leaves aren't sad and restless; the canyon isn't cooling so fast, darkening between its walls as the days shorten and the way narrows. I am not going back. There is no body made to take me back into itself.

Always in the in-between, at ease with my tongue in its pool, or taking a shocking first breath in the bright room in the hands of an expert. Lucky in-between, where friction finds me.

MR. DOOMS WOULD MEET US across the Bay Bridge at a restaurant that featured "Dancing Waters." Fountains in colored lights. He was a client of my father's; we were to be polite. Later, at his house, his daughters showed us porno pictures in a magazine and then we rode back to our hotel.

I learned about business—that it was a late-night, uneasy entertainment, chilled and full of sparkle. The lights on the bridge and from San Francisco on the dark bay, and the cold car and lack of fun were swept up in exchange for something I would never hear of, because the taboo deals were as delicate as ice in a glass against a glass toasting Friday.

•

This evening, here in Los Angeles, clerks and managers in their smooth, safe jackets ride the buses home where they turn on lights and TVs. I bend to the sink and as I close my eyes I know now, I am vulnerable now, in the dark of my own hands, in the pleasure of washing.

And in the loneliness of slippers and fear of comfort I breathe, I hold my breath. Tonight's anxiety melts into tomorrow's meeting, a few laughs, a loose thread, a demand flying on the city's own wind.

Doubt howls up from gutter drains to argue with brilliant offices and the determined pace echoes on hard expensive shoes across the parking garage under Pershing Square. I am in between, on edge, patient and gullible while mail is sorted at Terminal Annex and trucks make their way toward Grand Central Market, from Mexico with melons, with flowers from Leucadia.

Even though I lose my secrets repeatedly the unfinished and unseen dance with experience, what cannot be forgotten. Another car is hit head-on. Another friend says, "Don't look."

RESTLESS BEFORE THE CANARY, wave of traffic on an inhale, I can just barely see on a dark blue ground black arabesques. Music begs, "More." Toward Elysian Park the sky pinks, and whispers build into a Santa Ana breeze in the pepper tree. My day opens above the pale rivers of freeways, patterns of tongues and districts; a tapping energy quickens. I am moving.

Light and vibration double and double again. The last cool whirl of dust promises wishes will turn in rage, spin, widen and disappear. I know my hand on the door jamb, hot coffee passing my heart; I believe the stars are still up there.

WHEN MY HEART ASKED FOR A WAY FREE, it was led into this lightless room. In the back-neighbor's kitchen window a woman stands at the sinkboard eating eggs quickly. 11 o'clock night cat and traffic. Bamboo leaves and wind between here and a next place. It could be lonely. Cold business suits of tired men after airplanes from San Francisco mostly. Something for them to eat too and fewer stars. Awful lights, corridors, ugly ceilings. Gloom, spirited in comfort hills. Dark-shoed children in a playground. A smooth-faced dull girl with her blue dress dreams on something near the fence—stained patch of sand from last night's rain. Good friends talk about thunder. A letter to the corner leisure in an almost warm afternoon passing people as if it was Sunday. Then it's all memories. I could do something for you. You wouldn't know; you would feel better and I'd stay quiet as if it were fair.

WANDA COLEMAN

Wanda Coleman's work includes a
book of prose, *Native in a Strange
Land* (Black Sparrow Press, 1996),
and a book of poems, *Bathwater
Wine* (Black Sparrow Press, 1998).
Her many honors include
Guggenheim and NEA literary
fellowships.

© Susan Carpendale

"I was born at home, in the Watts
community of Los Angeles, in the
post-war California of November
1946. I have lived in Los Angeles
all my life. Over the years, I've dri-
ven the state from border to bor-
der performing my work in
venues as diverse as San Quentin's
writers' workshop to rock clubs to community centers, at political rallies and
in classrooms. I've spent considerable time in San Francisco and San Diego,
enough to drive the streets without a map. I've stared at the Big Sur moon
from the heights of Nepenthe's, dabbled my toes in Half Moon Bay, ridden
the wooden ponies of Cannery Row, and have scribbled poems in desperation
at Djerassi off Skyline Drive above Alice's Restaurant. I've hitchhiked Sir
Francis Drake Boulevard into Kentfield. I've been thrown out of Hollywood
night spots for being too rowdy, have picked cotton from the roadside in
Fresno, and was once pulled over by the CHP for swilling apple juice on the
roads of King City. I was stared at in Eureka. The tallest redwood in the state
fell over after my visit. Allen Ginsberg hugged me in Oakland. I've seen L.A.
riot twice. I've been blissed out at Mt. Shasta, stoned at Wolfgang's, and nau-
seated in Palm Springs. My heart lives in Lancaster, and my grief dwells in
the Russian River. I am a Black Californian. But I am forever married to a
New York Jew. I was born here. I intend to die here. At home."

April in Hollywood

cool brisk fingers in my hair
the fresh sweet bite of crisp red delicious apples
service stations with "sorry no gas" signs
palm trees. the american flag full mast and shouting
sun. the body shop in red black and white. wind
the black man in blue who's got to get to cerritos

on 55¢. latins stealing swigs of tequila from
a torn brown paper bag in the back of a bus
radios barking disco
dogs mute in the face of poverty
old white ladies with shopping bags as wrinkled
as their necks, in tattered wigs, black high-fashion
eyelashes and green mascara
crisp starched sagebrush narcs crawling campuses
for children dealing illegal drugs
sweaty gay runners in tennis shoes jogging up sunset
chinese japanese thai korean vietnamese and
soul food kitchen smells
the mindless roar of
traffic on the boulevards at rush hour
endless grey curbs of home

Dog Suicide

on the harbor freeway
heavy traffic 6 p.m. home to the pad
the kids in back and me watching, careful
the front and back
sweating behind r&b at the steering wheel
the dog
saw it standing there
about a mile up
cars/sudden slowing to keep
from hitting the dog
that threatened to
go out on the freeway
i slowed up with the flow
as i passed, it moved
toward me
i honked my horn
it went back, then
i watched to see what would happen
in the rear view mirror
it just walked out there
in front of the black buick

its body fell into a tumble
under impact
its flesh tore red and open
then another car hit it
and another and another
thought about it on
the way home
wondered if that dog knew something i didn't

Prisoner of Los Angeles (2)

in cold grey morning
comes the forlorn honk of workbound traffic
i wake to the video news report

the world is going off

rising, i struggle free of the quilt
& wet dreams of my lover dispel
leave me moist and wanting

in the bathroom
i rinse away illusions, brush my teeth and
unbraid my hair
there're the children to wake
breakfast to conjure
the job
the day laid out before me
the cold corpse of an endless grind

so this is it, i say to the enigma in the mirror
this is your lot/assignment/relegation
this is your city

i find my way to the picture window
my eyes capture the purple reach of hollywood's hills
the gold eye of sun mounting the east
the gray anguished arms of avenue

i will never leave here

Where I Live

at the lip of a big black vagina
birthing nappy-headed pickaninnies every hour on the hour
and soul radio blasting into mindwindow
bullets and blood
see that helicopter up there? like
god's eye looking down on his children
barsandbarsandbarsandbarsandbars
where i live
is the gap-filled mouth of polly, the old black woman
up the street whose daughter's from new orleans and who
abandons her every holiday leaving her to wander
up and down the avenue and not even a holiday meal. she
collects the neighborhood trash and begs kindness in
doorways/always in the same browns. purples
and blues of her loneliness—a dress
that never fades or wears thin
where i live
is the juke on the corner—hamburgerfishchilli smells
drawing hungry niggahs off the street and pimpmobiles
cluttering the asphalt parking lot. pool tables in the
back where much gambling and shit take place and
many niggahs fall to the knife of the violent surgeon.
one night me and cowboy were almost killed by a stray
bullet from some renegade low riders and me and
kathy used to go down and drop quarters
and listen to al green, and the dudes would hate
my 'sditty ways and call me a dyke
'cause i wouldn't sell pussy
where i live
is the night club working one to six in the morning.
cigarette burn holes in my stockings and wig full of
cigarette smoke. flesh bruised from niggahs pinching my
meat and feeling my thighs, ears full of spit
from whispers and obscene suggestions and mind full of
sleep's spiders building a hazy nest—eyes full of
rainbows looking forward to the day i leave this hell
where i live
avoiding the landlord on the first and fifteenth when he

comes around to collect the rent. i'm four months behind
and wish i had a niggah to take care of me for a change
instead of taking me through changes. this building which
keeps chewing hunks out of the sides of people's cars and
the insane old bitch next door beating on the wall, scaring
the kids and telling me to shut up. every other day she calls
the cops out here and i hope they don't run a make on me
and find all them warrants
where i live
the little gangsters diddy-bop through and pick up
young bitches and flirt with old ones, looking to
snatch somebody's purse or find their way into somebody's
snatch 'cause mama don't want them at home and papa
is a figment and them farms them farms them farms
they call schools. and mudflapped bushy-headed entities
swoop the avenues seeking death
it's the only thrill left
where i live
at the lip of a big black vagina
birthing nappy-headed pickaninnies every hour on the hour
the county is her pimp and she can turn tomorrow
swifter than any bitch ever graced this earth
she's the baddest piece of ass on the west coast
named black los angeles

GLOVER DAVIS

Glover Davis has published three books, *Bandaging Bread* and *August Fires* (Cummington Press) and *Legend* (Wesleyan University Press). His fourth book, *Cloud Trains,* has not yet been published. He is also the Director of the M.F.A. program at San Diego State University.

"I was born in San Luis Obispo, California. I have lived in Los Angeles, North Hollywood, Fresno, Felton, and San Diego. I am not sure how the landscape and environment helps shape my poems though I know they do. I use these place names along with images of heat, flowers, trees.

"I often think of Thom Gunn's poem 'Flying Above California,' where he describes California 'sinewed and tawny in the sun, and/ valley cool with mustard, or sweet with/ loquat.' There is 'a mixture of mediterranean and northern names./ Such richness can you drunk.' This is a place like the Mediterranean, and its poppies, oak trees, manzanitas enter my poems. For California is my world even if they continue paving it over, pave forever. It is *mi querencia* as those who speak Spanish call that special place they prefer."

August Fires

Drove all day from San Diego
up the great trail of ashes
in my rearview mirror the eyes
of truckdrivers benzedrined
a broken truck outside of Newhall
thousands of oranges spilled
a woman crying   I didn't stop.
Signs everywhere in the mountains
radar towers   smoke lookouts   mirror flashing
200 miles to go   I keep pushing
and think "a singing bird will bring
the message"   drops of oil fall

from his wings   down from Santa Barbara
where the beach gasps through its coating.
Firebird over Topanga
a shower of sparks two miles high
hot winds blowing in from the deserts
the mountains purifying themselves
and no one learns.

II

There's a red dot in a scrawl
of lines on the road map.
I touch the places where my friends live
hundreds of miles away.
I was lonely once and talked
to no one. I sat in the shade next
to my trailer through the afternoons
watching a squirrel or a hawk
and did not read or write.
The sand burned my feet and the
dry stalks whispered. I killed
a rattlesnake that summer
and the white hiss struck through the air.
Part of him was smooth
and the red lines crossed like diamonds.
I thought how he mapped the ground
with his belly. Grit in the flaps
and the thick coils looped over
a stick. I oiled the rifle
showered   and drove 500 miles.
Now I drive to the spot
where the red lines joint like a heart.

III

fog swirls down Golden State   fenders turning
into flares   the truck horns blaring past
Delano coming up   snow crust above
Grapevine   my breath clear as frost
at this altitude she smiled and touched
my forehead to see if I was tired
patches of ice beside the road
a smeared pine against the ridge   cold blue

and metal everywhere.
                        L.A. far below us
in a blanket of fumes   neon lights
like a glowing wind rushing toward
the sea   we paused in the clear streams
of air and watched the water
burning down the stone ducts of mountains.

IV
someone is grinding the faces
of the poor. their sweat rags smoking
their brows charred   a deputy
shows them the long way down into
the valley flowing with metal.
a little black dog smudges the air.
a man gnarled and tougher than a tree.
words break loose like the branches
of his life. the prayers of the poor go up
like smoke from the ghettos 30 miles south.

Eddie brought me here one morning   praising
with the eye of the painter   sweeping
his arms along the valley like brush strokes
the deep greens   the blond shadows sweeping in
from Malibu   this is for all of us
he said   I remember the swift hand
of his imagination striking
out fence posts   boundaries   the inked
poisons of real estate coming down
now in a rain of smoking paper.

V
leaflets of fire along the highway
near Ft. Tejon race toward the trees.
the dial on my speedometer flutters
like a pine needle. I watch   fire sparrows
stones melting   oak trees blessing
the flames and far below   a tract
of houses flares into dust
mesquite crackles toward the grove
and the wind turns.

smoke in my skin and hair
I pick the ashes from my collar.
I kneel in the ruined meadow
and find in a handful of earth
the three shining seeds of the poplar.
taillights at dusk
like candles to the sun.
the cars keep coming   and coming.

VI

Allan holds the book of changes
and the words change into ideograms
black lines   on snow white rags   steaming branches.
He says man is like a tree in the pale earth.
He holds a saucer up to the light
and points to the opaque moons
two pale wings in glass.
Behind us the hills are boiling
and the almond barely stirs.
We drink our tea. He says   the chinese
would have cherished these August Fires.
His eyes are like the eyes
of the sage on my tea cup   glowing eyes
that miss nothing   the radiant mass
of the mountains.   The pines exploding
20 miles away. He goes on praising
a petal from an almond tree.

VII

50 houses   puffed
like parchment   used cars
melted into grease   dogs
with a mottled thighbone
pipes   chimneys   twisted iron
of bedsteads   wind humming through a black refrigerator.
I touch the chalky feathers
of the pine   and reach for
the cypress cup where I drank
my own breath.   Blue fog
from my lungs beads the lips
of the men hand-loading   canvas hose

pickaxe   shovels and gunny sacks.
Rabbits streak from the red valleys.
And the rain behind my heart
full of swords months away
from the purple heart-shaped
fruit of the cactus.

VIII

There's a stained lunch sack
and a cup of coffee
in which a petal floats
but the workers sleep
in the shade until
a burning thistle drops
like a sword through their dreams.
They brush the grass
from their shirts and
take the path flung
through the heat like
a branch deflected on
the water. I watched
and dozed and read my book.
I did not see the veins
of an oak leaf in the
hide of a deer or the
butterfly who turned
white hot in a second.

IX

Let the manzanita go
like a prayer wheel tipped
with rockets   a burning rag
of the seagull flutter down.
Let the butane spread
through the stained air
of California   the oil slick
billow like a robe of gold
from the harbors   let the
barbed wire leap from its post
the eagle and the fox return
like pieces of light.

The Orphan

I saw her near Anaheim by the fence
in a black fur coat from the trash.
The wind ruffled her blond hair, tugged
at the black fur. She pointed with an oily wrench,
a streaked scepter, and her lips
murmured a song. I was five miles
down the freeway before I turned the car
and found among the packing cases, glass,
stripped fenders nothing but a piece of silk
and a crayon drawing on slate, a girl
with a glowing crown and a house
near a green river beyond acres of cars.
I remember the cheekbones tipped with rouge,
the tears blurred, and then the long ride
back to the orphanage, the cold sandwich
and the beating in front of everyone.
The locked room where she must kneel
under a thick belt and a sister's habit
unfurling like a pirate flag would rise
in a book full of crosses. Bells sound
in the stone courtyard where the children march
in robes and slippers, and the traffic stalls
forever in the calm lanes of the wind.

Children in the Arbor

Driving up highway 99
I look into the backyards and see
nopales, fig trees, grape arbors,
added-on scrap lumber lean-tos,
clotheslines with purple dresses, work shirts, darned socks.
Beneath trees as old as the state of California
there's a chaos of fruit and flowers
and the shade seems as valuable as water
in the valley's fierce heat.
There's probably a man who rises early.
He puts on a khaki shirt, takes a lunch sack

and walks to the corner where he smokes
in the warmth just after dawn,
waiting for a friend's pick-up,
a day in the fields that'll leave
his shirt stiff with sweat, a dark cheekbone
smudged where he wiped sweat with a glove.
Only his children have time for the yard.
I can see one or two in a fig tree,
or among the oranges, their faces blurred
by the bug smeared windshield.
They must be laughing there.
They must be free not knowing it.
The cars and trucks go by
muffled by branches.
The children move across a litter of leaves
and petals, mottled, scarcely visible, with toy cups
and saucers, carved wooden guns and horses.
For them there is no time
until a mother's voice
cuts through the afternoon
and I am miles away in minutes.
Fifty miles to go. I can't stop now.

JUAN DELGADO

Juan Delgado lives in San Bernardino and is an Associate Professor of English at California State University, San Bernardino. His books of poetry are *Green Web* (University of Georgia Press) and *El Campo* (Capra Press). He has also published a chapbook, *Change of Worlds*.

"In California our freeways connect and divide us at the same time. Freeways don't drive you through a downtown or neighborhood as much as drive you above, below, and around it. At times the freeway is more a tunnel than a road, more an exit or entrance chartering our time. When I first came to this state, I was struck by the beauty of the freeways, their centipede pillars, their practical geometry. I was born in Guadalajara, Mexico, and at some point in our family's journey to California we left a dark lane and merged into a three-lane freeway with off-ramps and on-ramps that spiraled. When a ramp veered back under itself and merged into another freeway, I recalled the image of a snake swallowing its tail on an ancient wall in Mexico. Our countless migrations are the scales of that snake, and its eyes are bent on driving a little farther on."

I-5 Incident

"Hit-run victim survives four days alone."

On the fourth day the phone wires talked,
replied like voices pressed to pillows,
trapped behind walls or dying in the wind,
then quiet as a priest who listens to sins.
All sorts of things I imagined; they kept me going.
No. I didn't see the car; I had my back to it.
I only heard its radio, you know,
American rock and roll. No.
I wasn't crossing; I stayed to the side.
When struck, I hit the rushing ground
and dragged myself toward the bushes
of an embankment, afraid they'd return.

In La Sagrada Familia, my neighborhood,
a man delivering Coke on his bike
fell at a corner and lifted his head
only to vanish under a city bus,
so I wasn't going near the road again.
Plus, I couldn't. Look at my legs.
My jeans were soaked in blood.
Dirt stuck to them. I patted my legs,
thinking they were part of the ground.
I was half dead, a lizard without a tail.
Luckily, I had the sprinkler's water;
its head was broken. I held its cool neck,
but my stomach groaned, all knotted up.
I shouted when I heard a car coming
and shook the bushes at the headlights.
Through the night I held on to a branch
and had a dream about a market place
where people drifted among the stalls.
Some glanced, keeping up with the crowd;
others haggled, then turned from the vendors,
walking away, seemingly losing interest.
I came upon a stall of toys: race cars,
dolls with eyes bright as hubcaps,
and puppets hooked, their limbs still
as if they had fallen through the sky.
A child stopped to tug the string of one
and tried to get his mother's attention
by having it dance and wave its arm,
but she was already several stalls ahead,
looking in front for him, shouting his name.
He ran dodging strangers and yelling, "Wait!"
I heard his voice over the crowd's
and woke to a semi and the rush of wind
that made the oleander's leaves tremble.

Awakened in a Field

I made car batteries new,
replacing their dead cells.

And once one exploded
on our work bench;
its acid ran down the wall,
a fire that peeled the paint,
a name with a heart beside it,
and a few phone numbers.
I carried your photo
inside my coat pocket
when I left for Stockton.
Now from a bed of corn husks,
I rise and brush the silk
away from my face and work.
My hands are heavy as clay.
My fellow workers are gone,
some to other fields and work;
a few returned to Mexico,
to their wives and children.
Did your father make it
through another dry season?
Is your brother leaving
the farm and coming up north?
I have work until summer,
so write when you receive this.
I loaded the corn in boxes
all day yesterday and today,
but between the company store
and the bar in town I can't
seem to save any money,
so I can't mail you anything.
Forgive me for leaving you,
for thinking I had to go.

Campesinos

A foreman drives by the fields counting his pickers,
their spines bent like the necks of clothes hangers.
What hangs on them is the harvest, the fields
and roads from crop to crop merging into
a circuit of hands working close to the ground.
Others are packing the cabbages into a truck,

cramping the boxes the way their coyote had them
hidden in his camper shell crossing the border;
he smuggled ten of them, his crop of wetbacks.
They sat, their heads rocking into a half-sleep
until a voice woke them, their new foreman,
calling and directing them to a line of tents.
Some tents had cots, old army surplus,
and others, the trash of the last field hands.

A driver starts his route with the packed cabbages,
coming upon tire tracks that went off the road.
The wreckage of a van is fenced off
with yellow tape, and the bodies on the ground
are covered with yellow sheets, a yellow unlike
any bush or stone viewed through a windshield.
The police direct traffic, waving the truck on,
and at a pothole a few cabbages fall,
a faceless green pushed aside.
The driver sees in his rearview mirror
the scattered bodies again, a receding yellow.
Their journey was a wrinkled map unfolding
a country shaded by the promise of work,
inviting as hands on a wheel, an open road.

La Llorona

1. Moon

Two girls walk to the river bank,
the yucca plants pointing the way.
Wiggling their toes in the sand,
they decide to swim toward the moon.
Their hands flutter above their heads;
the moon turns them into butterflies
gliding over the surface and reeds.
In the morning their bodies appear
where the laundry dries on the rocks.
The people have no one to blame
but the woman who walks the river.
They say she drowned her own son.
She sang him lullabies; he floated

like a lily until he could not hear
her song and feel his hand in hers.

2. Water

The clarity of the moon
begins to sway the reeds,
her children's hair.
She sees her children drift
into an eddy, swirl in moss,
the water's flesh.
She retraces her path, the steps
that led her children to the lake.
Her story is like water:
it takes the shape of the holder,
a storyteller's mouth.
She dips her hands and drinks.
Their voices fill her throat.

3. The Widening Sea

The pier she is on goes beyond
the waves to the rising swells.
Her clenched hands no longer feel
the strain of pushing the stroller.
She tucks in her baby's blanket,
then walks to the sounds of wheels
against the planks and the calls
of seagulls that whirl and scream.
A nylon line is tied to the rail
and dangles over the edge.
It vanishes, pointing to the sea.
She lifts her baby over the rail
and lets the bundle drop, undraping.
A gull gives chase to the wing,
the blanket's flapping corner.
She looks at the ripples, the ocean's
widening mouth, then she leaps,
her legs as stiff as a baby doll's.
With little light reaching the bottom,
her body darkens, half of her
a reported story, the rest a myth,
retold, shifting with the tide.

CHITRA BANERJEE DIVAKARUNI

A longterm resident of the San
Francisco Bay Area, Chitra Banerjee
Divakaruni now teaches at the Univer-
sity of Houston. She has four books of
poetry, the latest being *Leaving Yuba
City,* from which these poems are
taken. She has a collection of stories,
Arranged Marriage, and two novels,
The Mistress of Spices and *Sister of My
Heart.* Her awards include an Amer-
ican Book Award, two Pen Syndicated
Fiction awards, a California Arts
Council Award, a Pushcart Prize, an
Allen Ginsberg Poetry Prize, and a

Pen Josephine Miles Award. Her work has appeared in *The Atlantic, The
New Yorker, Ms, The Chicago Review,* and numerous other magazines. Active
in women's issues, Divakaruni helped found Maitri, the first south Asian
women's hotline on the West Coast.

"I have loved the Bay Area for twenty years, ever since I came as a graduate
student to U.C. Berkeley and, driving down from the airport, saw the olean-
ders that line the freeways—the same pink as in my grandfather's garden. I
took as my own all the beauties and terrors of the California landscape—the
slim, fragrant eucalyptus, the ascetic redwoods, the tendrils of fog curling
around the Golden Gate, the viscous horror of the mudslides, the ground ex-
ploding in earthquakes. I've put them all into my writings. And the cities and
towns, each with its wonderful diversity, they're in there too, Berkeley and
Oakland and Sunnyvale (where I lived for many years), and of course 'The
City'—is there any other? The imagined landscape of the past was of particu-
lar importance to me as I re-created the lives of my people in Yuba City, harsh
yet filled with hope. Now, in Houston, I find that I continue to write about
California, which pulls at my heart in the same way that India does. I think,
in a way, no matter where I live, it will be one of my homes."

The Founding of Yuba City

Let us suppose it a California day
bright as the blinding sea that brought them
across a month of nights
branded with strange stars
and endless coal shoveled
into a ship's red jaws.

The sudden edge of an eucalyptus grove,
the land fallow and gold to the eye, a wind
carrying the forgotten green smell
of the Punjab plains.

They dropped back, five or maybe six,
let the line straggle on. The crew's song
wavered, a mirage, and sank
in the opaque air. The railroad owed them
a month's pay, but the red soil
glinted light.
Callused from pounding metal into earth,
their farmer's hands
ached to plunge into its moisture.
Each man let it run pulsing
through his fingers,
remembered.

The sun fell away. Against its orange,
three ravens, as in the old tales. Was it good luck
or bad? They weren't sure.
Through the cedars, far light
from a window on a white man's farm.
They untied their waistbands,
counted coins, a few crumpled notes.
They did not fear
work. Tomorrow they would find jobs,
save, buy the land soon. Innocent
of Alien Laws, they planned their crops.
Under the sickled moon the fields
shone with their planting:
wheat, spinach, the dark oval wait
of potatoes beneath the ground, cauliflowers
pushing up white fists toward the light.

The men closed their eyes, turned their faces
to the earth's damp harvest-odor.
In their dreams their wives' red skirts flamed
in the Punjab noon. Slender necked women
who carried on their heads
rotis and *alu*,

jars of buttermilk for the farmers' lunch.
When they bent to whisper love
(or was it farewell)
their hibiscus-scented hair fell like tears
on the faces of the husbands
they would not see again.

A horned owl gliding on great wings
masked the moon. The men stroked the soil,
its soft warm hollows. Not knowing
how the wheels of history
grind over the human heart, they
smiled in their sleep.

> Note: Yuba City, settled by Punjab farmers around 1910, is now a thriving Indian
> community in Northern California. Until the 1940s, the Alien Land Laws precluded nonwhite
> immigrants from owning land, and immigration restrictions prevented their families from
> joining them. A number of the original settlers were never reunited with their families.

Leaving Yuba City

She has been packing all night.

It's taking a long time because she knows she must be very quiet, mustn't
wake the family. Father and mother in the big bedroom downstairs, he
sharp and angular in his ironed night-pajamas, on the bed-lamp side because
he reads the Punjabi newspaper before he sleeps. Her body like a
corrugation, a dark apologetic crease on her side of the wide white bed,
face turned away from the light, or is it from her husband, *salwar-kameez*
smelling faintly of sweat and dinner spices. Brother and his new wife next
door, so close that all week bits of noise have been flying through the thin
wall at her like sparks. Murmurs, laughter, bed-creaks, small cries, and once
a sound like a slap, followed by a sharp in-drawn breath like the startled
start of a sob that never found its completion. And directly beneath her
bedroom, grandfather, propped up on betel-stained pillows to help him
breathe, slipping in and out of nightmares where he calls out in his asthmatic
voice hoarse threats in a dialect she does not understand.

She walks on tiptoe like she imagines, from pictures seen in magazines, a
ballerina would move. Actually she is more like a stork, that same awkward
grace as she balances stiff-legged on the balls of her feet, her for-the-first-

time painted toes curling in, then out, splaying fuchsia pink with just a hint of glitter through the crowded half-dark of her bedroom. She moves back and forth between suitcase and dresser, maneuvers her way around the heavy teak furniture that father chose for her, Armchair. Dressing table. Narrow single bed. They loom up in the sad seep of light from her closet like black icebergs. Outside, wind moves through the pepper trees, whispering her name through the humid night. *Sushma, Sushma, Sushma.* She has been holding her breath, not realizing it, until her chest feels like there are hands inside, hot hands with fuchsia-pink nails scraping the lining of her lungs.

Yuba City School

From the black trunk I shake out
my one American skirt, blue serge
that smells of mothballs. Again today
Jagjit came crying from school. All week
the teacher has made him sit
in the last row, next to the boy
who drools and mumbles,
picks at the spotted milk-blue skin
of his face, but knows to pinch, sudden-sharp,
when she is not looking.

The books are full of black curves,
dots like the eggs the boll-weevil lays
each monsoon in furniture-cracks
in Ludhiana. Far up in front the teacher makes word-sounds
Jagjit does not know. They float
from her mouth-cave, he says,
in discs, each a different color.

Candy-pink for the girls in their lace dresses,
matching shiny shoes. Silk-yellow for the boys beside them,
crisp blond hair, hands raised
in all the right answers. Behind them
the Mexicans, whose older brothers,
he tells me, carry knives,
whose catcalls and whizzing rubber bands dash, mid-air,
with the teacher's voice,

its sharp purple edge.
For him, the words are a muddy red,
flying low and heavy,
and always the one he has learned to understand:
idiot idiot idiot.

I heat the iron over the stove. Outside
evening blurs the shivering
in the eucalyptus. Jagjit's shadow
disappears into the hole he is hollowing
all afternoon. The earth, he knows, is round,
and if he can tunnel all the way through,
he will end up in Punjab,
in his grandfather's mango orchard, his grandmother's songs
lighting on his head, the old words glowing
like summer fireflies.

In the playground, Jagjit says, invisible hands
snatch at his turban, expose
his uncut hair, unseen feet trip him from behind,
and when he turns, ghost laughter
all around his bleeding knees.
He bites down on his lip to keep in
the crying. They are
waiting for him to open his mouth,
so they can steal his voice.

I test the iron with little drops of water
that sizzle and die. Press down
on the wrinkled cloth. The room fills
with a smell like singed flesh.
Tomorrow in my blue skirt I will go
to see the teacher, my tongue
a stiff embarrassment in my mouth,
my few English phrases. She will pluck them from me,
nail shut my lips. My son will keep sitting
in the last row
among the red words that drink his voice.

Note: *uncut hair: the boy in the poem is a Sikh immigrant,
whose religion forbids the cutting of his hair.*

ANGIE ESTES

Angie Estes's collection of poems, *The Uses of Passion,* won the 1994 Peregrine Smith Poetry Competition and was published in the *Peregrine Smith Poetry Series* (Gibbs Smith, 1995). She has received grants from the California Arts Council, the National Endowment for the Humanities, and the Woodrow Wilson Foundation. Her poems have appeared in many literary magazines, including *AGNI* and *The Antioch Review,* and in the recent anthology *Queer Dog,* and are forthcoming in *American Literary Review* and *The Paris Review.* She is currently a professor of poetry and American literature at California Polytechnic State University, San Luis Obispo.

"Whatever other kind of place California may be, it has always loomed most forcefully for me as an edge, a place for departure—and arrival: high-dive of adolescence when my family left Virginia for Hawaii; elbowed coastal ledge I traced back from graduate school in Oregon to my first teaching job; author of the asphalt squiggle that points east; last place I set foot before lifting off to Paris.

"California: whatever else it might be, it's an edge, where something is always turning from something, to something, or into something. Landscape or poem, it is, after all, the hometown of love. It calls your name. It speaks to you first, before you even know you are being spoken to, the way the gray and white tabby was there by Laguna Lake when I walked by one evening, a few weeks ago, at the beginning of July. Pushing the reeds like saloon doors before her, she was Kitty on 'Gunsmoke': hard and soft, part of—and not—the frontier.

"It transforms you without even being asked to. I still walk that same path by the lake, though the cat hasn't appeared for some time. Each evening I pause, look into the undergrowth along the wet bank, and call 'Here, kitty; here, kitty kitty.'"

Nocturne

Shortly after midnight, certain creatures become what they really
Are, bats flex their nostrils and go out to map

The earth with shrieks while slugs outline the borders
Of the real with slime. Possums no longer pretend

To be everything they're not, and for once are just
Possums, while all that's human turns to dream.

Now boundaries realign, and only deer
Know the property lines to my backyard

And whose oak tree it really is.
At this hour nothing stops under street lights

Or for traffic lights for that matter—
Not the deer flicking back the black fleas

Of night, nor I in my sleep, throwing my arm
Across you, as if you weren't there.

Serenade

Yelling never works, but I'm told
                         that sometimes
a well-pitched shoe
               or the unusually stiff
beam of an ardent flashlight
                  will get them
to move on.
        I hear them warming up
each evening about five,
               while wooden spoons
turn around in their pots.
                After he has chased
the intruder away
           from the car door's mirror, flashing
the blankness held beneath wings,
              the mockingbird begins
to repeat everything he has ever heard
                you say: how it is time
to get to the table,
          how there will be seconds
for all, how at the beginning
             of June you are willing to pay
six times the going price
            for a basket of tomatoes that you will want

to give away at the end
                    of July.

When all the words that could be said
                              had been, when all
the verbs that could be moved
                              were, the mockingbird had to be
invented to remind us to be sure
                    to remember
everything we had wanted
                    to forget. So mockingbirds sing
the same songs each year,
                    and if, in repeating, a wrong note
is sung, mockingbirds know
                    like musicians
or lovers, to sing it again
                    so you think
that they meant it, to keep
                    doing it over
until they get it right.
                    And while they go on believing
that what's repeated long enough
                    does become
right, you lie awake imagining
                    sleep, how it will arrive
at last with the thick, humid scent
                    that remains
when the house is empty of everything
                    but darkness, and one
oblong bud of gardenia
                    spreads its thickened cream.

In the wide hour
                    before dawn, the bird calls
and raises, convinced
                    that the heart's full
deck has been played,
                    that a flush
beats a straight,
                    or two of a kind,

nothing,
            but before sleep moves in
like the final bet
                to be placed, the heart's tattoo
doubles, coaxed on
                    by what remains: memory's cadenza
of roses
        that go on climbing in the absence
of any frame, absence
                        dragged in and out
of the beak
            like song.

You Stand There Fishing

When the sun decides to comment
on the day, you are the first thing
it points to.

You are the one fact the waters refuse
to deny, and so they swerve around you
willingly, clasping your thighs.

In fact, this entire implacable river
flinging itself from side to side
takes the very tongue of your flashing whip
down to the bottom of its own desire.

Only the bees
gorging themselves in the clover
seem oblivious, and even they occasionally lift
their dripping chins and manage
a few dizzy hosannas.

I am already waist deep when you call my name—
halfway out to your swirling array
of lines and hooks, and as I float
toward you, lids gliding down over my eyes,
even the trout loosen their gazes
and rise.

WILLIAM EVERSON

William Everson was born in 1912, in Selma, a San Joaquin Valley town near Fresno. There he discovered the poetry of Robinson Jeffers and embarked on a poetic vocation that would span sixty years. Everson tended grapes with his wife on a small farm until World War II brought an end to both his marriage and his life in the Central Valley. He spent over three years interned at a camp for conscientious objectors at Waldport, Oregon, where he helped found the Untide Press and began his work as a fine printer. In 1948 Everson converted to Catholicism. He entered the Dominican order, and for nearly twenty years wrote religious poetry as Brother Antoninus. In 1969 Everson left the Dominicans to marry. He served as poet-in-residence at the University of California, Santa Cruz, where he gave his seminal *Birth of a Poet* lectures and created several masterpieces of fine printing at the Lime Kiln Press. Parkinson's disease forced his retirement from the university, but he continued to write and to inspire poets and printers alike. He was the author of some fifty books of poetry and criticism, including *Archetype West: The Pacific Coast as a Literary Region*. He died in 1994 at his home at Kingfisher Flat in the Santa Cruz Mountains.

A Canticle to the Waterbirds

Clack your beaks you cormorants and kittiwakes,
North on those rock-croppings finger-jutted into the rough Pacific surge;
You migratory terns and pipers who leave but the temporal clawtrack written on sandbars there of your presence;
Grebes and pelicans; you comber-picking scoters and you shorelong gulls;
All you keepers of the coastline north of here to the Mendocino beaches;
All you beyond upon the cliff-face thwarting the surf at Hecate Head;
Hovering the under-surge where the cold Columbia grapples at the bar;
North yet to the Sound, whose islands float like a sown flurry of chips upon the sea;

Break wide your harsh and salt-encrusted beaks unmade for song
And say a praise up to the Lord.

And you freshwater egrets east in the flooded marshlands skirting the sea-
level rivers, white one-legged watchers of shallows;
Broad-headed kingfishers minnow-hunting from willow stems on mean-
dering valley sloughs;
You too, you herons, blue and supple-throated, stately, taking the air majes-
tical in the sunflooded San Joaquin,
Grading down on your belted wings from the upper lights of sunset,
Mating over the willow clumps or where the flatwater rice fields shimmer;
You killdeer, high night-criers, far in the moon-suffusion sky;
Bitterns, sand-waders, all shore-walkers, all roost-keepers,
Populates of the 'dobe cliffs of the Sacramento:
Open your water-dartling beaks,
And make a praise up to the Lord.

For you hold the heart of His mighty fastnesses,
And shape the life of His indeterminate realms.
You are everywhere on the lonesome shores of His wide creation.
You keep seclusion where no man may go, giving Him praise;
Nor may a woman come to lift like your cleaving flight her clear contralto
song
To honor the spindrift gifts of His soft abundance.
You sanctify His hermitage rocks where no holy priest may kneel to adore,
nor holy nun assist;
And where His true communion-keepers are not enabled to enter.

And well may you say His praises, birds, for your ways
Are verved with the secret skills of His inclinations,
And your habits plaited and rare with the subdued elaboration of His intri-
cate craft;
Your days intent with the direct astuteness needful for His outworking,
And your nights alive with the dense repose of His infinite sleep.
You are His secretive charges and you serve His secretive ends,
In His clouded, mist-conditioned stations, in His murk,
Obscure in your matted nestings, immured in His limitless ranges.
He makes you penetrate through dark interstitial joinings of His thicketed
kingdoms,
And keep your concourse in the deeps of His shadowed world.

Your ways are wild but earnest, your manners grave,

Your customs carefully schooled to the note of His serious mien.
You hold the prime condition of His clean creating,
And the swift compliance with which you serve His minor means
Speaks of the constancy with which you hold Him.
For what is your high flight forever going home to your first beginnings,
But such a testament to your devotion?
You hold His outstretched world beneath your wings, and mount upon His
storms,
And keep your sheer wind-lidded sight upon the vast perspectives of His
mazy latitudes.

But mostly it is your way you bear existence wholly within the context of
His utter will and are untroubled.
Day upon day you do not reckon, nor scrutinize tomorrow, nor multiply the
nightfalls with a rash concern,
But rather assume each instant as warrant sufficient of His final seal.
Wholly in Providence you spring, and when you die you look on death in
clarity unflinched,
Go down, a clutch of feather ragged upon the brush;
Or drop on water where you briefly lived, found food,
And now yourselves made food for His deep current-keeping fish, and then
are gone:
Is left but the pinion-feather spinning a bit on the uproil
Where lately the dorsal cut clear air.

You leave a silence. And this for you suffices, who are not of the ceremonials
of man,
And hence are not made sad to now forgo them.
Yours is of another order of being, and wholly it compels.

But may you, birds, utterly seized in God's supremacy,
Austerely living under His austere eye—
Yet may you teach a man a necessary thing to know,
Which has to do of the strict conformity that creaturehood entails,
And constitutes the prime commitment all things share.
For God has given you the imponderable grace to *be* His verification,
Outside the mulled incertitude of our forensic choices;
That you, our lessers in the rich hegemony of Being,
May serve as testament to what a creature is,
And what creation owes.

Curlews, stilts and scissortails, beachcomber gulls,
Wave-haunters, shore-keepers, rockhead-holders, all cape-top vigilantes,
Now give God praise.
Send up the strict articulation of your throats,
And say His name.

The High Embrace

They stand in the clearing of Kingfisher Flat,
Twin giants, *sequoia sempervirens,* the ever-vernal,
And take in the arms of their upper branches
The last light crossing the bench-ridge west,
Sinking toward dusk.

   Standing between them
I look up the double-columned space to the soaring crown,
Where those red-ribbed branches clasp each other in a high embrace.
For hundreds of years they have stood here, serenely apart,
Drinking clear creek water through sequaceous pores,
Feeling the flake of mountains sift chalkstone gravel about their boles,
Watching giant grizzlies scoop gravid salmon on the spawning bars below,
And tawny cougars stalk for fawns in their leaf-dappled shade.
They heard the kingfisher chirr his erratic intemperate cry,
While over their tops the slow-wheeling condors circled the sun,
Drifting south to their immemorial roosting ledges in the Los Padres peaks.
And they felt the demon of fire lick its running tongue up their shaggy skin
And not flinched, scorched but unscarred in the long warfare,
The stress-tension shaping fuel to fire,
The life-flux of their kind.

   Tonight,
In the heat of the drought, we will forsake our bed,
Shutting the house-presence out of our thought,
Taking our respite in the open air. We will muse late,
And lay ourselves down by fir-bark embers,
Under the cape of the twin redwoods, swept back in time
A thousand years when this coast nurtured its kind—
The great beasts, the towering trees, the bird-flight migrations,
The shy coastal tribes. And in the sea-troughs of sleep

Our dreams will mirror the world above
Where stars swim over, and shadow the bloodstream's sibilance,
All through the foliage of the flesh, its fern-like fronds.

Up there above me the last light
Filters in as through stained glass windows,
Diffuse, glowing in the lofts of the upper branches,
Radiant and soft. And the mystery of worship
Descends on me, out of those far fenestrations.
And the God-awe, wake-wonder, envelops me,
Between the monumental straightness of columns
Bearing the sky, illuminate zone, twin towers
Conjoined above, clasped in the high embrace,
The soaring arch.

                    And the face of my son
Dawns between the gigantic boles
As he runs to meet me. And I ask in my heart
The graciousness of God, that he may grow in their presence,
As the tan-oak grows, as the fir-tree and fern,
As the chipmunk and the jay shelter under their span.

And I invoke their mystery of survival,
That the lightning-shattering years,
And the raw surge of fire,
May skim but not scar him—
As they themselves are scathed but unscarred—
Through the skip years of his childhood
And the leap years of his youth.

Make over our heads, then, the high embrace,
Like a blessing, the numinous descent, faith-fall,
Out of the heights, the leaf-light canopy,
The lofts of God, induplicate,
A gift regiven, the boon bestowed.

PETER EVERWINE

© Pat Wolk

Peter Everwine was raised in western Pennsylvania and educated in the Midwest. In 1962 he began a teaching career at California State University, Fresno. His books of poetry and translations include *Collecting the Animals, Keeping the Night, In the House of Light*, and *The Static Element*.

"Not long after I came to Fresno, transplanted from Pennsylvania and the Midwest, an old man took me into the upper reaches of the San Joaquin River in the Sierra. Long familiar with those mountains, he had found a way to reach an almost inaccessible section of the river, traveling cross-country through steep and difficult terrain. To guide himself he had placed, at odd intervals, a small stone marker that was all but invisible unless one deliberately looked for it. Even so, on later trips without him, I was often lost, blind to the marker or following a stone that led nowhere. The final marker lay close to a narrow granite chimney where he had made a ladder out of tree limbs and wire. Below this, a low shelf opened out to the river and his camp. From the first moment, I knew I had been given a rare gift.

"Over the years I often went back, in good weather and bad, sometimes alone, often with close friends, in time with my sons. We called it simply The Canyon, and to me it was not only our secret place-name but also an increasingly rich store of familiar rituals and wonderous moments. On one occasion the trees around the camp suddenly filled with countless numbers of gold finches, each one a tiny nervous flare of sunlight. I never again saw them, and now, years later, they seem more dream than fact.

"A place reveals itself slowly, if at all, and never completely. Something imminent draws us, and if a sense of place enters a poet's work then surely memory and desire are as close and as necessary as the eye's immediacy or the pronouncements of the tongue. In such a process, place and poem are interdependent, even if one is the shadow world of the other.

"Whitney Balliett once said of Lester Young: 'He kept the melodies in his head, but what came out was his dreams about them.' Change the context slightly: place as a given, poem as the dream about place. Then give Lester the last word: You have to tell a story."

Distance

The light pulling away from trees,
the trees speaking in shadows
to whatever listens...

Something as common as water
turns away from our faces
and leaves.

The stars rise out of the hills
—old kings and animals
marching in their thin tunnels of light.

Once more I find myself
standing as on a dark pier, holding
an enormous rope of silence.

From the Meadow

It isn't that you were ignorant:
star thistle, bloodroot, cruciform—
beautiful words, then as now,
unlike pain with its wooden alphabet,
its many illustrations, which are redundant.

You had imagined vistas, an open meadow:
on the far side, water trembles its lights;
cattle come down to their shadow lives
beneath the trees;
the language of childhood is invented anew.

But now you know, right? what lies ahead
is nothing to the view behind?
How breathtaking these nostalgias rising
like hazy constellations overhead!—

little to go by, surely,
though from the meadow where you stand looking
over your shoulder, that tiny figure you see
seems to be calling someone,
you perhaps.

Gray Poem

1

Another gray morning
in this month of valley fog.
Everything seems old, little threads and roots
sucking a cold sea.

When I look into it, the mirror
cups my face in its silver hands.
I hear my grandmother whispering
beneath her shawl—

Cloth of forgetfulness
Skull of the one night
Shag of wisdom
White grass of misery

In the yards, our children
are turning into clouds.

2

There are times when I shut my eyes.
I stand in a place
from which journeys are forever beginning—

in the distance
a small feather of smoke, a haze
where the earth falls off.

3

Now that I'm this far,
I've come to like things weathered—
all that is whipped and polished by wind
to the color of shirts hanging
in poor backyards,
the fever a long time in the slabs of barns,
water rubbing the first light,
salt crust of meat for a long march.

I think of the twilight's gray eyes—
they are so beautiful,
so grave with a longing I never quite understand.

4

The window darkens.
A man bends over me
and kisses my cheek.

When the sun rose, he says,
I turned up my hands to the light,
Every road was on fire.

I call him father.
He is gray
and his shoes are gray.

Just Before Sleep

In the poem that comes just before sleep,
I am walking out into
the darkness of summer fields,
drawing it close about me.
What I wanted to say
was the silence of olive groves,
the longing of a road white with dust.
I speak an old language, love—
the fields rising and falling,
the small beards of light
nodding over the earth.
I am entering your hair,
coming home.

Perhaps It's as You Say

Perhaps it's as you say
That nothing stays lost forever

How many times have I said No No
There is a darkness in the cell

And opened my hands to cup emptiness
Tasting its bitten face

I do not know if our loves survive us
Waiting through the long night for our step

Or if they will know us then
Entering our flesh with the old sigh

I do not know
But I think of fields that stretch away flat

Beneath the stars their dry grasses
Gathering a light of honey

The few houses wink and go out
Across the fields an asphalt road darkens

And disappears among the cottonwoods by the dry creek
It is so quiet so quiet

Meet me there

KATHY FAGAN

Kathy Fagan is the author of *MOVING & ST RAGE* (University of North Texas Press, 1999), winner of the Vassar Miller Prize for Poetry, and *The Raft* (Dutton, 1985), a National Poetry Series selection. She has received fellowships from the NEA, the Ingram Merrill Foundation, and the Ohio Arts Council. She currently teaches in the M.F.A. Program at Ohio State University, where she also co-edits *The Journal*.

© A. Estes

"Living in California intermittently as I do—for fourteen years now, primarily on the central coast and in Fresno—I have mixed emotions about calling the place 'home.' While I feel genuine, sometimes overwhelming affection for it—for its valleys, deserts, beaches, and mountains, for its towns and cities, for its malls and freeways alike—I have never developed any sense of belonging here. And it's precisely that distance, I think, that's been best for my work. It's in the California spirit, after all, to constantly re-invent oneself. In my writing life, as a kind of exile—an exile *of* and *from* California—California, the real and imaginary place, is most importantly alternative, even anti-home. It's the edge and surprise here, and what strikes me as California's infinite exotica, that helps keep me awake, attentive to language, to landscape, and to soul."

California, *She Replied*

It's driving into all that goldness makes
You blind, *she said*. The road oats, timothy,
The mustard hung beside the highway like
So many crowns thrown out, *she said*. That ma-
Ma cow who cools her thin blond ankles in
A shiny ditch? Her baby's bones hurt—it's
The newness. Poplars, too, they have their secrets
With each other. Seen them at it in my
Rearview, whisperin where the smoke trees get to
Once the mist's burnt off. Why, I was in a
'Nother country by the time I knew, myself,

Where I live comfortably, to this day,
She ended, without question.

Desire

How the melody of a single ice cream truck
can rise from the streets of your city
and bring with it every year you have ever known.
How it can bring forth children
and the promise that has always belonged to them
and the shining dimes and the rush of icy vapors
from the truck's freezer to the sky.
How it rises past the green froth of maple leaves
to your window as if to say, *Summer already,*
here for you and haven't they always been?
And haven't you given each one of them away,
your arms lifted, your mouth opened
for the cool winds of October?
Yes, you think, on the other side of the country
in the long tanned valleys of California,
the fiddlehead curls upon itself and crows pull
every living morsel from the soft ground.
And farther west, on the warming coastal rocks
of the Pacific, crabs raise their one good arm
to the sun—like the farmer in China you imagine
or the dusty pistils of tulips in Europe. But you
have to be here, listening to an incessant song and children
who want, who want, no more and no less than yourself.
Tell your sorrow to the gulls that flail outside
your window, too far inland for their own good.
They could be at any shore but they are here
and isn't that all they're good for:
to be screamed at, to scream back?
Tell it to the man who shares your bed
and he will weight his head more deeply
into his pillow, touching your hand out of habit,
taking you ever farther from the life you wanted
as if you ever wanted a life, as if your many mounting desires
led to no more than the final consolation of silence

and the long dreamless sleep of those who hunger for nothing.
That is the lie we tell ourselves—that we can do without
this life. For if night darkened our eyes and our very hearts
turned cold as the moon, then wouldn't you
take it all back if you could? Three thin dimes in your pocket
and the music of a truck close to your ear and the summer
already moist in your armpits—don't you want to wrap your lips
around the melting sweetness of it? Won't you pay
and keep paying for as long as you must, to know
it belongs, has always belonged, to you?

In California

one either believes in God
or believes one is
God. Like the freeway, you can't drive on
both sides at once.
Medians themselves are horticultural
phenomena. And from every direction there is
vista, there is grande.
There are places called
Vista Grande.
I have seen them myself,
have the photos to prove it.
I have stepped from my car in a glockenspiel
shirtfront and conducted
orchestras.
I have held in my hand a baton of sky,
while the hills looped gold
green silver black,
and the automatic tollbooths rang and rang,
lifting and letting fall
their braceleted arms.

In California there is more
land than ocean; we will not
discuss then, in this poem, the ocean.
Let us place coins where its eyes used to be
and insist instead,

as wisteria insists—
the insistent part of the wisteria—on
architecture. Consider
the bungalow, the overpass, the balcony
balustrade as muscular as any Mister
Atlas, tiny kites wound
round his triceps. And the palms:
it's not just headdresses with them
but mufflers, full-length
raccoon coats, that trailing
perfume of fennel and sage, a dust
that will not dust
off. Not off the palm, not off the grape,
not off the live oak or
the dead. Rolling the piers and streets and orchards,
only the fog can slick it down.

I take it back
about the kites. I see now the five points,
the pentagons of morning
glory choking the balcony,
and potted nasturtiums on the landing
gleaming. How our grandmothers favored them,
the old flowers, old edible
flowers. Like the old
stories, they have it all:
feet of clay, suits of mail,
coats of brine, hoops of gold....

Red Aster, who made you?
The Sun made me.
And who, Red Aster, ringed you with gold?
You have, Maestro, who planted me here.

DANA GIOIA

Dana Gioia is a poet, critic, trans-
lator, and anthologist. A contribu-
tor to *The New Yorker, The Hudson
Review, Poetry,* and *The Atlantic
Monthly,* Gioia was born and
raised in Los Angeles but spent
twenty years in New York (mostly
working as a businessman) before
returning to the West Coast in
1996. A full-time writer, Gioia
now lives in Sonoma County.

© *Star Black*

"A California poet almost in-
evitably feels the competing claims
of language and experience. I am
Latin (Italian, Mexican, and
American Indian) without a drop
of British blood in my veins, but English is my tongue. It belongs to me as
much as to any member of the House of Lords. The classics of English—
Shakespeare, Milton, Pope, and Keats—are my classics. The myths and im-
ages of its literature are native to my imagination. And yet this rich literary
past often stands at one remove from the experiential reality of the West. Our
seasons, climate, landscape, natural life, and history are alien to the world-
views of both England and New England. Spanish—not French—colors our
regional accent. The world looks and feels different in California from the
way it does in Massachusetts or Manchester—not only the natural landscape
but also the urban one. There is no use listening for a nightingale among the
scrub oaks and chaparral. Our challenge is not only to find the right words to
describe our experience but also to discover the right images, myths, and
characters. We must describe a reality that has never been fully captured in
English. Yet the earlier traditions of English help clarify what it is we might
say. California poetry is our conversation between the past and present out of
which we articulate ourselves.

"I was born and raised in Hawthorne, California, a tough working-class
town in southwest Los Angeles. Hawthorne was also my mother's home-
town. (Her mestizo father had fled his reservation in New Mexico to settle on
the West Coast.) My father's family had immigrated from Sicily at the turn of
the century and gradually made their way west. Surrounded by Italian-
speaking relations, I grew up in a neighborhood populated mostly by
Mexicans and Dust Bowl Okies. I attended Catholic schools at a time when
Latin was still a living ritual language. Having experienced this rich linguistic
and cultural milieu, I have never given credence to Easterners who prattle
about the intellectual vacuity of Southern California. Mine was a rich Latin
childhood, a mixture of European, Central American, Indian, and North

American culture, in which everything from Hollywood to the Vatican had its place.

"My adult life has comprised equal parts of wanderlust and homesickness. The first journey, from L.A. to Stanford, still feels like the farthest since I was leaving the world of the working-class and immigrant family for parts unknown. Since then I have lived in Vienna, Boston, Rome, Minneapolis, and New York, but I always called myself a Californian. I always knew I would return. In 1977 I went to New York with my girlfriend (now my wife), planning to stay two years. We remained for nearly two decades. In 1996 we finally returned to live in rural Sonoma County. It is too easy in our society for an artist to become rootless, but I believe that it is essential for some writers to maintain their regional identities—to speak from a particular place and time. What a pleasure and challenge it is to speak from California."

Cruising with the Beachboys

So strange to hear that song again tonight
Travelling on business in a rented car
Miles from anywhere I've been before.
And now a tune I haven't heard for years
Probably not since it last left the charts
Back in L.A. in 1969.
I can't believe I know the words by heart
And can't think of a girl to blame them on.

Every lovesick summer has its song,
And this one I pretended to despise,
But if I was alone when it came on,
I turned it up full-blast to sing along—
A primal scream in croaky baritone,
The notes all flat, the lyrics mostly slurred.
No wonder I spent so much time alone
Making the rounds in Dad's old Thunderbird.

Some nights I drove down to the beach to park
And walk along the railings of the pier,
The water down below was cold and dark,
The waves monotonous against the shore.
The darkness and the mist, the midnight sea,
The flickering lights reflected from the city—
A perfect setting for a boy like me,
The Cecil B. DeMille of my self-pity.

I thought by now I'd left those nights behind,
Lost like the girls that I could never get,
Gone with the years, junked with the old T-Bird.
But one old song, a stretch of empty road,
Can open up a door and let them fall
Tumbling like boxes from a dusty shelf,
Tightening my throat for no reason at all
Bringing on tears shed only for myself.

Becoming a Redwood

Stand in a field long enough, and the sounds
start up again. The crickets, the invisible
toad who claims that change is possible,

And all the other life too small to name.
First one, then another, until innumerable
they merge into the single voice of a summer hill.

Yes, it's hard to stand still, hour after hour,
fixed as a fencepost, hearing the steers
snort in the dark pasture, smelling the manure.

And paralyzed by the mystery of how a stone
can bear to be a stone, the pain
the grass endures breaking through the earth's crust.

Unimaginable the redwoods on the far hill,
rooted for centuries, the living wood grown tall
and thickened with a hundred thousand days of light.

The old windmill creaks in perfect time
to the wind shaking the miles of pasture grass,
and the last farmhouse light goes off.

Something moves nearby. Coyotes hunt
these hills and packs of feral dogs.
But standing here at night accepts all that.

You are your own pale shadow in the quarter moon,
moving more slowly than the crippled stars,
part of the moonlight as the moonlight falls,

Part of the grass that answers the wind,
part of the midnight's watchfulness that knows
there is no silence but when danger comes.

In Chandler Country

California night. The Devil's wind,
the Santa Ana, blows in from the east,
raging through the canyon like a drunk
screaming in a bar.
                            The air tastes like
a stubbed-out cigarette. But why complain?
The weather's fine as long as you don't breathe.
Just lean back on the sweat-stained furniture,
lights turned out, windows shut against the storm,
and count your blessings.
                            Another sleepless night
when every wrinkle in the bedsheet scratches
like a dry razor on a sunburned cheek,
when even ten-year whiskey tastes like sand,
and quiet women in the kitchen run
their fingers on the edges of a knife
and eye their husband's necks. I wish them luck.

Tonight it seems that if I took the coins
out of my pocket and tossed them in the air
they'd stay a moment glistening like a net
slowly falling through dark water.
                            I remember
the headlights of the cars parked on the beach,
the narrow beams dissolving on the dark
surface of the lake, voices arguing
about the forms, the crackling radio,
the sheeted body lying on the sand,
the trawling net still damp beside it. No,
she wasn't beautiful—but at that age
when youth itself becomes a kind of beauty—
"Taking good care of your clients, Marlowe?"

Relentlessly the wind blows on. Next door
catching a scent, the dogs begin to howl.
Lean, furious, raw-eyed from the storm,
packs of coyotes come down from the hills
where there is nothing left to hunt.

Planting a Sequoia

All afternoon my brothers and I have worked in the orchard,
Digging this hole, laying you into it, carefully packing the soil.
Rain blackened the horizon, but cold winds kept it over the Pacific,
And the sky above us stayed the dull gray
Of an old year coming to an end.

In Sicily a father plants a tree to celebrate his first son's birth—
An olive or a fig tree—a sign that the earth has one more life to bear.
I would have done the same, proudly laying new stock into my father's
    orchard,
A green sapling rising among the twisted apple boughs,
A promise of new fruit in other autumns.

But today we kneel in the cold planting you, our native giant,
Defying the practical custom of our fathers,
Wrapping in your roots a lock of hair, a piece of an infant's birth cord,
All that remains above earth of a first-born son,
A few stray atoms brought back to the elements.

We will give you what we can—our labor and our soil,
Water drawn from the earth when the skies fail,
Nights scented with the ocean fog, days softened by the circuit of bees.
We plant you in the corner of the grove, bathed in western light,
A slender shoot against the sunset.

And when our family is no more, all of his unborn brothers dead,
Every niece and nephew scattered, the house torn down,
His mother's beauty ashes in the air,
I want you to stand among strangers, all young and ephemeral to you,
Silently keeping the secret of your birth.

RIGOBERTO GONZÁLEZ

Rigoberto González received an M.A. from the University of California, Davis, and an M.F.A. from Arizona State University. His first book of poems, *So Often the Pitcher Goes to Water until It Breaks,* was a 1998 National Poetry Series Selection. His work also appears in the anthology *The Floating Borderlands: Twenty-Five Years of Hispanic Literature in the U.S.*

"I was born in Bakersfield, California, the son and grandson of migrant farm workers. From the age of six through high school,

I spent most summers with my family picking grapes, onion, green beans, and other fruits and vegetables within the Coachella Valley in Southern California. We lived so close to the U.S.-México border that we crossed back and forth frequently. The inhabitants of this meeting ground between the two countries haunted me more than the oppressive heat and farm labor. Who were these people and how was I one of them? The border did not separate or distinguish bodies and landscapes—it blurred and overlapped them. My California was not the sun and the crops that grew beneath it, but the sweat and the people that endured the pain of working the land."

Marías, Old Indian Mothers

Las Marías, our Indian mothers, have
disappeared. At the U.S.-México border, they used to walk
between our cars, with one child
attached to the ends of their braids
and four others peeling off
from their skirts like patches, like over-bellied pockets.

They used to hold up plastic cups for our coins,
closing their eyes with each thank you, offering
blessings too weak to take home.
Where did these women come from,

whose child-lumped backs trail off
into our rear view mirrors like ghosts or visions

from some long-ago vacation?
Are they from a hidden Mexican village
only the National Geographic could find?
Then how did they get here? Are they
husbandless, or are they married to that pair
of sandals too tight to let them walk far, too large

to fit back into the narrow pathways
of uncharted towns? Have they slept under newspaper
headlines to produce such sorry-eyed children
that yawn away each minute, meatless as
a bone? When the children are old enough,
they'll learn to stretch their toes

into their mothers' footprints, each foot
cross-flat and empty as their supper plate.
Some of these children will wander
out of the lines and get lost, searching
for their missing mothers. Some of them
will lag behind, checking under vehicles,

and inside policemen's boots, attempting
to detect the echo of the plastic cups.
People say the women found the same wind
that flew them here; the children were too heavy-eyed
to fly. Others say that the foreigners took them
and stuffed them, and dust them weekly

at city museums. And some say, the women simply
died, leaving nothing to the streets
except the smell of copper and the sound
of an arm coming down. But you and I know
they are indestructible, built to last
at least a century or two, rattling our coins

like pits, tolling our lucky
appetites. You and I know they are
where we last left them, waiting for us
to sew our hands back onto their skirts.

These Indian women have never gone
beyond our reach; it is we who have kept our arms

inside our cars and driven off
through that gate that divides us in half,
where we exchange our names, our eyes.
Now no one calls to us to look
back. Here, there is no one to lose—
there's no reason left to believe we have mothers.

Penny Men

for Emiliano, who came to live, and die, picking grapes

These are the men from México's boot, the ones
who fell out from a hole in its bottom. They are bony
but well-attached as scissors. When they become
hungrier, they will cut their own stomachs
in half. They come to live like loose change

in a country that drops its pennies
and leaves them there; in a country whose jingle
of coins muffles the sound of backbones cracking.
These men squeezed through the gate, that slot,
and found the backroads with crosses

on which the grapevines wave their leaves
like dollar bills. Green, edible, the vineyards
promise to feed—to stuff—their pockets
though the cups of wine aren't theirs
to drink. Thirst concerns the boss no more than heat,

nor how much of it garlands each head.
After work, their faces glow sun-flat; they resemble
copper centenarios with dust instead of a bridge
over the nose, with a rust-heavy hinge for a mouth.
These faces promise to reveal exotic lands

and languages. But the bridges are impassable,
distant as the waters of a river on a map,
and the tongues are too tired to speak.

They sit beneath the pines for shade,
their heat-suffused hair steaming off. Precipitations

of sweat clean off their arms, those thin pokers
that stir the ash all day. They express no
criticism here, no shame. Their ears build up dirt
into stones inside their wells, at times confusing
the memory of a woman who speaks inside their sleep.

To stretch out the afternoon breeze, they play
blackjack and twenty-one, gambling bottle caps
instead of silver. Slowly, the darkness in their eyes
blends with the shadows; the sparkle of the caps
and beer can tabs ascends into the canopy of sky.

Beds are too luxurious; back seats too cramped
and sticky in summer. Some men prefer cool car hoods,
their own hands for pillows, the privacy of twilight.
The moon, their second mother, knits their sleeping
coats, which always fade away with stars.

Some dawns, not all the men wake up so quickly.
One man might sink too deep in dreams, clinging
to the woman he wishes he had never left—the woman
who throws her voice toward the North, whose words
stir up a breeze for all the men below.

You and the Tijuana Mule

They're the dead ends
at this avenue's corners,
turning away the traffic
of tourists. They amuse only once
like a firehydrant in green
or an inside-out calf at the butcher's.

But this joke is more perverse:
the light pole painter's solution
to an excess of thick black, cream
and olive: stripes on mules—zebras!

Static as carousel horses
off the platform, they're heavier

at the belly, gravity
finally keeping their viscera
down; the rhythm of their head-shaking
is erratic, it's the wild hair
at the tail-tips. Each mule is irreplicable
in a coat of hand-painted stripes.

Take a second look. Next
to each mule stands a man.
Ignore his camera, forget about his
FIVE DOLLARS FOR A PICTURE.
Focus instead on his outline—
one-dimensional as a figure in chalk,

an upright paper cut-out.
Work your way outward to the fumes
melting the blue in the sky,
to the exhaust pipes and the glare
of cracked windshields, to the mule
taking away the eye from the dull

colors on the building behind it
and from the light pole in front.
If you follow further to the left,
you'll reach another mule.
Further on you'll find an entire pack
of cars, filtering out the gate

and across the border at donkey
speed. But you don't need to go
that far to consider this: this corner
is a vanishing point, the absence
of the man leaves a hole sucking up
concrete, flesh and air, like a drain.

And you are avoiding it,
scurrying off as far north as you can, turning
only to see how far you've gotten.
Put the man back in like a plug.

Let him stop the pull, sinking in
like a drenched rag in the mouth

of a gas tank. In one hundred degrees of heat,
let him be more threatening. Pay him
five dollars, take your picture next to
(or on) the mule. Place yourself
within the man's breathing space and wonder
why you shudder in the middle of June.

JANICE GOULD

Janice Gould has published two volumes of poetry, *Beneath My Heart* (Firebrand, 1990) and *Earthquake Weather* (University of Arizona, 1996). She is also the author of a chapbook/artbook entitled *Alphabet* (May Day, 1996). She lives in Portland, Oregon, where she is working on a new manuscript of poetry, teaching creative writing, and assiduously studying classical guitar.

© Margaret Randall

"The landscape of the north coast, the Sacramento Valley, and the northern Sierra Nevada is a map for me. The network of back roads, dirt roads, trails, and paths that lead to creeks or lakes, through oak groves or mixed conifer forests, is a constant part of my memory of California. The north part of the state is where I grew up and spent most of my life. I've always felt that my memory of California, my imaginative landscape, is not entirely my own but is embedded in the memory of many tribal people, my own tribe, the Koyangk'auwi Maidu, and in the other small nations of Indian people who inhabited California before it was ever named and was still Turtle Island."

Earthquake Weather

It's earthquake weather in California,
that hazy stillness along the coast
just before the Santa Anas howl
out of the east, hot and dry.

There were days in September when we drove
down the fault line south of Hayward.
We went where there were Spanish names:
Suñol and Calaveras,
la Misión de San José.
I remember seeing the cells of the padres,
their faded vestments,
the implements of wood and iron.

We were looking for another country,
something not North America:

a taste, a smell, a solitary image—
the eucalyptus on a bleached hill.
Its blue pungent leaves made you long
for another home.

That was what you wanted from me—
to be your other home,
your other country.
Being Indian, I was your *cholo*
from the Bolivian highlands.
I was your boy, full of stone
and a cold sunset.

At night, seated at your bedside,
I was remote. I often made you weep—
you in the guise of an *angelita*.
You lay on the low mattress,
a weaving beneath your head,
and watched me with your slow eyes,
your sadness.

When September comes with its hot,
electric winds,
I will think of you and know
somewhere in the world
the earth is breaking open.

Easter Sunday

Easter Sunday and my father plans a visit to one of the old missions along the Camino Real. After church we get on the highway and begin our journey. It is late March or early April. The sky is azure and clouds scud in from the Pacific, thick and white. They break apart as they pass over the coast range, and the broken fragments, still large, move swiftly over the land. The land is green, not the green of Germany as I have heard it reported, but a green full of sunlight and rapid change. If the winter and spring rains have been sufficient, the presence of last year's grasses will be hidden, their gray stalks covered by fresh growth. This spring the sturdy flowers have opened, and my mother reels off the endless list of names as we pass them by: lupine, California poppy, clarkia, larkspur, Indian paintbrush, owl's clover, buttercup, vetch, trillium, forget-me-not, columbine, fairy's lantern, pearly everlasting. The species are so mixed we hardly know the indigenous from the introduced, the native from the volunteer, the survivor from the parasite populations that have sprung up in the friendly habitat. This is California with its rich, false history. Whatever direction one goes, north or south, the flowers mark boundaries, the possibility of their appearance determined by many things: hills or gullies, rainfall or drought, ranches or subdivisions, the presence of other like-minded plants and trees.

We drive far south to the mission in the Los Padres Mountains. Here, at the far end of a long, fertile valley, the military has established a base. It is difficult to understand the need for weapons or to feel cheered by the hard-faced, uniformed men, armored vehicles, and what appear to be the underground houses for missiles. No one wants to talk about the war, which explodes somewhere else with wearisome regularity each night on television. It is Sunday, Easter; the family is enjoying a rare peace. The day is beautiful and the hills sacred. It is hard to imagine destruction. At the mission, the enclosed courtyard is dry and warm, bees buzz among the cactus and purple roses. In the small adobe cells, opened for our inspection, are the accoutrements of the Franciscans, solemn crucifixes nailed above their skinny beds. In other rooms the Indians worked, tanning leather, shoeing horses, cooking the padres' soup. In these troughs, the Indians were fed. Beyond the mission are the remnants of *hornos* and corrals, the fields of wild bulbs and clover the Indians longed to eat. Under one portico, a shiver moves up my spine: the dead, I know suddenly, are buried in the walls, among the arches, and beneath this well-tamped earth.

Across the mountains, not far as the raven flies, lies the ocean, the jagged edge of the continent.

I Learn a Lesson About Our Society

Late November on our way to work
you pulled the cord and the bus stopped
this side of the Alameda tube.
"I've got to get out of here,"
you told me abruptly.
"Please, don't follow me."
I looked in your face

but you wouldn't look back.
You were nervous,
your eyes moving everywhere.
"I'll phone," you said.
I watched you push your way
through the press of students,
secretaries, the eight a.m.
crowd on their way to work.
Eyes glazed, you stepped off the bus.

I didn't know then it was epilepsy
that jerked you to your feet,
and like a pistol against the skull,
compelled you to walk,
walk, making your way to 14th Avenue,
your jaw clamped as if it had been wired closed.
You knew places where you could abort the attack
with heroin: back porches
where men of every color shot up,
a hard gang of hard-asses, and you,
skinny and tough as the boy
you wished you could be.
Those were times of no time for you,
weeklong blackouts in which you lost
all trace of your history,
name, or family.
Your kids would be alone in the house,
eating cold hot dogs and white bread.
They were used to taking care of themselves.

After an attack, you woke here or there
and had to find your way home.
Sometimes you came to on the stone
cold floor of a cell.
Other times, like that day,
you ended up in the hospital
on some ward in the basement,
strapped down on a table.
The nurses and orderlies abused you,
kept the restraints on you for hours.
They despised you for being an addict,

a queer, at the mercy
of an illness.

It was then I learned things
I never knew before: that privilege
is a form of ignorance,
that the poor are the enemy of the state.
And not the poor alone, but the sick,
criminal, crazy, queer, young,
old, and disabled.
No matter what color we are,
no matter what language we speak.
Every person, I suppose, must come
to this understanding: it's not your right
to question the police, the army,
any number of authorities.
If you pass, sucker,
it's because they let you pass.

And I have you to thank for this, my friend,
though in the end we broke up like any couple
where jealousy is involved.
I, who thought I was so butch,
got tired of playing mistress
to your drugs. You were married
to a poison you loved
almost better than life itself.

It happened three weeks later,
Christmas nearly upon us,
fake ice in the windows, fake snow,
and the yellow glare of lights
around the lots of cut trees.
The usual cold fog
had rolled down from Sacramento.
Out on the Nimitz freeway
you began to pound my arm.
"Oh please, goddamn it,
please," you kept saying.
Then you cracked the windshield
with your fist, and I took

the next exit, obedient,
while you directed me to the house
on that particular dirty street.
I waited in the car watching the children,
the drunks, listening to sirens,
jet noise, the freeway.

When you came out you were happy,
calm as a butterfly
who had closed her wings.

FORREST HAMER

Forrest Hamer is an Oakland psychologist, candidate psychoanalyst, and lecturer at the University of California, Berkeley. His first book of poems, *Call & Response* (Alice James Books, 1995), won the Beatrice Hawley Award.

"I've lived in the Bay Area for twenty years, arriving here for graduate school with plans soon after to return to the East Coast. I found my home here, a community of people who've chosen this place to find each other, and I've found a place that allows me to write not only about my life here, but about growing up mostly in the rural South. Perhaps it is the contrasts in landscape, in climate, the history and the racial composition of its people, that California is westward to another ocean, which allows me to find all of my homes here. Or perhaps it is that when I fly away from the drunk pines of North Carolina toward the dry brown curves of the northern California hills, the bougainvillea is always so brilliant."

Berkeley, late spring

I'd been browsing the poetry section at Cody's

and as I walked out, the unexpected sun lighted the lips
of everyone in the Friday afternoon crowd along Telegraph,
and I imagined kissing them all: nestling mine
with pouted lips, wrinkling lips, some faded and practical,
others comfortably possessed. Though how funny
folks would think me if they knew, then how rare
in all our lives these reverences are (like being next
to another as they sleep, or rest); imagined what their smells
were, the sun now steaming the air around us:
and if the smells would matter, sweet or rank; decided
then to write of it, save in the spaces between words
elusive want.

and remembered kissing my first girlfriend inside a church
before aching out goodbye; remembered kissing my grandmother

three days dead and laid out for respects all night
before the funeral, her face cool and newly taut, the kiss
protecting me from fearing her spirit come back to sleep
    beside me;
remembered how a lover kissed, his tongue tracing desire
    along rivers
of my body (and now that he is dead, too, the traces make me
    anxious: as if
a spirit—his, or another's—walks with me along this street
and everywhere); remembered how at moments even now
    watching strangers kiss
goodbye leaves my lips just enough warm.

and I noticed that the poems that moved me
had mostly to do with loving and loss and the loss of love
and I wondered when it would be time to be moved by
    other poems
not haunted by fears of wanting and remembering.
And I noticed that this poem is not the one
I thought it'd be because the smells that move along rivers
in our breathing have mattered after all; because spaces
between all these words hold there more complicated wishes
than for casual prayers within a motley crowd.

Origins

Thinking he was asking about race, I told him I was black;
and, thinking he was asking where I come from, I told him
I was from the South and from here in California and, really,
I am from the people I love who love me; and, thinking
he was asking about my sexual orientation, I told him, yes,
I am sexually oriented, especially with some men; then,
thinking he was asking about my religion, I told him I had none
to speak of except for my awe of the spirit; and, hearing
him ask specifically where I was coming from, I told him then
I come from wherever it is strangers tell their lives
in ways far less specific than speaking to each other dreams,
which is how, if I had been thinking, I should have told him
about myself.

The Different Strokes Bar, San Francisco

Maybe I knew it wouldn't last long, that the joys of us
could vanish like ghosts having lost interest.
Maybe I knew there would be more
than the early twenties of this life, the body quicking.
Maybe I could see men dancing themselves invisible,
one by handsome one, that year before they began to go.
So when I told my friend to stop dancing,
stop with me in the middle of the floor and remember this,
how wondrous already it was, I must have known
how easy it is to forget, how easy it is not to notice,
the dancing going on all about
your new and hungry body, you taken away with it.

Charlene-N-Booker 4Ever

And the old men, supervising grown grandsons, nephews,
any man a boy given this chance of making
a new sidewalk outside the apartment building where
some of them live, three old men and their wives,
the aging unmarrying children, and the child
who is a cousin, whose mother has sent her here
because she doesn't know what to do with her,
she's out of control, she wants to be a gangsta, and
the old folks talk to her as if she minds them
and already has that respect for their years her mother
finally grew into. The girl who does not look
like them eats and eats and sleeps late, sneaks away
when they are busy, and tonight will write herself
all over the sidewalk while it is still wet but
the old have gone inside, and the grown gone home,
and her mother who is somewhere overseas thinks of
writing her that long long letter, but decides not to.

MICHAEL HANNON

Michael Hannon was born in Los Angeles in 1939. After graduating from high school in 1956, he served in the United States Air Force until 1960. He published his first book of poetry in 1972. Now entering his sixties, Michael has been widely published in journals and anthologies. He is the author of eleven poetry titles and the publisher of Impermanence Books. He lives with his wife, Nancy Dahl, in Los Osos, California.

"Thoughts rise from The Void and are tempered in the natural world. A native Californian, my first memories are of the sea and its cliffs—the land running out of land into the feminine, frightening and irresistible. My interest in poetry was first awakened by the work of Robinson Jeffers. Eventually I would practice my own version of the philosophical or religious investigation, grounded in the fact of what is. I have lived most of my life on the central coast of the state, near San Luis Obispo. My days and nights pass between the sea and the Coastal Mountain Range—hills really, green in winter, blond in summer. 'Homeless,' 'Subterranean,' and 'Temporary Heart,' are from that familiar country. Another sure source of poems for me, is the Eastern Sierra. 'Beneath Cold Mountain,' 'Beyond Freedom,' and 'Real Estate' have their origins there, where the sudden mountains rise from the desert, like the thoughts of a God made manifest."

Beneath Cold Mountain

for Joe Stroud

Sixty percent of the universe's energy is missing.
Science can't find it. The creek roars all night.

Yesterday, Coyote lay dead on the roadside,
Her corpse silvering in the overcast.
But you and I both know that Coyote's an Immortal,
and waits for us at the foot of Cold Mountain.

In the high country that we love, trails are steep.
We climb each mile, breath by breath,
and at the threshold of pain, bliss overtakes us.

This life on earth, who can say what it is?
On Cold Mountain, Coyote crosses the summit snow
and leaves no trace.

Beyond Freedom

Just short of the pass—juniper and spruce,
water boiling in a stone bowl, cold as it ever was.
The wind saying what the wind always says.

Up above the world, a single butterfly or leaf
turning in the mind's invention—
the day sky so deep, its night shines through.

Cottonwoods in their yellow begging robes,
prayer wheel of the blue locust, and the rockfall
sleeping under stopped waves of granite.

Turning in dream, Earth puts out the sun.
Her stone finger points just there and blots it.
Suspended in the halo, angels of ignorance and dust
are circling the habit of life.

In that wilderness, seeing was all that mattered,
seeing blinded by the eternity in the moment—
a vision of happy death in the serious mountains.

Homeless

In the parking lot where the path to the sea begins,
Impermanence has been living out of an old Chevy van—
frayed lawn chairs, six-pack vertebrae, grey jockey shorts,
and a rusty oil drum, sawed off for fire.

On the beach, white chaos seizes the year's drowned hair,
and lifts it against the wrecked horizon—cold,
county sized cumulous, streamed out and crumbling.

The feral Mexican boys are bathing in chrome,
thralled in Neptune's shock, howling for the sun.
And the sun comes out—tentative at first, just brushing
at crest or slatey trough. Then light, the real thing,
suddenly and at full strength, blinds and reveals.

Homeless...homeless...homeless,
the conscious stones cry out.

Real Estate

In the hall of The Mountain King,
the alders are spending their gold,
gold it is death to spend, and spending it gladly.

Already they have purchased the sky,
and its promise of oblivion.

Immortal Self, say the Vedas.
Snow, says the wind.

Subterranean

The drought seems to go on forever.

Horses come down through mallow and sheen
to dry lake beds, large bodies of water folded
and tar-mopped into tinder.

If I could read the cracks in these ghosts
I might surprise the secret of secrets.

I cannot read them.

Silenced by lust, the vineyards wish they could sleep,
the grasses wish they could wake in the wind's hut.
This logic is not easy to explain.

I meant this to be the thing itself,
and not a description—the blur in the raga,
the nothing that brings the good news.

But it's just another poem made out of language.
How could it hope to succeed? How imagine water,
flowing everywhere beneath the trance of living?

Temporary Heart

These hills were once mountains,
now only a few big bones poke through.
I've come up here to listen to the wind,
and what the wind can't say.

Hawk sets an ambush in the dusty pine,
Crow hops around the carcass of a crow.
What doesn't exist pretends I'm alive.

C. G. HANZLICEK

C. G. Hanzlicek is Professor of
English and Director of Creative
Writing at California State
University, Fresno. He is the au-
thor of seven collections of po-
etry, the most recent of which is
Against Dreaming (University of
Missouri Press, 1994).

"I first came to Fresno in August
of 1966. The city was near the
end of a spell of something like
forty days of temperatures above
100 degrees. The pavement radi-
ated heat all night long. The air
was dirtier than it is now. There
was one particular, though, that
had strong appeal for a trans-
planted midwesterner: outside
my kitchen door was a tree filled
with ripening oranges. I would have to wait until the following spring to
drive alongside a hundred acres of orange blossoms on a hot night with the
windows down.

"It turned out there was more to the valley than oranges. There was, for
one thing, a community of poets who would be my lifelong friends, and away
from the city I found an unsuspected landscape. The foothills are green as
Ireland during the winter rains and then bake to pale gold early in June.
Yosemite is close by, but since I like my landscapes as unpopulated as possible,
Kings Canyon National Park has become my favorite stop in the mountains,
where I can peer over a ledge at the ribbon of river 4,000 feet down or trace
the peaks for fifty miles southward. A drive three times longer gets me to the
central California coast, which has also become an important oasis in my life
and work.

"I could not tell you the day or even the year when I ceased thinking of
myself as a midwesterner and became a man of the west, but that is what I've
become. Daydreaming or in sleep, the backdrop for the movie in my mind is
a western one—the great table of the Central Valley, coastal cliffs hammered
by surf, or the backlit ridge of the Sierra at dawn. It is in these places that I
take my own measure. I can't see myself anywhere else."

Feeding Frenzies

The last time it was shearwaters.
They appeared out of the fogbank
Like a second fogbank,
Only darker.
It took five minutes of their move toward shore
Before we could tell they were birds,
Thousands of them
Wildly circling inches off the water.
In five more minutes we could see
That they were riding herd on a school of fish,
Driving them to the beach,
And then suddenly they were there,
Right in front of us,
And the anchovies were boiling
And popping out of the water,
Even onto the sand,
And the shearwaters were moaning
And crooning and squealing
In the madness of appetite
That surely, this time, would be slaked.
They gorged until the fish-stir stopped,
And then were gone, back to the open sea.

This morning the red snappers were running,
Right off the end of the pier,
And there were cormorants
Who could relax and make shallow dives,
Half a dozen harbor seals
Rolling under and then bobbing up again,
Looking almost bemused at the easy life,
And what looked to be nearly a hundred
Dive-bombing brown pelicans.
Each time a pelican dove
A little band of skuas hit the water
Beside it, screaming,
Trying to rob its pouch.
All morning this dark cloud of birds
Rose and fell over the water

Like a swarm of midges,
And watching it was as good as breakfast.

For over twenty years we've come here
When the valley heat became too much,
And little has changed.
I'd like to point you to this place,
I really would,
But you'd come here,
Which would be all right
Until you'd slip and tell some idiot cousin
With an interest in real estate,
And your cousin would find Flo,
Poor, weary Flo, at last
Sick of her sausage and egg breakfast place,
And she'd sell in a minute,
And it wouldn't be breakfast anymore,
The cousin would open the place
For three meals a day,
Backhoe the succulent garden next door
To put in a barbeque pit,
Tear out the walls of the upstairs apartment
For an oyster bar,
And it would be a whole new world.

There was a moment around noon
When those feeding birds
Suddenly, mysteriously,
Took a break and came to rest on the water,
And then some broken link
In the human chain
Drove his boat right through the flock.
It took fifteen minutes
For the birds to gather their thoughts,
And even then everything they did
Looked ragged, almost random.
Because we were human we mourned.
We mourned the man in the boat
Who could never be our brother,
Not even a distant cousin,
And we mourned Flo,

Who someday may hold her head
Over her mistake,
And we mourned the pelican,
Who must always have one eye open
For the skua-thief,
And we mourned the skua,
Who has become the model for realtors,
And we mourned you,
Whose cousin barred you from this place,
Because if we told you where it is
We'd have nowhere,
Literally nowhere,
To feed.

Moment

The moments pass,
Moment by moment,
Like they're on a fast track to somewhere
Worse than Oblivion Depot,
But once in a while,
On a lucky day,
The bullet train stops
And lets you on board.
This day was solid overcast
Except for one thin band
On the eastern horizon,
Where it looked like the gallery
For Chinese landscapes was open for viewing.
The scroll was painted lengthwise,
A long stretch of snowfields
In the high Sierra pure white
In the new sun.
Most days the cloud cover
Will drop back down in minutes,
But we decided to drive east
Until the curtain fell.
One road led into another,
And still the scene held.

Finally we were in foothills
Smeared with mustard flower and fiddleneck,
On a paved road that turned to gravel
At the gate across someone's driveway.
I wonder what it feels like
To come home each evening
To the literal end of the road?
We turned around.
At the crest of the first hill,
A meadowlark perched on a strand of wire
No more than five feet from the car.
He had the yellowest breast
I'd seen on a lark, so I braked
And lowered the window for a clearer look.
He squirted out a quick
White poop as if in greeting,
And then began what may be
The loveliest bird song of all.
Another joined him and then another,
And Dianne rolled down her window,
And I killed the engine,
And suddenly the songs of a whole field
Of larks, fifty of them maybe,
Filled the car.
Fifty meadowlarks singing to each other,
Or maybe singing one to one,
In the early morning,
In the middle of our lives,
In the middle of the San Joaquin Valley.
There were only two houses nearby,
And for a moment I envied
The people who lived there,
In the middle of that sound each morning,
But then I thought maybe it was we
Who should be envied,
For whom the larks sang deeper,
And even, stretching all the way from there
To this very moment,
Sang longer.

On the Road Home

In a valley of leafless scrub oaks
Greened by mistletoe,
A magpie
Hauls his long iridescent tail
Home through the dusk.
It has been a full day for him,
Scavenging at the roadside,
Yakking with friends.

I too had a full day:
A five-hour drive
Yakking through lunch with friends,
Then reading poems for an hour.
It seemed to go well,
Though one, nervous,
Clearly upset about something else,
Perhaps a love grown too complex,
Nagged me for being simple.

The magpie builds its broad nest
Well hidden in mistletoe.
Even this most sociable of birds
Wants, at day's end,
Privacy, silence,
And I, less loquacious,
Secretly longed all day for this moment,
No car ahead of me,
No car in the mirror,
Just me, driving between hills
In the slanting shadows of evening,
Just me and this other
Simple bird.

Sierra Noon

for Larry Levis

Each time I come over a rise,
The mirage in the next dip
Looks like I'll be up to the windows
In water, stalled,
Having to wade to high ground.
The red-tailed hawks won't hunt
When it's 106;
You can size their territory
By how far apart they perch, solitary,
Crowning the oldest oaks.
Ground squirrels siesta,
Belly-flopped on shaded boulders,
Dreaming long lives.
The poppies and baby blue eyes
Dropped their seeds months ago;
What's left is grass
Bleached to pale gold.
I park the car in a turnout,
Sidestep a trap door spider
As I cross the road,
Then join the cattle across the fence.
In one minute, their curiosity
About me ends, and they lower
Their heads and plod along their path
That switchbacks up a slope.
A piece of granite as big as my car
Has been cleanly split
By a glacier or some heave of the earth;
A fence lizard curls
Out of the rift and onto yellowed lichen.
When he sees me,
He does a dozen nervous pushups.
Don't worry, son of rock
And of the sun itself,
I've only come to look back down
On the valley orchards and vineyards,
And to mourn my friend, another son

Of that valley and these burned hills,
Hills that rolled through his first
Memories and stayed,
No matter what cities he found himself in,
No matter what hotel he checked out of,
The one geography of his life.
So many times he seemed to me
A solitary, peering down
From an oak older than both
Our ages combined, a century tree,
But as a man of place
Placed among men of property,
I'm sure the last landscape he drew
Was bordered by these hills,
Oak by oak, rock by rock,
All the way past timberline.

JAMES HARMS

James Harms is the author of two collections of poetry, *The Joy Addict* (1998) and *Modern Ocean* (1992), both from Carnegie Mellon University Press. He has received the PEN/Revson Fellowship, creative writing fellowships from the Pennsylvania and West Virginia Arts Commissions, the John Ciardi Fellowship from The Bread Loaf Writers' Conference, and two Pushcart Prizes. He directs the Creative Writing program at West Virginia University.

"I've now lived away from California for more than ten years, first in Indiana, then in Ohio and Pennsylvania, presently in West Virginia. I find, however, that the landscape of my poems remains the landscape of my dreams, the landscape of my childhood: the foothills of the San Gabriel Mountains, the beaches south of Los Angeles, the deserts east of Redlands. I'm not sure why this is, but I recently read an interview with Robert Hass, one of California's finest poets, that touched on the subject, and which made sense to me. Hass says that 'the places where we grow up become a kind of vocabulary, a semantics of [the] inner life....In an early way, we are always making a human vocabulary out of the nonhuman world.' He goes on later in the interview to talk about the changes that occur in our language, in our modes of discourse, when we begin to address a landscape that is in some way alien, and by alien he means any landscape other than the one we grew up in. Moving away from that originating place, both figuratively and literally, actually changes the shape of our voice, the way we interact with our subjects, changes the way we sound, which isn't always a bad thing. But since I'm not much interested in the *activity* of describing the natural world in and of itself, I don't find myself defaulting to the immediate landscape—the one right outside my door—when I write a poem. Instead I feel the tug of dreams, the pull of the past, which ends up locating language in the place that I feel made me, a place that is now completely within me. That relationship, between language and place, is everything to me as a poet. In all honesty, most of what happens in my poems is invented, engendered in fact, by the struggle to wrestle language from that place within. This is an old and tired argument if we take it much further (with respect to language: did I make the poem or did the poem make me?), and I don't spend much time thinking about it. But I know that my poems stick pretty close to the western edge of the continent, that words like manzanita, eucalyptus, chaparral, arroyo, river oak, oleander, bougainvillea, and names such as Altadena, San Onofre, Catalina, Anacapa, Balboa, and Mendocino have a talismanic power over my writing process; they literally fuel the strange symbiosis between memory and imagination that makes the poem possible.

"I miss California a lot less than I used to, and I'm sure that has to do with all sorts of things: my wife is from the southeast, my son was born in West Virginia, I feel at home in these hills. But I also don't doubt that my long and careful crafting of an inner landscape, one that resembles California, albeit burnished with the golden light of a perpetually setting sun, has sustained me in ways that are as true to the spirit as actual residence in the place."

Dogtown

Venice, California

Funny how the kid you always punched
remembers you fondly.
Standing at the taco stand
exchanging numbers, laughing,
he keeps looking around, keeps
shrugging for no good reason.
He says, "Do you remember when…"
then leaves mid-sentence
to answer a ringing payphone.

Around you it's Sunday.
A tattooed fat man sells postcards
of himself. The Spanish shawl
glides by on her Schwinn.
A little boy kneels to strap his sandal,
the ocean a blue terrace behind him.

Some days, when the smog
blows inland at dusk,
you stare out where Japan should be
and count backward the people who love you.
The sun sprays kites across the water,
a V of pelicans drops softly behind the waves.
You see islands in the channel, a boat
or two coming home from sea.
Evelyn, your neighbor, walks her parrot

every evening, first down the strand
then to O'Pepe's for a beer.
When she sees you she stops, squats down
beside her bird.
She lifts his beak until he's looking,
and she points, says your name.
Some days, she says it three or four times.

Elegy as Evening, as Exodus
North of Malibu

The Pacific is nothing like its name.
For one thing, there are no silences,
despite the palm trees leaning into stillness.

Poppies rise like fire from the chaparral
on the bluffs, the manzanita, the oil in its leaves.
And every few yards a stubborn yucca,

late blossoms struggling to catch up at the edge
of whatever, this modern earth, tectonic rafts
slipping north and west, the ocean torn into white lace.

Tan knees tucked beneath my chin,
tan knees like a boy's, I sat watch
through the afternoon, staring at the islands:

Anacapa, San Miguel, Catalina to the south.
I heard a phone ring, a buoy bell, sun dissolving
into sea. I heard a name escape its word,

the wind between waves. The islands were rose and gray
in the last light of a last Tuesday,
the rock around me dark and trembling, volcanic.

I sat in the splash zone, black urchins
tucked into wet crevices at my feet,
a keyhole limpet next to my left hand.

And though you would suppose the islands
would vanish into the channel when the sun did,
for hours I could see their shapes, like whales

sleeping peacefully on the horizon,
like ships. Ships waiting for enough light,
for safe passage, for cargo. For all of us.

Los Angeles

"The days change at night."
X

I drove today along the foothills
looking for relief in distances.
I found the distances.

•

In late spring in Los Angeles—
in the air beneath a streetlight,
above a swimming pool, a breeze
sweetened by jasmine and orange blossoms—
there is nothing to know
except the stillness that follows loss,
the quiet in the blood.

•

Sunlight in the canyons.
The rustle of doves
in the palm trees, squirrels in the ivy.
Half of what I hear or see
is memory; the other half is what
I'm now ignoring and eventually will dream.
And like the last lingering smoke
that curls away toward the desert,
it's easy enough to choke
on what's left of my city.

•

I drove today as if to somewhere.
I spun the dial left to find a song.
And the space between stations
was a thousand throats clearing,
the sound a phone makes
when you've answered out of habit

or hope and no one's there,
it hasn't even rung.

•

In Los Angeles in late spring,
what's unknowable is always an angel,
always quiet. And in my latest dream
of leaving, I couldn't hear her
when she spoke, couldn't
hug her for the wings.

Sky

Last night a few years ago my sister
waited by the phone with a wooden spoon
and when it finally rang she beat it
and began to cry. Neither I nor
my mother made attempts to get near
that phone. Our house those years
was a block away from Christmas Tree Lane,
a row of deodars that ran without break
from Woodbury Street to Altadena Drive.
Indigenous to Nepal, the deodar is fine
in the thin air of the himalayas, less adept
at discerning CO_2 from the solitary
molecule of smog. So now there
are gaps in the lane where the dying
trees have been cut up and dragged away.
The lights at Christmas are more obvious
and somehow garish, shocking, hanging free
where once were branches. When I was twenty
I considered lying down in front
of the crane used to remove my parents'
enormous eucalyptus. It robbed the garden
of water, they said, it would kill them
one day, drop a limb through the roof.
Instead of protest, I took a lawn chair
and a six-pack on the patio and watched the men
work their way down from the delicate

top branches, chopping for hours, finally
sawing off the trunk at the ground.
In a few years my sister's baby
will be old enough to listen attentively.
I'll walk with her through the backyard
beyond the terrace, her hand up high
in mine like a child at the fair attached
to a balloon. We'll step onto the stump,
flush now to the earth and ringed
with St. Augustine. There will be room
enough to dance with one so small.
And when she asks how tall it was,
the bluegum eucalyptus that held and hid
the stars I looked for from my
bedroom window, and caught the few that fell,
it will be easy enough just to point
at a particular spot in the sky.

ROBERT HASS

Robert Hass is the author of four collections of poems—*Field Guide,* which won the Yale Younger Poets Prize, *Praise, Human Wishes*, and most recently, *Sun Under Wood.* His many honors include a MacArthur Fellowship and the 1984 National Book Critics Circle Award in criticism for *Twentieth Century Pleasures.* Beginning in 1995, he served for two years as Poet Laureate of the United States. He teaches at the University of California, Berkeley.

© Barbara Hall

Meditation at Lagunitas

All the new thinking is about loss.
In this it resembles all the old thinking.
The idea, for example, that each particular erases
the luminous clarity of a general idea. That the clown-
faced woodpecker probing the dead sculpted trunk
of that black birch is, by his presence,
some tragic falling off from a first world
of undivided light. Or the other notion that,
because there is in this world no one thing
to which the bramble of *blackberry* corresponds,
a word is elegy to what it signifies.
We talked about it late last night and in the voice
of my friend, there was a thin wire of grief, a tone
almost querulous. After a while I understood that,
talking this way, everything dissolves: *justice,*
pine, hair, woman, you and *I.* There was a woman
I made love to and I remembered how, holding
her small shoulders in my hands sometimes,
I felt a violent wonder at her presence
like a thirst for salt, for my childhood river

with its island willows, silly music from the pleasure boat,
muddy places where we caught the little orange-silver fish
called *pumpkinseed*. It hardly had to do with her.
Longing, we say, because desire is full
of endless distances. I must have been the same to her.
But I remember so much, the way her hands dismantled bread,
the thing her father said that hurt her, what
she dreamed. There are moments when the body is as numinous
as words, days that are the good flesh continuing.
Such tenderness, those afternoons and evenings,
saying *blackberry, blackberry, blackberry.*

Palo Alto: the Marshes

For Mariana Richardson (1830–1891)

1

She dreamed along the beaches of this coast.
Here where the tide rides in to desolate
the sluggish margins of the bay,
sea grass sheens copper into distances.
Walking, I recite the hard
explosive names of birds:
egret, killdeer, bittern, tern.
Dull in the wind and early morning light,
the striped shadows of the cattails
twitch like nerves.

2

Mud, roots, old cartridges, and blood.
High overhead, the long silence of the geese.

3

"We take no prisoners," John Fremont said
and took California for President Polk.
That was the Bear Flag War.
She watched it from the Mission San Rafael,
named for the archangel (the terrible one)
who gently laid a fish across the eyes
of saintly, miserable Tobias
that he might see.

The eyes of fish. The land
shimmers fearfully.
No archangels here, no ghosts,
and terns rise like seafoam
from the breaking surf.

4

Kit Carson's antique .45, blue,
new as grease. The roar
flings up echoes,
row on row of shrieking avocets.
The blood of Francisco de Haro,
Ramon de Haro, José de los Reyes Berryessa
runs darkly to the old ooze.

5

The star thistles: erect, surprised,

6

and blooming
violet caterpillar hairs. One
of the de Haros was her lover,
the books don't say which.
They were twins.

7

In California in the early spring
there are pale yellow mornings
when the mist burns slowly into day.
The air stings
like autumn, clarifies
like pain.

8

Well I have dreamed this coast myself.
Dreamed Mariana, since her father owned the land
where I grew up. I saw her picture once:
a wraith encased in a high-necked black silk
dress so taut about the bones there were hardly ripples
for the light to play in. I knew her eyes
had watched the hills seep blue with lupine after rain,
seen the young peppers, heavy and intent,

first rosy drupes and then the acrid fruit,
the ache of spring. Black as her hair
the unreflecting venom of those eyes
is an aftermath I know, like these brackish,
russet pools a strange life feeds in
or the old fury of land grants, maps,
and deeds of trust. A furious dun-
colored mallard knows my kind
and skims across the edges of the marsh
where the dead bass surface
and their flaccid bellies bob.

9

A chill tightens the skin
around my bones. The other California
and its bitter absent ghosts
dance to a stillness in the air:
the Klamath tribe was routed and they disappeared.
Even the dust seemed stunned,
tools on the ground, fishnets.
Fires crackled, smouldering.
No movement but the slow turning
of the smoke, no sound but jays
shrill in the distance and flying further off.
The flicker of lizards, dragonflies.
And beyond the dry flag-woven lodges
a faint persistent slapping.
Carson found ten wagonloads
of fresh-caught salmon, silver
in the sun. The flat eyes stared.
Gills sucked the thin annulling air.
They flopped and shivered,
ten wagonloads. Kit Carson
burned the village to the ground.
They rode some twenty miles that day
and still they saw the black smoke
smear the sky above the pines.

10

Here everything seems clear,
firmly etched against the pale

smoky sky: sedge, flag, owl's clover,
rotting wharves. A tanker lugs silver
bomb-shaped napalm tins toward
port at Redwood City. Again,
my eye performs
the lobotomy of description.
Again, almost with yearning,
I see the malice of her ancient eyes.
The mud flats hiss as the tide turns.
They say she died in Redwood City,
cursing "the goddamned Anglo-Yankee yoke."

11

The otters are gone from the bay
and I have seen five horses
easy in the grassy marsh
beside three snowy egrets.

Birds cries and the unembittered sun,
wings and the white bodies of the birds,
it is morning. Citizens are rising
to murder in their moral dreams.

San Pedro Road

Casting, up a salt creek in the sea-rank air,
fragrance of the ferny anise, crackle of field grass
in the summer heat. Under this sun vision blurs.
Blue air rises, the horizon weaves above the leaden bay.
Rock crabs scuttle from my shadow in the silt.

Some other day the slow-breathing, finely haired mussels,
on the shore, under rocks, buried thick-clustered in black mud
would be enough, blended in a quick formal image
with butter, tarragon, a cool white Napa Valley wine.
Today in the ferocious pointless heat I dream,
half in anger, of the great white bass,
the curious striper, bright-eyed, rising to the bait,
flickering in muddy bottoms, feeding the green
brackish channels where yachts wallow in the windless air.

My hands are tense.
                A carcass washes by, white meat,
spidery translucent bones and I think I understand,
finally dumb animal I understand, kick off boots, pants, socks,
and swim,
                thrashing dull water to a golden brown,
terrorizing the depths with my white belly, my enormous length,
done with casting, reeling in slowly, casting...

The Return of Robinson Jeffers

1

He shuddered briefly and stared down the long valley where the headland
    rose
And the lean gum trees rattled in the wind above Point Sur;
Alive, he had littered the mind's coast
With ghosts of Indians and granite and the dead fleshed
Bodies of desire. That work was done
And, whether done well or not, it had occupied him
As the hawks and the sea were occupied.
Now he could not say what brought him back.
He had imagined resurrection once: the lover of a woman
Who lived lonely in a little ranch house up the ridge
Came back, dragged from the grave by her body's need
To feel under ashen cloud-skies and in the astonishments
Of sunrise some truth beyond the daily lie
Of feeding absolute hunger the way a young girl might trap meadow mice
To feed a red-tailed hawk she kept encaged. She wanted to die once
As the sun dies in pure fire on the farthest sea-swells.
She had had enough and more of nights when the brain
Flickered and dissolved its little constellations and the nerves
Performed their dumb show in the dark among the used human smells of
    bedsheets.
So she burned and he came, a ghost in khaki and stunned skin,
And she fled with him. He had imagined, though he had not written,
The later moment in the pasture, in moonlight like pale stone,
When she lay beside him with an after-tenderness in all her bones,
Having become entirely what she was, though aware that the thing
Beside her was, again, just so much cheese-soft flesh

And jellied eye rotting in the pools of bone.
Anguish afterwards perhaps, but he had not thought afterwards.
Human anguish made him cold.
He told himself the cries of men in war were no more conscious
Nor less savage than the shrill repetitions of the Steller's jay
Flashing through live oaks up Mal Paso Canyon
And that the oaks, rooted and growing toward their grace,
Were—as species go—
More beautiful.

2

He had given himself to stone gods.
I imagine him thinking of that woman
While a live cloud of gulls
Plumes the wind behind a trawler
Throbbing toward the last cannery at Monterey.
The pelicans are gone which had, wheeling,
Written Chinese poems on the sea. The grebes are gone
That feasted on the endless hunger of the flashing runs
Of salmon. And I imagine that he saw, finally,
That though rock stands, it does not breed.
He feels specific rage. Feels, obscurely, that his sex
Is his, not god-force only, but his own soft flesh grown thick
With inconsolable desire. The grebes are gone.
He feels a plain man's elegiac tenderness,
An awkward brotherhood with the world's numb poor
His poems had despised. Rage and tenderness are pain.
He feels pain as rounding at the hips, as breasts.
Pain blossoms in his belly like the first dark
Stirrings of a child, a surfeit of the love that he had bled to rock
And twisted into cypress haunts above the cliffs.
He knows he has come back to mourn,
To grieve, womanish, a hundred patient years
Along this fragile coast. I imagine the sky's arch,
Cloud-swift, lifts him then, all ache in sex and breasts,
Beyond the leached ashes of dead fire,
The small jeweled hunger in the seabird's eye.

ELOISE KLEIN HEALY

Eloise Klein Healy is Chair of the M.F.A. in Creative Writing program at Antioch University, Los Angeles. The author of four books of poetry and the associate editor/poetry editor of *The Lesbian Review of Books,* she has received fellowships from Dorland Mt. Colony, The MacDowell Colony, and the California Arts Council. She holds an M.F.A. in Creative Writing from Vermont College. *Artemis in Echo Park* is available on CD and audiotape. Her most recent collection, *Women's Studies Chronicles,* is a chapbook from The Inevitable Press (The Laguna Poets Series #99). Her work has been anthologized in *Intimate Nature: The Bond Between Women and Nature; The Key to Everything: Classic Lesbian Love Poems; Ladies, Start Your Engines: Women Writers on Cars and the Road; Grand Passion: The Poets of Los Angeles and Beyond; HERS: Brilliant New Fiction by Lesbian Writers*, and *The Arc of Love: An Anthology of Lesbian Love Poetry.*

"What is a poem but a place? For me, poems have in their inception the pressure of weather, the air of rooms, the lay of the land, the light and space surrounding the scene. Things happen *somewhere*. Perceptions and feelings are contextualized by locale. Even language is flavored by the vistas the poet surveys with her senses. 'How close' and 'how far' have been guiding words for me about feelings, and not just in a metaphorical sense. Perspective is not solely related to what is commonly known as 'point of view.' From where I stand, my opinion also means *exactly* what it says—where my beliefs begin and end is *embodied*.

"My book, *Artemis in Echo Park,* was written to engage the notion that the landscape is intrinsically linked to human history. In this case, I wanted to talk about the enduring pressure of landscape, the fact that what rivers have formed or earthquakes have pushed up still determines everything about life in a modern megalopolis. Also, where I live, in Los Angeles, corridors of wilderness penetrate into urban areas, and animal life—wild animal life—intermingles with human activity. Often I have awakened to find a skunk or opossum in my yard, or I see deer grazing along the margins of a five lane freeway on my way to and from work. Then there's a hawk I've been observing for about a year who incorporates the 405 into its glide path. What kind of poetry comes out of that mix? That's what's of interest to me."

Artemis in Echo Park

I turn out the driveway, point down the street,
bend where the road bends and tip down the hill.
This is a trail, even under asphalt.
Every street downtown cuts through adobe
and the concrete wears like the curve
of a bowl baking on a patio or the sway of a brick wall
drying in the sun.
The life before cement is ghosting up
through roadways that hooves and water
have worn into existence forever.
Out to Pasadena, the freeway still behaves
like a ravine, snaking through little valleys.
The newer roads exist in air, drifting skyward,
lifting off the landscape like dreams of the future.
We've named these roads for where they end—
Harbor Freeway, Ventura Freeway, Hollywood Freeway—
but now they all end in the sky.

Moroni on the Mormon Temple/Angel on the Wall

Moroni is a foreigner
and not one of the angels living here.

He was imported to point at heaven.
His name is hard and final,

not like Angel, soft *n* and soft *g*
whose name is sprayed down the street

eye-level, arm-level on a building,
quick and at night

to say, *I am no foreigner,*
this is my barrio,
something old, something here.

The City Beneath the City

I own a print of cows on a green hill,
brown-and-white cows
like peaceful wooden cutouts
who dream me through the wall,
through my neighbor's house, straight back
to old Pasadena—Rancho San Pasqual,
Rancho Santa Anita, and the wild cows
with arching horns, their spines knobbed
and hairy, 3-D and mean.

Their hides, I know, became chairs a century ago,
the hair reddish brown and white wore smooth.
The extra hides shipped down to the harbor
were traded for furniture carted home
to the main house on the two-wheeled *carettas*
up the track that's now the Harbor Freeway
out the ravine to Pasadena.

Little black olives pocking the dust
were picked and pickled in brine.
In the *zanjas*, horses drank
and scum floated on the water
green as neon.
From los ranchos to Sonora,
young ladies traveled in society.
The population of Chinese workers
was kept small—no women allowed—but
under the Governor's mansion, while
his daughter gave piano recitals and sang,
the Chinese dug tunnels north
from Olvera Street where their wives would live
in hiding. Under the cover of night
they spread out the secret earth to dry.

Some days still the ground shivers, splits
open the face of an unmined seam.
The city beneath the city dances
like a *calavera* in the ballroom of the dead.
The old bones shake when a shovel

strikes an amber bottle
or excavations uncover stone canals
mysterious as the mountains on the moon.

Two Centuries in One Day

The couple painted on the Bridal Shop
on Broadway are six-stories high
and done up in a bright blue wash.
I like to think they're in the nineteenth century
and feeling close to the ground.
The twentieth century wants to get off the planet
but you'd never know it
from the traffic on this street.
Titulos en Español. Discos Latinos.
Soft tacos with shredded beef.
This is Alta California,
land of the tomato, apple of love.

The couple looms above and can look
into the offices of the *Los Angeles Times.*
Their wedding reception swirls
on the street below, and in the parking lot
one hundred years ago today
the horses doze in the sunlight.

In this sunlight it's all a wedding today,
never mind the century.

Wisteria

This pale winter the wisteria looks like an empty
nest. When I look deeper, there is an empty nest
inside her. The reason the mockingbird kept flying in.
I have to do some talking with this plant. In the summer
it's such an argument I just stay away. She wants
to be playful and slap my arms when I trim her.
She's like a twelve-year-old girl, and she stings me with
the venom in her leaves. Now is the only time

I can handle her. Asleep and slow, she's just a brown plan
which will become complicated again.
I'll have a good talk with her while she dozes.
Convince her she's simply a wild girl, that what she needs
is a good haircut, a fresh outlook, another chance
to really show her stuff.

BRENDA HILLMAN

Brenda Hillman has published five collections of poetry, all from Wesleyan University Press. Her most recent collection is *Loose Sugar*. She teaches at Saint Mary's College in Moraga, California.

© Ethan Michaels

"California and the idea of California affect my work prominently in at least three parts of a method. (1) I have since 1985 been interested in postmodernist and innovative poetic techniques—among them, the fragment, discontinuity, oblique and indeterminate syntax and diction, experiments of a purely aural and spacial nature—meanwhile trying to maintain a sense of the ongoingness of the lyric impulse and to find alternatives for conventional autobiographical narrative structures. This combination of efforts seem to reflect the unpredictable and rugged nature of the land shifts, vegetation, and climate as well as the many forms of play and peril in a popular culture that are located specifically in this state. I was trying to demonstrate this directly in 'A Geology,' which shows with the several different types of syntactic breaks and upheavals a similarity between struggles for reality, the formation of a specialized linguistic life and the formation of the earth over millions of years. The corner words 'anchor' the rest of the lyric to the page and signal it to focus. Language is the separate and real nature we inhabit most; in using it, we reach far across the gap to the 'place' beyond, no less real, no more real than words themselves. (2) California as an idea of itself provides an inner world of astonishment; imagination is often the 'subject matter' for writers who live here. Figurative space is full of its infinite possibilities. In *Death Tractates, Bright Existence,* and *Loose Sugar* I was trying to explore particularly Californian spiritual systems that would combine gnostic wildness and alchemical imagery with investigations of a generalized psychological or collective human nature; probably this is more a feminine project in *Death Tractates,* a book equipped with much that is particular to the Bay Area scenery. (3) In recent poems, and the poems I'm working toward, like 'El Nino Orgonon,' I'm trying to engage less in metaphysical inquiry than in social and political subjects; I hope always to be devising different methods to break with the predictable or the expected perceptions. In other poems, ontogenic claims are made on the artist by creation itself. These seem directly related to the idea of California as a place for hanging off of everything, at the edge, for creating itself. There is an excited so-much-ness and a fertile blankness in the plurality of living between California city and country life.

"A poem, like California, proudly calls for the thing it cannot do."

A Geology

What we love, can't see.

If Italy looks like a boot to most people, California
            looks like the skin of a person about to sit
            down, a geology.

Consider the Coast Range. We can achieve
            the same results by pushing a pile of wet
            papers from the left and finally
            they were just in love with each other.

Consider the faultline; with only two sides of it,
            how come you never thought of one of them.

A place we love, can't see.   A condition

            so used   to becoming....

(Those who have straddled reference know a map
            will stand for wholeness)

When you were trying to quit the drug and broke
            in half you said...

And you had to trust it   (that is, needing it)

Landforms enable us to scare. Where
            Berkeley is, once a shallow sea with
            landforms to the west, called Cascadia.
            No kidding. I read this.

A geology breaks in half to grow. A person whose drug like
            a locust jumps across someone's foot, singing—;
            we disagree with D, who hates similes.

The Transverse Ranges holding Los Angeles spit out
        a desert on their hazard side, a power
        transformed from a period of thrall into
        an ordinary period of lying here.

There are six major faults, there are skipped
        verbs, there are more little
        thoughts in California. The piece of coast
        slides on the arrow; down is
        reverse. Subduction means the crust

goes underneath the continent, which is
        rather light. It was my friend. I needed it.
        The break in the rock shows forward; the flash
        hurts. Granite is composed of quartz, hornblende
        and other former fire. When a drug

is trying to quit it has to stretch. Narrow comes.
        from the same place as glamor.

A scarp hangs over the edge as it does from
        Monterey to Santa Barbara. When we
        were trying to quit it had to shout.
        (The rest of our party had gone up ahead.)
        Exaggeration has no effect upon silence.

It took my breath, I gave it willingly, I told
        it to, and the breath listened—

Consider the place of I-80 towards outcroppings.
        When you've gotten to Auburn, a whole
        dog-shaped ground has broken through,

the rock struggling with features, its bachelor joy, caused
        by the power that has kissed you.

silence   re-used

What happened, happened a lot. Not to glamorize
              what can't be helped. A bunch of fiery
              islands floated over and sutured themselves to us

a hundred million years ago. I liked

to hold one. Just, really, light it. Put my
              mouth on it.

It's appropriate to discuss features when we speak of California,

daylight's treatment of a sudden

movement in rock. It pretended not to mind. You
              passed him on the path. Miocene lava
              smiled as it ordered the darker

color to sit down,

When he was trying to quit he based his reasoning
              on the way mountains slip. California's
              glaciers never reach the sea. The drug

was trapped in you, and fit. The Klamath mountains love
              the veins of excellent stress, see figure 12.
              Between the time two mountains slip, nothing.
              Between two points of resolution, nothing
              less. A little more
              almost and the slip happened; it happened
              a lot just 30 million years ago.

I saw between the flames four types of instruments:
              with one they touched my mouth,
              with another you touched
              her feet. Rocks of the oldest

time are barely represented. This is the voice
              from the cave, Oleiria. He was coming
              to fuck me but my face had been removed.

The fault went under artichokes in 1982. She talked
        to the permanent fire about it;

what pushes up from under isn't
        named. Or is that "What makes you do this
        to yourself."—What makes you…A language
        caught up under, like a continent.
        She was inhaling though they told her not to.

In the Gabilan Range, small volcanoes erupted
        softly, then this throw-rug-over-the-carpet
        in-a- bowling-alley type of effect. A California

is composed of moving toward, away, or past; a
        skin is not separate; a poem is

composed of all readings of it. Elements
        redeem themselves plenty, alchemists say so.
        I gave my breath quite easily, then. Sorry it's

ashes, sorry it's smoke all the way down. Gravity
        has to practice. The disciple of angles
        smashed planet after planet, rubbing the cave
        of chalk onto his cue, and put them
        into corners like Aquinas's five
        proofs for the existence of God. Nice
        touch on that boy, nice touch on those
        who sleep till noon, sleep the sleep
        of the uninsured till noon and wake with maps
        of Sacramento on their hands.

What made the Sierra lift from the right. Telluric Poptart.
        Geologists refer to the range as
        trapdoorlike. It made him cry, he gave it
        willingly, the bartender brought him

free drinks and sent him out into the pale
wrong proud civilian night—

A geology can't fix itself. Nor can description.
        Horses run upside down in
        the undermath. A power has twinned itself
        in that place. We follow it until we are
        its favorite, and then we live. Does the drug
        recover? The Pacific Plate

began this recent movement 20 million years ago. Fresno
        was underwater; the small creatures
        barely noticed.

She smelled it till it stopped looking pretty; let's call a spoon
        a spoon. We dig right down into ourselves
        for the rocks of the middle kingdom. Gold

folded into the Motherlode often twinned
        with quartz. They seemed to like each other.
        Addicts stay on the porch together, lighting them,

and elsewhere, lighthouse cliffs recall the tremors
        that brought them there. Cascadia…I *whered*
        the wheel and the continent moved over

but I still wanted it.

Los Angeles cheap bedding. You'd allow her
        to go first and then you'd go, pull the youngest
        blanket over her—bang. If that's
        how you like it, fine. Like warm sandstone.

We're living at the dawn of creation as far as
        California is concerned. The skin
        goes first. Most beaches are losing sand,
        it drifts south to Mexico. He sold it, she mixed it, we

proud   civilian

bought the pfft in 198x, trying to endure
          the glassfront curve in the unaccountable
          ghostman's pleasure. Get down

off that ladder, you. Ceiling stars. Little fiery

islands were light as they ordered Nevada
          to move over. The white thing took
          her breath, she let it slide, it recognized
          what to do; after it started no
          change, seeing you was methodone
          for seeing you.

The number of faults in middle California
          is staggering—that is, we stagger
          over them till it's
          difficult to follow our own. Each tremor
          is the nephew of a laugh—
          sandstone, shale, chert from the Triassic
          near I-Forgetville. He lined
          them up, they made white sense,

stretchmarks on her body like
          public transportation, very coastal,
          very Sierra traintracks that click click
          down the sides of thighs, stretchmarks
          where the soul has grown too quickly
          from inside—

But in a way, not really. A geology

has its appetites. New islands are forming
          to get the gist of it. Much of the coast
          moved on its own to get free. Sometimes
          he'd just pass it to you, the prince of stains,—
          the universe cried through him. The sea

stars   Mexico

was glassing itself over Half Moon Bay. Should have
                dropped again suddenly, in the service
                of some burnt out Eden.

It's appropriate to discuss what can't be
                helped. Phyllites, schists, cherts,
                marbles. An angel in the annunciation,
                little subzero Mary kneeling
                before you in the bathroom while you were
                burning your skin off.

You went east and you went south. They
                took out their little fear schedules. The Pacific
                Plate on the left moving north while
                the right stands still if you
                look down on it. There's no way

to say progress had been made. I never did

not think about lighting them, not one day,
                as if a requiem could help how chords
                fell out the bottom, Cascadia breathed, I tried
                program, H tried program after program,
                D tried specific harvests
                of bubbles. 12 step ashes. Extra metal

on the stove. The rest of our party
                had gone on ahead. Don't name it. The lithosphere
                likes to float on the aesthenosphere, the soft
                mobile voice of the unseen. *I slide*

below you sweet and high. It wants

to hear you. It wants to touch you. It wants
                to be happy and it wants to die.

Phyllites, shales, cherts, marbles. Press #
        when you are finished. No one knows why
        the arc of minor islands sewed themselves
        to us in that way. When I put it

to my mouth I had no ability to stop it.
        The sea ate the colors a hundred million years ago.

A geology is not a strategy. When an addict tries to leave
        the desire to make himself over shifts from
        what it felt like to have been a subject;

L.A. will dwell beside San Francisco eventually.

Tempting to pun on the word *fault*. All right,
        say *plot*. All right, *happens*. The tendency
        to fault relieves the strain. New islands
        were forming to get the gist of it. We wanted
        the extraordinary stranger in our veins.

Whether it's better not to have been held by something.
        The oldest limestone, prevalent between Big Sur
        and Calaveras, is not "better than," say,
        any other kind. The suffering wasn't luckier,
        it wasn't a question of asking.

In the instead hour, the minutes of not recovering
        from the difference of what we loved;
        sameness is also true: stone like a spider

sucking the carapace the same color as itself.

In the expiation of nature, we are required to
        experience the dramatic narrative of matter.

The rocks under California are reigning in their little world.

This was set down in strata so you could know
        what it felt like to have been earth.

JANE HIRSHFIELD

Jane Hirshfield is the author of
four books of poetry, most recently
The Lives of the Heart (Harper-
Collins, 1997), as well as a collec-
tion of essays, *Nine Gates Entering
the Mind of Poetry* (HarperCollins,
1997). She has received fellowships
from the Guggenheim and
Rockefeller Foundations, The
Poetry Center Book Award, and
other honors, and has taught at
University of California, Berkeley,
the University of San Francisco,
and elsewhere.

© *Jerry Bauer*

"I arrived in northern California in
a red van with tie-dyed curtains in
June 1974 and have lived here steadily since then—in a canyon in the middle
of a national forest, in a city, in a windowed cabin overlooking the ocean, and
now in a small house on the hem of Mount Tamalpais. It took about four
years before the California landscape came sufficiently into my psyche to
enter my poems. I had to hike, plant, listen my way into the place where I'd
come to live—had to cut firebreak, to sleep by a stony and powerful creek
where mountain lions walked at two in the morning, to put miles of climbing
and descending its ridgelines into my legs. To care about such things is, per-
haps, one small marker of coming to be of this place.

"A few days ago, I placed a beloved border collie into the ground she had
walked for almost fifteen years. Digging her grave with a friend, I realized
how intimately I know this soil—know exactly the depth the rocks begin,
know where the roots are, know the scent and texture of the good soil that
holds all. She is buried next to a seedling I was given, offspring of the only
tree in the city center to survive Hiroshima: a *Pawlonia tomentosa*. The tree is
an exotic, my dog is an exotic, as am I—but still the ground takes what is
given. That is part of California's nature, too."

Invocation

This August night, raccoons,
come to the back door
burnished all summer by salty,
human touch: enter secretly & eat.

Listen, little mask-faced ones,
unstealthy bandits whose tails
are barred with dusk:
listen, gliding green-eyed ones:
I concede you gladly
all this much-handled stuff,
garbage, grain,
the cropped food and cropped heart—
may you gnaw in contentment
through the sleep-hours
on everything left out.

May you find the house
hospitable,
well-used,
stocked with sufficient goods.
I'll settle with your leavings,

as you have settled for mine,
before startling back into darkness
that marks each of us so differently.

Letter to Hugo from Later

Dear Dick: In order to xerox your book I had to break
the spine. Somehow that felt right, because to get
the life of anything it seems you have to let some part
be broken. Here, now, it is spring. It must be there
as well, if you can see it. And the poppies are
stringing themselves out the way they do in California,
and the indian paintbrush dabbing itself in. Also,
the horses are sick with strangles. That's true, although
I also think you'd like the way the word leaps out,
the way the lump does also under the jaw of the sick ones,
making your stomach fall. And maybe I say it too because
it's hard to speak the rest until you've loosed what sticks
in the throat. Watching a small white moth as it goes stitching
across the trees—that helps as well. The particular does.
I envy the way you managed to pack so many parts of the world
in such a little space, the way you'd go from pouring a glass

of beer to something American and huge. I don't write much
about America, or even people. For you, people were what there was:
you talked with and about them and stayed up late
to love those high-lobbed lives. I'd often enough rather
talk to horses. I lived not far from you that summer the book
came out—in Lolo. I knew you were in town, but never thought
to knock or ask to join a class. I wonder what might have happened,
if I'd have come to love the barrooms more, the haze of smoke
and talking. I was young and might have. I'm planning to give
your poem to a workshop in Kansas City, along with Horace and Komachi
and maybe this one if I'm feeling brave. I bet you'd like to know
the book sells higher now than when it was first published.
And like knowing it's still cheap: five bucks, a bargain.
Poems shouldn't cost a lot, we'd both agree, except for how
the spine breaks when you try to pin them down. It hurts but not
too much, and anyhow, one thing no poet does is look away.
And now you're past it. You wrote: *I want my life inside to go on
as long as I do*, and it did. The big fish are almost gone now
from the places you once went to, but clean or dirty, water keeps on
pouring. Today I bait the hook with you, as you did with Denise
and Jim and Gary. We throw each other in and hope the line bends.
I'm sorry to have pulled up such a small one—I'll throw it back, I
promise, while it's still alive and able to swim on. I'm sorry too
I missed you in this life, and send you blessings. Please do
what you can for the horses. Your tardy friend.

J.

Rain in May

The blackened iron
of the stove
is ticking into coolness
when the first drops
start against the roof.
It is late: the night
has darkened into this
like a fruit—
a sudden pear-aroma fills the room.

Just before dawn
it comes up harder again,
a white, steady drum of day-rain
caught in the moon's deep pail.
A battered tin-light
overspills ocean and sky,
hill opens to facing hill,
and I wake to a simple longing,
all I want of this ordinary hour,
this ordinary earth
that was long ago married to time:
to hear as a sand-crab hears the waves,
loud as a second heart;
to see as a green thing sees the sun,
with the undividing attention of blind love.

GARRETT KARU HONGO

Garrett Karu Hongo is the author of *Volcano: A Memoir of Hawai'i* and two poetry collections, *Yellow Light* and *The River of Heaven*, which was the 1988 Lamont Selection of the Academy of American Poets. A recipient of fellowships from the Guggenheim Foundation and the NEA, he has edited *Under Western Eyes: Personal Essays from Asian America; Songs My Mother Taught Me: Stories, Memoir, and Plays by Wakako Yamauchi;* and *The Open Boat: Poems from Asian America.* Currently, he is at work on an essay on the movement for Native Hawaiian sovereignty. He is Professor of Creative Writing at the University of Oregon.

© *Shuzo Uemoto*

"I write from the small tract home my parents bought for us in Gardena, near Los Angeles, its symmetrical grid of suburban streets, its corner gas stations and liquor stores, the barbed wire around my high school, the razor wire around wrecking yards and auto shops, the tiny Japanese *okazuyas* and gaudy poker parlors, the rat-nests of palm trees, and the long, cooling, fog-banked and wind-tunneled seaward-bound road at the center of town. I write from my memories of all of us in high school—black kids bused in from Compton, Chicanos from 'The Tracks' near Gardena Boulevard, and us *Buddhaheads* from all over town, worried about dress and the latest dances, worried about *cool* and avoiding addiction to glue and Robitussin even as we hoped we were college-bound. I write about the summer evening Festival for the Dead at Gardena Hongwanji and the intimate spaces of dinnertime cooking my mother and grandmother made, my father watching football and boxing on the TV, exhausted after work and stymied by his social isolation. I write from people who work and want better for themselves and their children.

"And I write from what was an intellectual native ground—my years away at Pomona College, where I studied literature, languages, and philosophy and was allowed to develop my deep love for learning and reflection. I found 'the better nature' of literary practices there, sponsored in my soul a feel for the finish of language, the finer tone of contemplative emotions. What was better than reading Keats and Kawabata in the mornings, hearing a lecture on jazz operas and *Moby Dick* by the fiery and signifying Stanley Crouch, browsing through the home library of the poet Bert Meyers and listening to him hold forth on the Spanish civil war and the last poems of Miguel Hernandez? What was better than reading *A Primer of Tu Fu* late at night, having a cup of burgundy, and practicing ideograms until I fell asleep over the smearing ink on the soft, absorbent pages of my copybook? A rhyme from Yeats runs through my head as I walk across the yellowing grass of the college soccer field. In the distance, I see the moon ascend over a snow-streaked Mt. Baldy, and I feel a studious complacency rousing into passion in the late spring twilight.

"In the end, I believe that writing from the ache of love for place exceeds all the praise and lyric description anyone can muster. Poet, take nothing from this world but awe and a longing to return to the magnificent beginnings of first things."

from Cruising 99

for Lawson Fusao Inada and Alan Chong Lau

I. A Porphyry of Elements

Starting in a long swale between the Sierras
   and the Coast Range,
Starting from ancient tidepools of a Pleistocene sea,
Starting from exposed granite bedrock,
From sandstone and shale, glaciated, river-worn,
   and scuffed by wind,
Tired of the extremes of temperature,
    the weather's wantonness,
Starting from the survey of a condor's eye
Cutting circles in the sky over Tehachapi and Tejon,
Starting from lava flow and snow on Shasta,
   a head of white hair,
   a garland of tongue-shaped obsidian,
Starting from the death of the last grizzly,
The final conversion of Tulare County
   to the internal-combustion engine,
Starting from California oak and acorn,
   scrubgrass, rivermist,
   and lupine in the foothills,
From days driving through the outfield clover
   of Modesto in a borrowed Buick,
From nights drinking pitchers of dark
   in the Neon Moon Bar & Grill,

From mornings grabbing a lunchpail, work gloves,
 and a pisspot hat,
From Digger pine and Douglas fir and aspen around Placerville,
From snowmelt streams slithering into the San Joaquin,
From the deltas and levees and floods of the Sacramento,
From fall runs of shad, steelhead, and salmon,
From a gathering of sand, rock, gypsum, clay,
 limestone, water, and tar,
From a need or desire to throw your money away
 in The Big City,
From a melting of history and space in the crucible
 of an oil-stained hand—
Starting from all of these, this porphyry of elements,
 this aggregate of experiences
Fused like feldspar and quartz to the azure stone
 of memory and vision,
Starting from all of these and an affectionate eye
 for straight, unending lines,
We hit this old road of Highway Ninety-Nine!

IX. Confession of the Highway/The Hermit Speaks

I know the rituals, the spells of grapes,
the ceremonies of tomatoes, celery, and rice.
I know the color of wind dressed for fiesta,
and the names of carnivals in Spanish and Japanese,
I am familiar with the determination of *campesinos*
who migrate up and down the stretch of the state
in search of crops ready for harvest.
It's all a dull ache in my back,
small cuts on the throats of my fingers,
and the alkali of a dry lake in my lungs.
For me, the oracle of the giant orange
always predicts good fortune,
yet, it never comes true.
My stomach is full of sand and tar,
a little bit of paint, a few crickets.
I stand in swampwater up to my hips,
and the stink of rotting figs
escapes from my armpits in small brown clouds.
Scrub oak and tumbleweed sprout from my scalp,

make a small grove behind my left ear.
I don't know why sparrows and starlings
refuse to approach me, to take the grass seed
tucked in the cuffs of my trousers.
Maybe it's the stain of asphalt around my ankles,
this copper sheen of sweat on my back.
Sometimes, when the valley heat
makes the bones in my feet
start to hiss and burn,
the desire to escape comes over me again.
I can't help it.
My arms pull down a few telephone posts,
my shoulders churn against the bindings.
I feel myself wanting to sit up,
begin to walk again, and thresh my way
across rice fields and acres of alfalfa.
For once I'd like to lift my face
straight above Shasta into the sky,
shout in unison with thunder,
roar with the assurance of Santana wind,
leap out of these bonds of copper and steel,
slough off this skin of cement,
and walk south or north or even west
into the weather and the sea.

Off from Swing Shift

Late, just past midnight,
freeway noise from the Harbor
and San Diego leaking in
from the vent over the stove,
and he's off from swing shift at Lear's.
Eight hours of twisting circuitry,
charting ohms and maximum gains
while transformers hum
and helicopters swirl
on the roofs above the small factory.
He hails me with a head-fake,
then the bob and weave

of a weekend middleweight
learned at the Y on Kapiolani
ten years before I was born.

The shoes and gold London Fogger
come off first, then the easy grin
saying he's lucky as they come.
He gets into the slippers
my brother gives him every Christmas,
carries his Thermos over to the sink,
and slides into the one chair at the table
that's made of wood and not yellow plastic.
He pushes aside stacks
of *Sporting News* and *Outdoor Life*
big round tins of Holland butter cookies,
and clears a space for his elbows, his pens,
and the *Racing Form's* Late Evening Final.

His left hand reaches out,
flicks on the Sony transistor
we bought for his birthday
when I was fifteen.
The right ferries in the earphone,
a small, flesh-colored star,
like a tiny miracle of hearing,
and fits it into place.
I see him plot black constellations
of figures and calculations
on the magazine's margins,
alternately squint and frown
as he fingers the knob of the tuner
searching for the one band
that will call out today's results.

There are whole cosmologies
in a single handicap,
a lifetime of two-dollar losing
in one pick of the Daily Double.

Maybe tonight is his night
for winning, his night
for beating the odds

of going deaf from a shell
at Anzio still echoing
in the cave of his inner ear,
his night for cashing in
the blue chips of shrapnel still grinding
at the thickening joints of his legs.

But no one calls
the horse's name, no one
says Shackles, Rebate, or Pouring Rain.
No one speaks a word.

Winnings

It's Gardena, late Saturday afternoon
on Vermont Avenue, near closing time
at the thrift store, and my father's
left me to rummage through trash bins
stuffed with used paperbacks, 25¢ a pound,
while he chases down some bets
at the card clubs across the street.

The register rings up its sales—$2.95,
$11.24, $26.48 for the reclaimed Frigidaire—
and a girl, maybe six or so, barefoot,
in a plaid dress, her hair braided
in tight cornrows, tugs at the strap
of her mother's purse, begging a few
nickels for the gumball machine.

She skips through the check-stand,
runs toward the electric exit, passing
a fleet of shopping carts, bundles
of used-up magazines *(Ebony* and *Jet)*
stacked in pyramids in the far aisle,
reaches the bright globe of the vendor,
fumbles for her coins, and works the knob.

My father comes in from the Rainbow
across the street, ten hands of Jacks
or Better, five draw, a winner

with a few dollars to peel away
from grocery money and money to fix
the washer, a dollar for me to buy
four pounds of Pocket Wisdoms, Bantams,

a Dell that says *Walt Whitman, Poet
of the Open Road*, and hands it to me,
saying "We won, *Boy-san!* We Won!"
as the final blast of sunset kicks through
plate glass and stained air, firing through
the thicket of neon across the street,
consuming the store, the girl, the dollar bill,

even the Rainbow and the falling night
in a brief symphony of candied light.

Yellow Light

One arm hooked around the frayed strap
of a tar-black patent-leather purse,
the other cradling something for dinner:
fresh bunches of spinach from a J-Town *yaoya,*
sides of split Spanish mackerel from Alviso's,
maybe a loaf of Langendorf; she steps
off the hissing bus at Olympic and Fig,
begins the three-block climb up the hill,
passing gangs of schoolboys playing war,
Japs against Japs, Chicanas chalking sidewalks
with the holy double-yoked crosses of hopscotch,
and the Korean grocer's wife out for a stroll
around this neighborhood of Hawaiian apartments
just starting to steam with cooking
and the anger of young couples coming home
from work, yelling at kids, flicking on
TV sets for the Wednesday Night Fights.

If it were May, hydrangeas and jacaranda
flowers in the streetside trees would be
blooming through the smog of late spring.
Wisteria in Masuda's front yard would be

shaking out the long tresses of its purple hair.
Maybe mosquitoes, moths, a few orange butterflies
settling on the lattice of monkey flowers
tangled in chain-link fences by the trash.

But this is October, and Los Angeles
seethes like a billboard under twilight.
From used-car lots and the movie houses uptown,
long silver sticks of light probe the sky.
From the Miracle Mile, whole freeways away,
a brilliant fluorescence breaks out
and makes war with the dim squares
of yellow kitchen light winking on
in all the side streets of the Barrio.

She climbs up the two flights of flagstone
stairs to 201-B, the spikes of her high heels
clicking like kitchen knives on a cutting board,
props the groceries against the door,
fishes through memo pads, a compact,
empty packs of chewing gum, and finds her keys.

The moon then, cruising from behind
a screen of eucalyptus across the street,
covers everything, everything in sight,
in a heavy light like yellow onions.

LAWSON FUSAO INADA

Although born in mid-Fresno (Burnett Sanitarium, 1938) and incarcerated in east Fresno (fairgrounds, 1942), Lawson Fusao Inada is from West Fresno, the West Side, "Chinatown," where he lived from 1945 to 1960 and never really left. His latest books are *Legends from Camp* and *Drawing the Line*.

"California. What about it? I'm still trying to comprehend my small portion of the state—West Fresno (designated by surveyors as the *exact center* of the state)—and even though it's a definable place geographically, its history is immense, churning with a multitude of cultures. Thus, even my immediate neighborhood, composed of only a few blocks, remains a mystery, shrouded in mist, and I'm learning more about it all the time.

"For instance, out of the blue recently, a childhood friend told me that my neighborhood (my block alone had Japanese, Chinese, Mexican, Italian, German, and black residences) used to be called 'the hill of tin roofs' by German immigrants who arrived via the Ukraine.

"Or, over on that corner, if you looked around the nicely landscaped grounds of that black Baptist church, you'd find an elongated building next to the main structure, and in the blink of an eye you'd realize you're looking at a barrack that was moved there by a previous congregation from the fairgrounds across town after the war and after their incarceration.

"For that particular congregation alone, the painted barrack was their *third* church over the decades in West Fresno; my mother went to three, I went to two, and the new manifestation in Clovis makes four. Now multiply that by any number of denominations and sub-denominations and peoples and cultures, and factor in house-churches and storefront places of worship, and you get a sense of one facet of West Fresno.

"I'm fascinated by the facets, the facts, because they all add up to our individual and collective selves who have been shaped by factors we may not recognize or know. I didn't even know that this space called 'California' is actually composed of seven distinct geographic areas with distinct histories until I read *The Seven States of California* by Philip Fradkin. Or, do you know where Yokohama, California, is? That's the title of a book by Toshio Mori. A new book, *Central Avenue Sounds,* edited by Bryant et al., provides a vision of the 'Harlem Renaissance' of South Central L.A.

"However, fittingly enough, I've learned the most about California by reading about pre-California in the publications of Heyday Books. That 'California' was really something, with such powerful poetry. May this collection be worthy of that tradition."

Concentration Constellation

In this earthly configuration,
we have, not points of light,
but prominent barbs of dark.

It's all right there on the map.
It's all right there in the mind.
Find it. If you care to look.

Begin between the Golden State's
highest and lowest elevations
and name that location

Manzanar. Rattlesnake a line
southward to the zone
of Arizona, to the home
of natives on the reservation,
and call those *Gila, Poston.*

Then just take your time
winding your way across
the Southwest expanse, the Lone
Star State of Texas, gathering
up a mess of blues as you
meander around the banks
of the humid Mississippi; yes,
just make yourself at home
in the swamps of Arkansas,
for this is *Rohwer* and *Jerome.*

By now, you weary of the way.
It's a big country, you say.
It's a big history, hardly

halfway though—with *Amache*
looming in the Colorado desert,
Heart Mountain high in wide
Wyoming, *Minidoka* on the moon
of Idaho, then down to Utah's
jewel of *Topaz* before finding
yourself at northern California's
frozen shore of *Tule Lake*...

Now regard what sort of shape
this constellation takes.
It sits there like a jagged scar,
massive, on the massive landscape.
It lies there like the rusted wire
of a twisted and remembered fence.

from Legends from Camp

Prologue

It began as truth, as fact.
That is, at least the numbers, the statistics,
are there for verification:

10 camps, 7 states,
120,113 residents.

Still, figures can lie: people are born, die.
And as for the names of the places themselves,
these, too, were subject to change:

Denson or Jerome, Arkansas;
Gila or Canal, Arizona;
Tule Lake or Newell, California;
Amache or Granada, Colorado.

As was the War Relocation Authority
with its mention of "camps" or "centers" for:

Assembly,
Concentration,
Detention,

Evacuation,
Internment,
Relocation,—
among others.

"Among others"—that's important also. Therefore, let's not forget con-
tractors, carpenters, plumbers, electricians and architects, sewage engi-
neers, and all the untold thousands who provided the materials, decisions,
energy, and transportation to make the camps a success, including, of
course, the administrators, clerks, and families who not only swelled
the population but were there to make and keep things shipshape
according to D.C. directives and people deploying coffee in the vari-
ous offices of the WRA, overlooking, overseeing rivers, cityscapes,
bays, whereas in actual camp the troops—excluding, of course, our
aunts and uncles and sisters and brothers and fathers and mothers
serving stateside, in the South Pacific, the European theater—pretty
much had things in order; finally, there were the grandparents, who
since the turn of the century, simply assumed they were living in
America "among others."

The situation, obviously, was rather confusing.
It obviously confused simple people
who had simply assumed they were friends, neighbors,
colleagues, partners, patients, customers, students,
teachers, of, not so much "aliens" or "non-aliens,"
but likewise simple, unassuming people
who paid taxes as fellow citizens and populated
pews and desks and fields and places
of ordinary American society and commerce.

Rumors flew. Landed. What's what? Who's next?

And then, "just like that," it happened.
And then, "just like that," it was over.
Sun, moon, stars—they came, and went.

And then, and then, things happened,
and as they ended they kept happening,
and as they happened they ended
and began again, happening, happening,
until the event, the experience, the history,

slowly began to lose its memory,
gradually drifting into a kind of fiction—

a "true story based on fact,"
but nevertheless with "all the elements of fiction"—
and then, and then, sun, moon, stars,
we come, we come, to where we are:
Legend.

III. The Legend of Protest

The F.B.I. swooped in early,
taking our elders in the process—

for "subversive" that and this.

People ask: "Why didn't you protest?"
Well, you might say: "They had *hostages.*"

XX. The Legend of Home

Home, too, was out there.
It had names like
Marysville, Placerville,
Watsonville, and Lodi—
and they were all big cities
or at least bigger than camp.

And they were full of trees,
and grass, with fruit
for the picking, dogs
to chase, cats to catch

on streets and roads
where Joey and Judy lived,

Imagine that!
The blue tricycle
left in the weeds somewhere!
And when you came to a fence,
You went around it!

And one of those homes
not only had a tunnel
but an overpass
that, when you went over,

revealed everything
going on forever up to
a gleaming bridge
leading into neon lights
and ice cream leaning
double-decker.

Imagine that!

The Fresno Truth

For Malcolm Margolin

A proud associate told me—
"I'm moving to the upper West Side"—
but I wasn't all that impressed.

After all, I moved *from*
the upper West Side
of Fresno, that prominent plateau
overlooking the grand metropolis…

Fresno, being Fresno—
that visionary, planned community,
role-model of the Western world—

continually serves to uphold itself
as a point of reference and comparison.

Thus, all the lesser, aspiring Fresnos
of the Great Valley,
from Bakersfield to Redding—

"the poor man's Fresno,"
"Fresno gone amok," etcetera—

and so on up and down the Coast:

San Francisco ("Gateway to Fresno"),
L.A. ("Backdoor to Fresno"),
Seattle ("Wet Fresno")…

Then there's New York
("Fresno in a vise"),

Chicago ("Half of Fresno
flooded by a lake"),

and other unfortunate places:

Venice ("Fresno
without drainage"),
Paris ("Fresneaux
without parking"),
and that crumbling
Anglo-Fresno
known as London…

As kids growing up in Fresno,
thanks to its proto-cosmopolitan ambience,
we knew what the rest of the world
was really all about;

and even as projected "larger than life"
on the silver screen,
that world and that life
shrank into realistic scale outside—

fitting, befitting, familiar Fresno
in black-and-white, technicolor,
animation, whatever,
all to the uncannily synchronized
soundtrack of outright Fresno life…

Consider: "The Wizard of Oz"
            ("white-trash Fresno"),
            "Citizen Kane"
            ("deluded East Fresno"),
            "Casablanca"
            (actually filmed in Fresno),
            "Gone With the Wind"
            ("historical Fresno"),
            "Snow White"
            ("political Fresno")—
and all Westerns are obviously Fresno.

Moreover, "subliminal Fresno" surfaced
in Bergman, Kurosawa, Fellini, Ray…

Which brings us to the Fresno Truth:

There has always been, and always will be,
a Fresno—and even before its present name
it was there, worthy of any gathering

in need of fresh food, fresh water,
fresh music and fresh Fresno companionship
on fresh Fresno land under the fresh Fresno sky!

JEAN JANZEN

Jean Janzen has lived in Fresno since 1961. Born in Saskatchewan, Canada, and raised in the midwestern United States, she and her pediatrician husband, Louis, have raised four children in the San Joaquin Valley. Jean teaches poetry writing at Fresno Pacific University and Eastern Mennonite University in Virginia. Her published collections of poetry are *Words for the Silence, Three Mennonite Poets, The Upside-down Tree*, and *Snake in the Parsonage*. She received an NEA grant in 1995, and her work has been included in numerous anthologies.

"To claim California as home is to claim both immensity and looseness. The open spaces of this great valley and the fine clay dust breathe an unsettledness for me, while the grand Sierra on one side and the ocean on the other shape the wild borders. It is an awesome home, one for which I have spent years trying to find language.

"But home is an imaginary construct, some say, the place where we most truly live. These poems, which investigate the deprivations as well as the plenitude of this valley, recognize that we are indeed east of Eden, and what we most desire is somewhere else. Meanwhile, the velvet summer nights and the fragrance of magnolias modulate the harsh realities of labor and loss, and the mockingbird celebrates desire, singing for us our origins and our destiny."

At Summer's End

The sweet run ends with the shutdown
gates at Pine Flat Dam.
And Fancher Creek begins its slow drain
into silence. It is inevitable,
the mountain's gift of snow-water
measured out. And then
what has been lost and discarded
reveals itself in the empty bed—
bicycle, mattress, the carcass of a dog.

I want the creek to run all year,
the singing that carries secrets away
to the sea, and buries them.
But even the Pacific returns
the lost—a diver, once, on the beach
where my children played, his black
suit glistening like a seal.
This spring a seven-year-old girl
spilled out into the lake
and hasn't been found. She had been
dragging her hands in the icy blue,
laughing, and no one saw what the clouds
held until the wind was unleashed.
That lake feeds the creek where I walk,
the sinking creek, that green music
which can't keep its secrets
because it has to stop. Because
a gift must be received to be a gift.
The whole thing. The truth of it.

August Nights

These nights when first
fermentations sour the air,
I hear the semis churn
their loads in a great
continuous groan.
And I know that thousands
of pickers lie exhausted
under the meteor showers.
All day in the sun's
brutal press, the tails
of debris flared over them,
unseen, over the vineyards
where they knelt
in the suffocating rows,
knives flashing.
But when we lie down
at last, each of us

in our separate weariness,
we see the burning flowers,
some traveling the whole arc
of the sky. We forget
about the jagged mass
of stone and metal,
a mile wide, riding loosely
in an orbit over us.
But sometimes in our dreams
that cold weight sweeps close,
and we awaken with clenched
hands, praying for the sun
and its labors to blind us
through another day.

Claiming the Dust

Like nomads we came
to this subtropical valley,
our borrowed space
under the sun. Once
an ancient lakebed,
the July ground powders
under our feet, lifts
in puffs to welcome us.
The children rise, then
run out to pound acorns
under the oaks, calling
to each other from
their rings of stones.
Pale bird-of-paradise leans
out of its gravelly bed.
It takes dynamite to plant
an orange tree, our neighbor sighs.

This is our new home,
this valley's layered clay
which offers its sunbaked surface
to the scuffing of our feet,

as if our fragile lives
are enough to rouse the ages.
The slightest breeze, and the dust
becomes skittish, whirls
to settle in the next yard.
But mostly, stillness,
so that the beige siftings
are almost imperceptible
Fig leaves in a talcum haze.

It is the night we finally learn
to claim. At dusk the children
float their sheets like flattened tents
and sprawl face-up into the warm
darkness, and we join them
in this rehearsal—a summer
night travel, the sky's black
curtains pinned back with stars.
That open stage.
This hard earth not our final holding
place after all, but the air
into which we sail,
breath by dusty breaths,
toward a different shore.

Pomegranate

This long valley caught
between two ranges,
this ancient seabed.
Nothing stirs in the scorched
fields, and still
our gardens swell, drinking
deeply from hidden
wells and streams.
So that in autumn a ripeness
hangs sweet and heavy
among brittle leaves—
seedy fig like a scrotum

in my hand, olives and walnuts
dropping as flocks
of starlings feast
and bicker in the trees.
The pomegranates won't fall;
their hides split and open
like books, rows
of ruby seeds clinging
to parchment. I clip one
and begin the crush,
suck the dark astringencies,
spit the seeds.
And I do a little jig,
clapping the air
with my stained hands.

MARK JARMAN

© Rebecca Walk

Mark Jarman's latest collection of poetry, *Questions for Ecclesiastes,* was a finalist for the 1997 National Book Critics Circle Award and won the Lenore Marshall Award from the Academy of American Poets. His book of essays, *The Secret of Poetry,* is forthcoming from Story Line Press, as is his next collection of poetry, *Unholy Sonnets.* He teaches at Vanderbilt University.

"My parents were Angelenos who thought of Redondo Beach as the sticks. When they were growing up in the 1940s, dairy farms and orange groves still separated where they lived, in South Central Los Angeles, from the beach towns like Redondo, Hermosa Beach, and Manhattan Beach to the southwest. My parents traveled to Kentucky, where my father went to seminary and I was born, then to Scotland, where my father served a church. When they came home to the states, my father took a church out in the sticks, in Redondo Beach. But by that time, 1961, the freeway system had filled in the rural spaces between Los Angeles and the lower part of Santa Monica Bay, where Redondo was located. Redondo wasn't the sticks anymore, though you could see Chicano graffiti on walls around town for a car club called *Los Tules.* Though still fairly seedy, Redondo was connected to the big busy world by miles and miles of freeway cities.

"Geographically, however, it remained distinct. A low range of coast hills protected it, keeping it cooler and its air cleaner than the rest of the L.A. Basin. On the south end of town, the Palos Verdes Peninsula hid the silhouette of Catalina Island. To the north, we could see the hazy serrations of the Santa Monica Mountains, descending toward Malibu. The beach break in Redondo was perfect for surfing, though the city attempted to extend its beaches one year, pouring miles of sand that ruined the waves. The ocean ate it all back eventually. Eventually I grew up and left for college at U.C. Santa Cruz (everyone I knew in the Basin wanted out, wanted to go to Northern California), then for graduate school in Iowa, and then many places, until coming to rest in Nashville, Tennessee, another kind of sticks a far cry from *Los Tules.*

"Redondo Beach remains one of two points of origin for me, one of two grounds of being. The other is a linoleum factory town on the North Sea, another sort of beach town. Many of my poems return to Redondo, to the ocean there, to the life I lived there and would happily live again.

"Recently, I returned to Redondo Beach on a summer day with my family. It had been hot and smoggy in Los Angeles, where we were staying. We exited the San Diego Freeway at 190th, and as soon as that long, long exit topped the rise between Dominguez Park and South Bay Hospital, the air changed. In a few blocks we could see King Harbor and the Pacific Ocean. We drove south on Catalina Avenue and parked at the beginning of the Esplanade. It was early evening, and people who had been at the beach all day were leaving, others were taking walks before supper. The air was cool, there was a light onshore breeze, the water was gray and clear, the red tile roofs of the houses on the P.V. Peninsula were as vivid as the Riviera. And I wondered, as I walked along with my wife and two daughters, why I had ever left or wanted to leave."

Ground Swell

Is nothing real but when I was fifteen,
Going on sixteen, like a corny song?
I see myself so clearly then, and painfully—
Knees bleeding through my usher's uniform
Behind the candy counter in the theater
After a morning's surfing; paddling frantically
To top the brisk outsiders coming to wreck me,
Trundle me clumsily along the beach floor's
Gravel and sand; my knees aching with salt.
Is that all that I have to write about?
You write about the life that's vividest.
And if that is your own, that is your subject.
And if the years before and after sixteen
Are colorless as salt and taste like sand—
Return to those remembered chilly mornings,
The light spreading like a great skin on the water,
And the blue water scalloped with wind-ridges,
And—what was it exactly?—that slow waiting
When, to invigorate yourself, you peed
Inside your bathing suit and felt the warmth
Crawl all around your hips and thighs,
And the first set rolled in and the water level
Rose in expectancy, and the sun struck
The water surface like a brassy palm,
Flat and gonglike, and the wave face formed.

Yes. But that was a summer so removed
In time, so specially peculiar to my life,
Why would I want to write about it again?

There was a day or two when, paddling out,
An older boy who had just graduated
And grown a great blonde moustache, like a walrus,
Skimmed past me like a smooth machine on the water,
And said my name. I was so much younger,
To be identified by one like him—
The easy deference of a kind of god
Who also went to church where I did—made me
Reconsider my worth. I had been noticed.
He soon was a small figure crossing waves,
The shawling crest surrounding him with spray,
Whiter than gull feathers. He had said my name
Without scorn, just with a bit of surprise
To notice me among those trying the big waves
Of the morning break. His name is carved now
On the black wall in Washington, the frozen wave
That grievers cross to find a name or names.
I knew him as I say I knew him, then,
Which wasn't very well. My father preached
His funeral. He came home in a bag
That may have mixed in pieces of his squad.
Yes, I can write about a lot of things
Besides the summer that I turned sixteen.
But that's my ground swell, I must start
Where things began to happen and I knew it.

Cavafy in Redondo

Our ruins run back to memory.
Stucco palaces, pleasure bungalows, the honeycomb
of the beachcombers' cluster of rentals—
I remember them, filings in sand
pricking up at the magnet of nostalgia,
a sigh of dusty filaments. Our ruins
wear the as-yet-unruined like coral crowns.

Night life blows through the boardwalk's
conch-shell coils of neon, skirting the water.
This was never—Ask my parents—a great city.
It had its charm, like a clear tidal shallows,
silted-in now, poldered, substantial, solid,
set for the jellying quake everyone expects.

I walked these streets one night with a new lover,
an as-yet-to-be lover—it took a whole night
of persuasion. I had been gone a year,
and walked as sea mist compounded the dew.
My legs ached by the time bed was agreed to.
How sentimental it was, to flatter, listen,
cajole, make little whining endearments,
plodding ritualistically among landmarks,
sandy shrines in alleys, the black meccas
of plate-glass windows fronting the beach
where white froth reflected in the night.
I kept that ache, not love's, after we parted.

We did not part to history with its glosses;
we were not even footnotes. Our ruins
will bear out no epics or histories here,
footprints compounded of dew and fog
and under them, maybe a rusty antique
that, boiled in acids, will tell a tale.
After all, ships passed, broke up on the point.
Mainly, the beach eroded in great ridges
until ground cover belted it back. A pleasure dome
was dismantled, certain fashions
of dress and of love. History builds to last,
crumbles to last, shakes off its dust
under the delicate excavating brush—to last.

Built above the beach was a colossus,
humped and strutted and roaring with many voices.
Winds chased through it screeching and then
it stood silent. People flocked to it, entered it,
and though not lost, screamed as if tortured.
I am joking. There was a roller coaster
of some note and no small size. Where did it go?

Ah, yes, lost in the coral make-up
of that teetering lover who walked beside me,
tired of my harangue, the persuasive underlove
that wanted to rise to the lips, those lips
colored by fuming street lamps.

Young, my parents drove out from a distant city,
through tawny hills medallioned with oak.
I have seen their worn postcards of the town,
a tide pool of neighborhoods mantled around
by semi-wilderness and orange groves.
Missiles came to squat above our house
on a benchmarked hill, turned obsolete,
and floated away on flatbeds, ruptured patios in their places.
We, too, left that house that heard,
in every lath and windowpane, the industry of phosphorus,
grinding out the waves in the late darkness.
My parents—all of us—have come and gone and left
no ghosts here, and that is our good fortune,
to give it all to the ocean, the troubled sleeper.

The Supremes

In Ball's Market after surfing till noon,
we stand in wet trunks, shivering
as icing dissolves off our sweet rolls
inside the heat-blued counter oven,
when they appear on his portable TV,
riding a float of chiffon as frothy
as the peeling curl of a wave.
The parade m. c. talks up their hits
and their new houses outside of Detroit
and old Ball clicks his tongue.
Gloved up to their elbows, their hands raised
toward us palm out, they sing,
"Stop! In the Name of Love" and don't stop
but slip into the lower foreground.

Every day of a summer can turn,
from one moment, into a single day.
I saw Diana Ross in her first film
play a brief scene by the Pacific—
and that was the summer it brought back.
Mornings we paddled out, the waves
would be little more than embellishments:
lathework and spun glass,
gray-green with cold, but flawless.
When the sun burned through the light fog,
they would warm and swell,
wind-scaled and ragged,
and radios up and down the beach
would burst on with her voice.

She must remember that summer
somewhat differently, and so must the two
who sang with her in long matching gowns,
standing a step back on her left and right,
as the camera tracked them
into our eyes in Ball's Market.
But what could we know, tanned white boys,
wiping sugar and salt from our mouths
and leaning forward to feel their song?
Not much, except to feel it
ravel us up like a wave
in the silk of white water,
simply, sweetly, repeatedly,
and just as quickly let go.

We didn't stop either, which is how
we vanished, too, parting like spray—
Ball's Market, my friends and I.
Dredgers ruined the waves,
those continuous dawn perfections,
and Ball sold high to the high rises
cresting over them. His flight out of L.A.,
heading for Vegas, would have banked
above the wavering lines of surf.
He may have seen them. I have,

leaving again for points north and east,
glancing down as the plane turns.
From that height they still look frail and frozen,
full of simple sweetness and repetition.

The Black Riviera

for Garrett Hongo

There they are again. It's after dark.
The rain begins its sober comedy,
Slicking down their hair as they wait
Under a pepper tree or eucalyptus,
Larry Dietz, Luis Gonzalez, the Fitzgerald brothers,
And Jarman, hidden from the cop car
Sleeking innocently past. Stoned,
They giggle a little, with money ready
To pay for more, waiting in the rain.

They buy from the black Riviera
That silently appears, as if risen,
The apotheosis of wet asphalt
And smeary-silvery glare
And plush inner untouchability.
A hand takes money and withdraws,
Another extends a sack of plastic—
Short, too dramatic to be questioned.
What they buy is light rolled in a wave.

They send the money off in a long car
A god himself could steal a girl in,
Clothing its metal sheen in the spectrum
Of bars and discos and restaurants.
And they are left, dripping rain
Under their melancholy tree, and see time
Knocked akilter, sort of funny,
But slowing down strangely, too.
So, what do they dream?

They might dream that they are in love
And wake to find they are,

That outside their own pumping arteries,
Which they can cargo with happiness
As they sink in their little bathyspheres,
Somebody else's body pressures theirs
With kisses, like bursts of bloody oxygen,
Until, stunned, they're dragged up,
Drawn from drowning, saved.

In fact, some of us woke up that way.
It has to do with how desire takes shape.
Tapered, encapsulated, engineered
To navigate an illusion of deep water,
Its beauty has the dark roots
Of a girl skipping down a high-school corridor
Selling Seconal from a bag,
Or a black car gliding close to the roadtop,
So insular, so quiet, it enters the earth.

STEPHEN KESSLER

Stephen Kessler's poems, transla-
tions, essays, criticism, and jour-
nalism have appeared variously in
the independent literary and alter-
native press since the late 1960s.

© David Alexander

"Born (1947) and raised in Los
Angeles, I lived for more than
twenty years in the Santa Cruz
area and since 1992 have resided
on the south coast of Mendocino
County. While I seldom set out to
write 'about' any particular land-
scape, the geography of coastal
California—southern, central, and northern—is the natural habitat of my
imagination, the sensory reservoir from which my writing draws some of its
richest resources. There's no great mystery to this; when I lived in New York
City for a couple of years my poems reflected that environment. But my his-
toric roots in California nourish the work in more pervasive ways. At best, I
think my native L.A. sensibility with its urban edges and jumpy associations
informs and transforms my apprehension of the more tranquil rustic land-
scape I now call home. Even 'nature poetry,' in my experience, thrives on the
vital anguish of the city."

Cigarette Case

When you come to smoke
with me in the mountains
I like the spark in your eyes
when we light up

the mist over the river reminds me
of the drift our friendship follows
through years of dinners in town
at Chinese restaurants where the beer
in our frosted mugs cooled and seduced
our tongues as we talked

in the pavilion of moonlit religion
tobacco was our sacrament

and the taste of gossip
left us reckless
with useless and beautiful
bad habits

Jack's Last Words

That last afternoon
when the nurse came in
and sucked the liquid out of his lungs
with a plastic tube down his nose
plugged in the wall
my father said
when she was done
"Give her a dollar"

he always was the big tipper
maybe because his sister
when their old man didn't come home
had to quit school and take a job as a waitress
he knew it was tough to work
and so he tipped

he barely spoke that day
the sun of L.A. blazing mid-July
cool room shady
facing the Hollywood Hills
Hamburger Hamlet across the street
where we ate
waiting for him to die

each of us had our turn
to be with him alone
lying there dignified
silent in the white sheets
face hollowed out and bald head glowing
radiation tanned
I told him he looked beautiful
and he groaned

the bandage around the i.v.
was too tight

after the nurse fixed that
he had a couple of hours
I was there for a while
the two of us just quiet
until he said with a shrug
in his tired voice
"I paid for it"

Marty's Mother

She wanted her ashes scattered
at Dodger Stadium
every time someone slides into third base
a puff of her dust
would float toward the floodlights

Vivian's voice had a tough
but affectionate edge
sweetened by watching Maury Wills
beat out cheap hits in 1962
and who knows what Yiddish history
absorbed in her Brooklyn youth

when we were kids
and we came over
she said as we left
"It was nice having had you"

years later
Maury got popped for coke
and Marty became a shrink
and I whom it was nice having had
a poet and former infielder
small but slow
with a nose for form
and no arm

Vivian it's been 30 years
missing you isn't the issue
but I want for a moment to go back
with your boy
to the real grass of our adolescence
secretly seeding at 2 a.m.
your memory in the gameless dark

CAROLYN KIZER

Carolyn Kizer has published eight books of poetry, two books of essays, and has edited two books: *The Essential Clare* (the first American edition of John Clare's poetry) and *100 Great Poems by Women*. *YIN* won the Pulitzer Prize for Poetry in 1985. She recently won the Aiken Taylor Prize for lifetime achievement from *The Sewanee Review*. She lives in Sonoma—and some of the time in Paris—with her husband, John Woodbridge, an architect and architectural historian.

© *Robert Turney*

"Although I was born and grew up in the Northwest, my ties to California go back almost to my birth. My mother was a Californian; so was my grandfather, Dr. Ashley, who ran a tuberculosis sanitarium in Newhall for the State of California; so were four of my uncles, two of whom worked for my grandfather. I visited 'the San' as soon as I was old enough to travel, and went there with Mother for part of eight years, usually at Christmas. Mother earned her graduate degree from Stanford in biology (in 1910!), and headed the biology department at Mills, and later, at San Francisco State. My younger daughter is also a Stanford graduate. And I've lived in California for the past twenty-two years, first in Berkeley and for the last ten years in Sonoma. So I feel perfectly at home here, though I don't know as many people here as in New York or Washington, D.C., or Seattle. My older daughter lives in Los Angeles with her doctor-poet husband and their three children.

"Although there is a reference to California in an early poem ('Tying One on in Vienna': 'the scent of orange groves in the sweet San Fernando Valley / North of Los Angeles where I spent my childhood') California didn't really creep into my poetry until the late seventies, when I'd been living here for a year or two. These poems don't focus on California as such, but to me they breathe the atmosphere of California and would not have existed had I not lived here. California exists as daydream, as myth, as the home of my husband and one of my best friends (who was born and raised in the St. Francis hotel), as a fantasy I shared with another dear friend. In particular, the time I spent in Sausalito in the sixties, where I was happy and unhappy at the same time, has left an indelible mark. I think it was both my ambivalent feelings and the great fun of Sausalito in those days—alas, no more—that made that time so memorable. Having lived with Seattle rain for seventeen years, I think of lovely sunlight first, when I think of California; then I see the tawny hills punctuated with the occasional dark oak; then the odor of pepper trees and eucalyptus; then the Golden Gate Bridge; then Palo Alto and memories of Mother; then....There's more, much more, but that's enough."

Afternoon Happiness

At a party I spy a handsome psychiatrist,
And wish, as we all do, to get her advice for free.
Doctor, I'll say, I'm supposed to be a poet.
All life's awfulness has been grist to me.
We learn that happiness is a Chinese meal,
While sorrow is a nourishment forever.
My new environment is California Dreamer.
I'm fearful I'm forgetting how to brood.
And, Doctor, another thing has got me worried:
I'm not drinking as much as I should...

At home, I want to write a happy poem
On love, or a love poem of happiness.
But they won't do, the tensions of everyday,
The rub, the minor abrasions of any two
Who share one space. Ah, there's no substitute for tragedy!
But in this chapter, tragedy belongs
To that other life, the old life before *us*.
Here is my aphorism of the day:
Happy people are monogamous,
Even in California. So how does the poem play

Without the paraphernalia of betrayal and loss?
I don't have a jealous eye or fear
And neither do you. In truth, I'm fond
Of your ex-mate, whom I name, "my wife-in-law."
My former husband, that old disaster, is now just funny,
So laugh we do, in what Cyril Connolly
Has called the endless, nocturnal conversation
Of marriage. Which may be the best part.
Darling, must I love you in light verse
Without the tribute of profoundest art?

Of course it won't last. You will break my heart
Or I yours, by dying. I could weep over that.
But now it seems forced, here in these heaven hills,
The mourning doves mourning, the squirrels mating,
My old cat warm in my lap, here on our terrace
As from below comes a musical cursing
As you mend my favorite plate. Later of course
I could pick a fight; there is always material in that.
But we don't come from fighting people, those
Who scream out red-hot iambs in their hate.

No, love, the heavy poem will have to come
From *temps perdu,* fertile with pain, or perhaps
Detonated by terrors far beyond this place
Where the world rends itself, and its tainted waters
Rise in the east to erode our safety here.
Much as I want to gather a lifetime thrift
And craft, my cunning skills tied in a knot for you,
There is only this useless happiness as gift.

An American Beauty

As you described your mastectomy in calm detail
and bared your chest so I might see
the puckered scar,
"They took a hatchet to your breast!" I said. "What an
Amazon you are."

When we were girls we climbed Mt. Tamalpais
chewing bay leaves we had plucked
along the way;
we got high all right, from animal pleasure in each other,
shouting to the sky.

On your houseboat we tried to ignore the impossible guy
you had married to enrage your family,
a typical ploy.
We were great fools let loose in the No Name bar
on Sausalito's bay.

In San Francisco we'd perch on a waterfront pier
chewing sourdough and cheese, swilling champagne,
kicking our heels;
crooning lewd songs, hooting like seagulls,
we bayed with the seals.

Then you married someone in Mexico,
broke up in two weeks, didn't bother to divorce,
claimed it didn't count.
You dumped number three, fled to Albany
to become a pedant.

Averse to domesticity, you read for your Ph.D.
Your four-year-old looked like a miniature
John Lennon.
You fed him peanut butter from the jar and raised him
on Beowulf and Grendel.

Much later in New York we reunited;
in an elevator at Sak's a woman asked for
your autograph.
You glowed like a star, like Anouk Aimée
at forty, close enough.

Your pedantry found its place in the Women's Movement.
You rose fast, seen suddenly as the morning star;
wrote the ERA
found the right man at last, a sensitive artist;
flying too high

not to crash. When the cancer caught you
you went on talk shows to say you had no fear
or faith.
In Baltimore we joked on your bed as you turned into
a witty wraith.

When you died I cleaned out your bureau drawers:
your usual disorder; an assortment of gorgeous wigs
and prosthetic breasts
tossed in garbage bags, to spare your gentle spouse.
Then the bequests

you had made to every friend you had!
For each of us a necklace or a ring.
A snapshot for me:
We two, barefoot in chiffon, laughing amid blossoms
your last wedding day.

For Ann London

For Jan as the End Draws Near

We never believed in safety
certainly not in numbers
and little more alone.

Picking peas in California
was our old jest of how we'd end our days
when we knew there was no providence,
not any.

We didn't need a reason to be foolish!
Now it turns out that serious theorists
were more improvident than we.

The ones with everything to lose
will mind it most.

I whisper this in some uncertainty:
I don't believe that they grow peas
in California, even on the coast.

Who knows? There may not be a California.

To us it meant a hellish kind of heaven,
a kind that unbelievers could believe in;
a warm land, where we would be
companionable crones

in our little shack, a stinking stove,
a basin of warm water for cracked feet,
each other's hands to stroke
our twisted spines;

our twin grins cracking leather
as we dish out dinner
on our pie-tin plates.

Well, we were a pair of feckless girls!
Depression children, idealists and dreamers
as our parents and grandparents were.

Of the two of us, you had the darker view.
As it turns out, it wasn't dark enough.

Now the sun shines bright in California
as I shell peas for supper.
Our old-crone fantasies have moved much closer
to an obscure isle in Greece
though we well know that there's no hiding place
down here.

Meanwhile, we've had nearly forty years
to crack our dismal jokes and love each other.
This was our providence, this was our wisdom.
The present is this poem, O my dear.

Promising Author

Driving on the road to Stinson Beach
I remember your witty gap-toothed face
Half-ruined in a dozen shore-leave brawls,
And the straw hair and softening gut
Of a beat-up scarecrow out of Oz.

I drove this road with you
Some sixteen years ago
Skidding on curves between the pepper trees.
You whipped the wheel as though it were a helm
And laughed at my nauseated pleas.

Once at the beach you made the finest soup
I've ever tasted: scallops, peas and leeks,
And I pictured you, the cook on some old tramp

Scudding through Conrad seas,
A boy still dazzled by his luck and grace.

Later that week, in Sausalito's
Bar with no name, I watched you curl your lip
As you ran down every writer in the place,
Unkinder with each drink,
Till I fled up the hill to the French Hotel.

After that you married Beth, so rich
She bought you monogrammed silk shirts,
A dozen at a clip,
You wore as you sneered at your shabby friends
Who had lent you money.

You became glib as any Grub Street hack,
Then demanded help
To write the novel you would never write:
As I turned you from the door
You cursed me, and I cursed you back.

Once I believed you were the great white shark,
Slick predator, with tough scarred hide.
But now I know you were a small sea-lion,
Vulnerable, whiskery, afraid,
Who wept for mercy as you died.

LARRY KRAMER

Larry Kramer was born in Newton, Iowa, and grew up in Amarillo, Texas, and Columbia, Missouri. A graduate of Ohio State University and the University of Iowa Writers' Workshop, he is currently Professor of English at California State University, San Bernardino. His first book, *Strong Winds Below the Canyons,* was published by The Quarterly Review of Literature Press in 1984. His second book, *Brilliant Windows,* was published in The Miami University Press Poetry Series in 1998.

"I think of myself as a writer of place. The poems start as place. 'Brilliant Windows' was an attempt to make a poem out of walks I took down Wilshire. It took a long time to catch the fantastic feeling; finally a dead woman had to show me. I want to speak, like Frost, out of a landscape, instead of toward it. Otherwise, he'd have been just another local color writer. I don't want to write about Wilshire, but to discover the universal in it, particularly the unique, apocryphal light of L.A.

"In the flat, desolate boom town of Amarillo, where I grew up, the great highway seemed to point only west, and the far towns appeared fabulous, even Barstow and San Bernardino. Years later, when I accepted a job in San Bernardino, Alice Notley, then a young poet and friend, who had grown up in Needles, expressed dismay, even fear. 'Well, maybe it will work out,' she said. My California is the shadowland of the glamorous coast, an inland, raw, dramatic place of rugged, delicate landscapes and equally outrageous human dissatisfactions and hopes. After arriving, I met the local writer. 'There used to be some poets here,' she said, 'but they turned to writing pornography.' When I laughed, she looked sternly at me, 'There's not much difference you know.' In time I have come to love this place, would be lost anywhere else. I have, I hope, become its voice, of the precipitous, craggy slopes of Cajon Pass where I live, with its fierce winds tossing semi-trailors like cardboard boxes; the desperate power of its citizens, who will try anything; yes, even the freeway, that reckless, wonderful, perverse river of life. I have found here what I most wanted, myself—a terrain twisted by immense forces of wind, water and fault, folded, upthrusted, fantastic, a desertous landscape, strangely sweet-scented, of desire and love."

Brilliant Windows

On Wilshire I lunched with a woman dead
The year before, her young face abraded,
Chipped like a child's game marble.
She'd been sent to inform, she said—
A bayonet slope her residence now,
Roots like air to breathe and nothing
To eat but grinds and tastes like stone.
She set a smile on all my fears,
Studied my Superburger like a shaman
Reading entrails and warned me
Of the living death. I didn't know,
Couldn't dare ask, and small talk
Seemed like proving angels. I thought
She'd want to be let in—the story
Lines of our wild friends—but no,
A walk was her desire. Outside, the sun
Was grayish flesh, the sputtering
Low resolution of a decayed black
And silvering flick, blotting up
The busy people. My hand in hers
Less clasp than knot, we paused
Before such heavens as we are given,
The Missa Solemnis of a bakery shop,
Then she laughed, trying on, in a glance,
Vast windows of our highest fashioned
Spectral dresses. We strolled among
The dry, rough riverbed of faces as
New windows, far above, gazed outward,
Brilliant, blank, some smoke, some
Golden as the ancestors, nothing
To worship, nothing to understand.
In the amazing corrosions of sunset
Fire cars budged by like crippled
Dirigibles, and in plate glass
I found myself dimmed, old, more
Outline than figure, lavish with all
The jewels within. I needed no one

At elbow, none of the junk eternal,
Save any minute where my life had been.

Images of the San Francisco Disaster

Everyone in Genthe's famous photographs of the San Francisco earth-
quake and fire is well dressed. The shock occurred near dawn; the peo-
ple, thrown from their beds, found themselves in listing, broken,
burning houses, then, instead of rushing pell-mell into the streets, ap-
parently dressed as if going to church. In the most famous image two el-
egant Victorian ladies on the heights overlooking their ruined city have
turned from the disaster laughing; one even appears to skip or dance.
We must not imagine them to be only frivolous or uncomprehending,
nor is theirs merely the happiness of having survived; rather we see in
them our own youthful fatalism delighted by proximity to disaster and
the finally unsuppressed powers of the earth, by our primitive feelings
of invulnerability and the unsuspected depths of the gambling spirit in
us all; but—this most important—we are struck by the fact that we, like
the earth after the sudden release of centuries of tension and pressure,
are already, countershock by countershock, beginning to right our-
selves.

Strong Winds Below the Canyons

Like a rubber tire another
night bears down; the wind
turns around, now its first piston
striking the chapparal rolls back
the chilling fog. I come
toward the window, a moon
suddenly fills: how plain
my life has become, how terrible.
Below my city composes, a wheel
laid out by Latter Day Saints,
a Zion of accelerating violence
driving so many men toward murder;
on any week, behind the hills

coyotes dig up some vague remains,
a dog drags home a human skull:
thus even now as a snowy arm & fist
thrust skyward off Mount San Bernardino,
my face luminous through the broad window
impresses itself on thousands upon
thousands of low houses that descend
like steps toward the sea.

                      On ponds
we once appeared naked, & we shone,
then we suffered so easily a wind's
gentle erasure. Love, remember our
true country, we gathered blueberries
from puritan graves; my hat full
we turned back through the amber light
then softened into evenings
that were watery green. There, beyond
the congruence of old house
& rapids, on ancient ruts
of syrup wagons drawing us through
abandoned apple trees bears twisted
then tore into bonsai we found
a way, disconnected, often
completely obscured, that always
further on, doubling back, &
doubling back would appear again
would never, though losing purpose, end.
& when against the midnight cold
we made love, when rats began to drum
on the low tin ceilings, we heard
only each other.

                  Tonight you hold
your face aside in strict profile
recalling the coins I collected
as a child; they were foreign—
the poor alloy of nations overrun,
one curiously large prewar cent:
like us they came to represent
values lost. Love, I press toward you

my own grave image struck on the smog
silvered air of San Bernardino;
now when we speak, or even touch,
it is metal, against metal.

The Night Bird

We look up into the stars, stitch in the constellations,
Old signs on a flat surface portending sense.
Walk along, remembering the misplaced tenor, our magnificent
Local artist whose work, at his death, was piled
And burned, the great unlucky ones. Notice the expansive weeds,
And cry of a night bird, the stones, the reasons everywhere.

DORIANNE LAUX

Dorianne Laux is the author of two collections of poetry from BOA Editions, *Awake* (1990) and *What We Carry* (1994) which was a finalist for the National Book Critics Circle Award. She is also co-author, with Kim Addonizio, of *The Poet's Companion: A Guide to the Pleasures of Writing Poetry* (W.W. Norton, 1997), which has been chosen as an alternative selection by Book of the Month Club, Quality Paperbacks, and Writer's Digest. Among her awards are a Pushcart Prize for poetry and a fellowship from the NEA. She is Associate Professor and Director

© Jeanne C. Finley

of the University of Oregon's Program in Creative Writing. Presently she is at work on a libretto with composer Wally Brill of San Anselmo, as well as a new book of poems tentatively titled *Music in the Morning*.

"I grew up in San Diego, where we moved from Quonset huts and Navy housing into a pastel pre-fab house on a suburban cul-de-sac. My family settled on the curved end of the key hole situated at the edge of a series of canyons called Tecolote, a zigzag chain that extended to the Mexican border and beyond. In front of our house, at the hem of a frayed skirt of grass, the sidewalk, manufactured from a mixture of crushed granite and quartz quarried from the canyons, sparkled in the sun.

"The canyon was my backyard. Every day after school I threw my books in a corner, changed my clothes, unlocked the sliding glass door and ran over the graveled patio, past the trash cans and under the clothesline, through the rusted bars of the swingset, beside the tetherball pole sunk in cement, leaped over the portable pool, the cardboard fort, the bike on its side in the dirt, climbing the crossties of the redwood fence to lift the hasp that opened the gate to the canyon. If I close my eyes now, I can smell it, caliche dust lining the inside of my nose. I can see the oceanic gray-blue expanse, scrubby and tough, its waves of glossy shale and sagebrush tumbling down the rocky slopes.

"The canyon offered me its poetry, its life, its clarity of light. I'd sit under a manzanita bush, ruddy bark scoured black by lightening, and listen to my heart, waiting for a blue-bellied lizard or tanned horned toad to skitter over my splayed fingers, or settle in the sun, like a blessing, on the torn toe of my sneaker. I'd watch whole families of quail strut through the brush to peck or scratch at a pebble. I was witness to vicious stink bug fights, their armored tail ends lifted in defense, and privy to the small brittle deaths of birds and squirrels, their jeweled insides left glistening on a stone. I never learned the names of the tiny flowers, flicks of yellow flame that burned close to the ground, existing on little but dust and air. I didn't need to know what they were called. It was enough that they were willing to survive on the canyon's tough terms, short brutal lives worth each starry bloom.

"The Tecolote canyons taught me to be still. To listen. To look closely at the ground, to merge with its textures and subtle colors, to raise my head toward the roiling sky, enormous domed house of the gods of rain and thunder. And when I spoke into the depths of those canyons, they spoke back to me. Even now they echo my secret name."

Fast Gas

for Richard

Before the days of self service,
when you never had to pump your own gas,
I was the one who did it for you, the girl
who stepped out at the sound of a bell
with a blue rag in my hand, my hair pulled back
in a straight, unlovely ponytail.
This was before automatic shut-offs
and vapor seals, and once, while filling a tank,
I hit a bubble of trapped air and the gas
backed up, came arcing out of the hole
in a bright gold wave and soaked me—face, breasts,
belly and legs. And I had to hurry
back to the booth, the small employee bathroom
with the broken lock, to change my uniform,
peel the gas-soaked cloth from my skin
and wash myself in the sink.
Light-headed, scrubbed raw, I felt
pure and amazed—the way the amber gas
glazed my flesh, the searing,
subterranean pain of it, how my skin
shimmered and ached, glowed
like rainbowed oil on the pavement.
I was twenty. In a few weeks I would fall,

for the first time, in love, that man waiting
patiently in my future like a red leaf
on the sidewalk, the kind of beauty
that asks to be noticed. How was I to know
it would begin this way: every cell of my body
burning with a dangerous beauty, the air around me
a nimbus of light that would carry me
through the days, how when he found me,
weeks later, he would find me like that,
an ordinary woman who could rise
in flame, all he would have to do
is come close and touch me.

Finding What's Lost

In the middle of the poem my daughter reminds me
that I promised to drive her to the bus stop.
She waits a few beats then calls out the time.
Repeats that I've promised.
I keep the line in my head, repeat it under my breath
as I look for my keys, rummage through my purse,
my jacket pockets. When we're in the car, I search
the floor for a Jack-in-the-Box bag, a ticket stub,
a bridge toll dollar, anything to write on.
I'm still repeating my line when she points
out the window and says "Look, there's the poppy
I told you about," and as I turn the corner I see it,
grown through a crack between the sidewalk and the curb.
We talk about it while I scan driveways for kids
on skateboards and bikes, while the old man who runs
the Rexall locks up for the night and a mangy dog
lifts a frail leg and sprays the side of a tree.
Then we talk about her history essay and her boyfriend,
and she asks again about summer vacation, if we're
going somewhere or just staying home. I say
I don't know and ask what she'd rather do, but by now
we're at the bus stop and she leans over
and, this is so unlike her, brushes her lips

quickly against my cheek. Then, without looking back,
she's out the door, and the line, the poem,
is gone, lost somewhere near 8th and G, hovering
like an orange flower over the gravel street.

If This Is Paradise

> The true mystery of the world is the visible...
> *Oscar Wilde*

If this is paradise: trees, beehives,
boulders. And this: bald moon, shooting
stars, a little sun. If in your hands
this is paradise: sensate flesh,
hidden bone, your own eyes
opening, then why should we speak?
Why not lift into each day like the animals
that we are and go silently
about our true business: the hunt
for water, fat berries, the mushroom's
pale meat, tumble through waist-high grasses
without reason, find shade and rest there,
our limbs spread beneath the meaningless sky,
find the scent of the lover
and mate wildly. If this is paradise
and all we have to do is be born and live
and die, why pick up the stick at all?
Why see the wheel in the rock.
Why bring back from the burning fields
a bowl full of fire and pretend that it's magic?

What Could Happen

Noon. A stale Saturday. The hills
rise above the town, nudge houses and shops
toward the valley, kick the shallow river
into place. Here, a dog can bark for days

and no one will care enough

to toss an empty can or an unread newspaper
in his direction. No one complains.
The men stand in loose knots

outside Ace Hardware, talk a little, stare
at the blue tools. A few kids
sulk through the park, the sandbox full
of hardscrabble, the monkey bars

too hot to touch. In a town like this
a woman on the edge of forty
could drive around in her old car, the back end
all jingle and rivet, one headlight

taped in place, the hood held down with greasy rope,
and no one would notice.
She could drive up and down the same street
all day, eating persimmons,

stopping only for a moment to wonder
at the wooden Indian on the corner of 6th and B,
the shop window behind it
filled with beaten leather, bright woven goods

from Guatemala, postcards of this town
before it began to go under, began
to fade into a likeness of itself.
She could pull in at the corner store for a soda

and pause before uncapping it,
press the cold glass against her cheek,
roll it under her palm down the length of her neck
then slip it beneath the V of her blouse

and let it rest there, where she's hottest.
She could get back in her car
and turn the key, bring the engine up
like a swarm of bottle flies, feel it

shake like an empty caboose.
She could twist the radio too high
and drive like this for the rest of the day—
the same street, the same hairpin turn

that knocks the jack in the trunk from one wheel well
to the other—or she could pass the turn
and keep going, the cold soda
wedged between her legs, the bass notes

throbbing like a vein, out past the closed shops
and squat houses, the church
with its bland white arch, toward the hills,
beyond that shadowy nest of red madrones.

CAROL LEM

Carol Lem lives in Temple City and teaches creative writing, literature, and composition at East Los Angeles College. Her poems have been published in *The Asian Pacific American Journal, Blue Mesa Review, Chrysalis, Hawaii Pacific Review, Lucid Stone, The Seattle Review,* and many others. Her books include *Searchings, Grassroots, Don't Ask Why, The Hermit, The Hermit's Journey: Tarot Poems for Meditation,* and *Moe, Remembrance.* Her work is also featured in *What Will Suffice: Contemporary Poets on the Art of Poetry,* edited by Christopher Buckley and Christopher Merrill, and *Grand Passion, Poets of Los Angeles and Beyond,* edited by Suzanne Lummis and Charles H. Webb. Her poem "Office Hour" won an award in the "Poetry in the Windows" contest, sponsored by the Arroyo Arts Collective of Highland Park.

"I was born in Los Angeles in 1944, which identifies me as a member of the baby boomer generation, and grew up in the sixties, which qualifies me as a survivor of sorts. Not quite a hippie or a yuppie, a radical or establishment, and not quite Asian or American, I survived the border mentality that comes with living in an urban environment such as Los Angeles all of my life. Also, teaching at East Los Angeles College, in which living on the borderlands is both a geographical and psychological reality for the majority of the students, has given me a shared identity with the Chicano population there. This is the reason why many of my poems, including 'Office Hour' and 'So Now You're Chicana,' arise from a self-conscious awareness of being Chinese, a middle-aged woman, teaching street-wise young Latinos and Latinas how to write and, as a result, how to think. But always, it is the poetry, the literature, the universal life experiences that bring us together.

"Home comes out of this imagined place in the heart, something I create for myself each day. Maybe it's not by accident that I live on a forked street as the poem 'Temple City Blvd. & Ellis Ln.' describes. Again, the images of ethnicity and identity appear, and the need to forge a life out of my 'kingdom of sweat' and 'seasoned roots.' Because I live in a semi-industrial area, where heavy trucks rumble by, and near the railroad track, it is normal to feel the house shake, so when I wrote 'Just Another Temblor, October 1, 1987,' on the occasion of a real *temblor,* I was reflecting on a more metaphysical shaking, in which my *home,* where 'I cut and splice the heart/on a board of plenty,' was being threatened. This living on the edge of things happening, this quaking metaphor, is felt again in 'California Dreaming' (thank you, The Mamas and the Papas), but besides the familiar urban images, the juxtaposition of cut lawns and rising smoke presents the confusion of inhabitants whose questions go on unanswered, 'No one knows if it's another fire or riot/or cares because answers come like aftershocks.' But always, it's the pen that keeps me steady, this daily sitting, that brings me home."

California Dreaming

Traveling Highway 101
as far as Big Sur, the Esalen retreats
I let Chant guide me back
down the winding curves of the Pacific Coast
through San Luis Obispo, Santa Barbara, Oxnard
through the yellow haze of L.A. high rises,
back to Temple City and the small factories
of transient workers who survive
in a borrowed language, who eat my peaches
and use my front yard as a park,
while I sit in my room
contemplating the sound of one hand
amidst the sounds of loading trucks, Murray's Lunch Wagon,
rap booming out of low riders, the sounds of a mother
calling her children home and shutting up the dog,
tricycle wheels screeching to a halt,
the imperceptible sounds of jacaranda leaves
falling on cool patio tile, as they merge
with the sound the heart makes
when it finds a phrase that can live on the page
until the next day, at least,
when it all starts up again:

These messages of hope hugging the curb,
the daily inventions; who am I? asks the freeway flyer
with a smile on his window shade,
passing blocks of cut lawns, sprinklers going on at once
and questions rising like smoke.
No one knows if it's another fire or riot

or cares because answers come like aftershocks,
and each finds himself
sitting on a porch or in the frame of a door
with a shopping cart of belongings
or beside a pool sipping a margarita.
Or here in this room above the garage
pushing one word against the other
in a mad internal dance to make the wind speak
and waves murmur back some song to sing
each to each.

Office Hour

after Philip Levine

My student says he wrote a poem
about me, but not as I am, not
this tired maestra talking to the blackboard
deafened by the echo of her own voice
but as a poet blowing her bamboo flute
on a hill. My student, a Chicano, is sitting
in my office, his eyes focused
on shelves of books, "Do you read all these?"
I don't say these are only textbooks,
my real books are at home, nor do I name
all the poets I love. He can take in
only a few now—Baca, Soto, Rodriguez.
The fluorescent lights above us
hum a broken tune, something like
"America the Beautiful" or "Time on My Hands."
It is late. Everyone has gone home
to shore up their other lives, and East L.A.
is quiet again. What a dream—
a teacher and student meeting at the edge
of a battle zone where drivebys and tortillas,
quinceañeras and someone's mijito cycling a future
on blood-stained sidewalks go on.
"I want to write," he says, "but I can't leave
my turf." I don't say you won't
even when you're a thousand miles from here.

What a dream—a young Chicano
crosses the border to me, a Chinese,
three decades away, to give me a poem,
knowing we are both Americans with a song
to pass on, even if it's still out of tune.
We hear the music in the attention of this hour.
What a dream—When I drove home
the 10 East was jammed with trucks and exhaust
and the San Gabriel mountains a vague vision.
That hill will have to stay in a poem
for a while. But think, without
the blaring horns and broken glass, without
these messages of hope spread across my desk
and the shadow who fills the barrel
of this pen, I could have missed it all.

So Now You're Chicana

> The Tao is nowhere to be found,
> yet it nourishes and completes
> all things.   *Tao Te Ching*

She says,
seeing me read at a festival
where Indio blood merges
with the streets of East Los Angeles.
My hair is black and my eyes
are small almonds.
My roots are gray strands.
Those who call me Carolina or Mei Ling,
I answer, because I drink
where the spirit water flows.
I am an empty tea cup waiting to fill.

My father used to hide a gold coin
under his mattress.
I once asked why. He simply said,
so no one could find it.
My mother was raised by the tracks
on Alameda, remembered lost baseballs
between the wheels.

Her father was the first herbalist
in Chinatown. I never knew him.
My leaves are gray.

Today, I do Tai Chi
and ask the I-Ching
what move to make next?

Does this mean I'm Chinese
or simply lost?
Tonight I read my poems of journey,
or making do.

Though I do not speak Spanish or Chinese
I read to those who know, too,
the way back begins here.
Tomorrow I will play my bamboo flute
at Zenshuji Temple in Little Tokyo.

So don't ask who I am.
My blood flows with the Tao.
Though you cannot see it,
it is always here.

Temple City Blvd. & Ellis Ln.

Along railroad tracks
I jog past Crown Plating, Nater
Manufacturing, the nameless
shops, the sheeted windows
past the resignation
of sewing machines.
If I could say
how this sun follows me
around, if I told every bone
43 laps are enough
go in now
before you burn up,
I would hear cars
groaning towards heaven
neighbors cursing

corn husks on front lawns,
Tecate beer and late mail
as they sit on porches
washed by afternoon sprinklers,
I would count gray-haired angels
hoisting the flag on any holiday
Chevy vans and 7-11's,
blond cheerleaders twirling
a future into shape.

So I don't say
how the sun makes its daily plea
how eternity gets lost in an hour
how this small body
has entered the kingdom of sweat
and returned like seasoned roots
for this is only a boulevard
crossed by trains.
I still don't know
which way the whistle blows.

Soon May will come.
I will grow another year.
The air will smell of jasmine
and when the man at the Chinese
market asks where you from,
I'll say
where the road forks.

PHILIP LEVINE

Philip Levine lives in Fresno, where he taught at the university until his retirement. He has received many awards for his poetry, including the Lenore Marshall Award, The National Book Critics Circle Award, the American Book Award, The Ruth Lilly Poetry Prize, and most recently, The National Book Award for *What Work Is* and The Pulitzer Prize for *The Simple Truth*. His most recent books are *Unselected Poems* (Greenhouse Review Press, 1997) and *The Mercy* (Knopf, 1999).

© Frances Levine

"My first night in California was spent in a motel in Squaw Valley. In August '57, I was on my way to study with Yvor Winters on a grant from Stanford. I turned on a little radio I'd brought with me and caught Kenneth Rexroth on KPFA from Berkeley talking psychoanalysis and literature in 'the voice God uses to lecture Jesus Christ.' Even more astonishing than a poet on the radio was the landscape itself. In southeastern Michigan, anything taller than a basketball center is man-made. The tallest hills I can recall were the slag heaps outside the foundries of Ford Rouge, which burned night and day, so that my friends the Strempeks, housed in a wretched project for Ford workers, lived in a kind of perpetual nightmare or film noir that—because of the pollution and the flames—was never light or dark.

"My own capacity to adapt to the aura of Detroit was amazing: smoke stacks, freight yards, huge gray-bricked single story buildings with their windows shattered, acres piled with war material, the immense wastes of snow-covered parking lots, all this was home. In the fall of '95, forty years after leaving Detroit, I took a bus ride from the picturesque village of Bellagio on Lake Como to the city of Como. Before the bus discharged us it passed through a small industrial neighborhood, and I felt utterly at home. Though I've lived in Fresno far longer than anywhere else, I've never completely surrendered the notion of Detroit as home—not the Detroit of today, but the magical city of a boy's memories.

"Socially and economically Detroit and Fresno are similar. Their structures were fixed decades ago: the field hands of this valley have about as much chance of becoming something else as the factory workers of Detroit have of owning GM and Ford. *The* difference between the two places is the Sierra Nevada east of Fresno, those same mountains in which I spent my first night in California. They possess some mystery I've never defined. Why else would I go into them so often only to return to the valley awed but unfulfilled? In my thirties and early forties I drove there at least once a week on a series of motorcycles I owned, at first alone and later with my wife or one of my sons. In spring the wildflowers were an Eden of colors; in winter when the valley was shrouded in fog the air was crystalline, the sky a deep calm blue. At any time I could come around a tight corner and suddenly the world would explode in a panorama so vast I had to pull over and look away. I felt as though I were fighting to contain this enormity, and it literally filled me to overflowing. It was on one of these solitary rides that I reached the conclusion that if I stuck with poetry I would have to reach for the largest work possible. In the face of this landscape it seemed petty to do anything else. I realized even then that if my energy and talents were not up to it the decision was a foolish one, but I took comfort in Blake's proverb: 'If the fool would persist in his folly he would become wise.'"

The Water's Chant

Seven years ago I went into
the High Sierras stunned by the desire
to die. For hours I stared into a clear
mountain stream that fell down
over speckled rocks, and then I
closed my eyes and prayed that when
I opened them I would be gone
and somewhere a purple and golden
thistle would overflow with light.
I had not prayed since I was a child
and at first I felt foolish saying
the name of God, and then it became
another word. All the while
I could hear the water's chant
below my voice. At last I opened
my eyes to the same place, my hands
cupped and I drank long from
the stream, and then turned for home
not even stopping to find the thistle
that blazed by my path.
                  Since then
I have gone home to the city
of my birth and found it gone,
a gray and treeless one now in its place.

e house I loved the most
        missing in a row of houses,
ᴜ.ᴄ park where I napped on summer days
fenced and locked, the great shop
where we forged, a plane of rubble,
the old hurt faces turned away.
My brother was with me, thickened
by the years, but still my brother,
and when we embraced I felt the rough
cheek and his hand upon my back tapping
as though to tell me, I know! I know!
brother, I know!
                Here in California
a new day begins. Full dull clouds ride
in from the sea, and this dry valley
calls out for rain. My brother has
risen hours ago and hobbled to the shower
and gone out into the city of death
to trade his life for nothing because
this is the world. I could pray now,
but not to die, for that will come one
day or another. I could pray for
his bad leg or my son John whose luck
is rotten, or for four new teeth, but
instead I watch my eucalyptus,
the giant in my front yard, bucking
and swaying in the wind and hear its
tidal roar. In the strange new light
the leaves overflow purple and gold,
and a fiery dust showers into the day.

28

At 28 I was still faithless.
I had crossed the country in a green Ford,
sleeping one night almost 14 hours in a motel
above Salt Lake City. I discovered
I'd had a fever all that day and thus the animals
that dotted the road, the small black spots

that formed and unformed crows, the flying pieces
of slate that threatened to break through
the windshield…were whatever they were.
I took two aspirins and an allergy pill—that was all
I had—and got into bed although it was light out.
That was 28 years ago. Since then I have died
only twice, once in slow motion against
the steel blue driver's side of a Plymouth
station wagon. One moment before impact I said
to myself, seriously, "This is going to hurt."
The kids in the Plymouth's back seat gaped
wildly, shouted, leaped, and the father held firm
to the steering wheel as I slipped through the space
that was theirs, untouched, skidding first
on the black field of asphalt and broken glass
that is California 168, Tollhouse Road, and over
the edge of the mountain, the motorcycle
tumbling off on its own through nettles and grass
to come to a broken rest as all bodies must.
Often when I shave before a late dinner, especially
on summer evenings, I notice the white lines
on my right shoulder like the smeared imprint
of a leaf on silk or the delicate tracings
on a whale's fins that the smaller sea animals carve
to test his virtue, and I reenter the wide blue eyes
of that family of five that passed on their way
up the mountain.
                    But at 28 I was still faithless.
I could rise before dawn from a bed drenched
with my own sweat, repack the green Ford
in the dark, my own breath steaming
in the high, clear air, and head for California.
I could spend the next night in Squaw Valley
writing a letter to my wife and kids asleep hours
behind me in Colorado, I could listen to Rexroth
reminiscing on a Berkeley FM station in the voice
God uses to lecture Jesus Christ and still believe
two aspirins, an allergy pill, and proper rest were proof
against the cold that leaps in one blind moment
from the heart to the farthest shore to shudder

through the small sea creatures I never knew existed.

It seems the sun passing back and forth behind clouds
this morning threatens to withdraw its affections
and the sky is as distant and pale as a bored child
in the wrong classroom or a man of 28
drilled so often on the names of fruit-bearing trees
that he forgets even the date palm. Here in New England,
no longer new or English, the first frost
has stained the elms and maples outside my window,
and the kids on their way hunch their shoulders
against the cold. One boy drops his lunch box
with a clatter and mysteriously leaves it there
on the pavement as a subtle rebuke
to his mother, to a father holding tight to a wheel,
to a blue Plymouth that long ago entered the heaven
brooding above Detroit. If only they had stopped
all those years ago and become a family of five
descending one after the other the stone ledges
of Sweet Potato Mountain and found me face down
among the thistles and shale and lifted me to my feet.
I weighed no more than feathers do or the wish
to become pure spirit. If I had not broken my glasses
I could have gone on my way with a thank you,
with a gap-toothed smile.
                    28 years ago, faithless, I
found the great bay of San Francisco where the map
said it would be and crossed the bridge from Oakland
singing "I Cover the Waterfront" into the cold winds
and the dense odor of coffee. Before I settled
in East Palo Alto among divorcees and appliance salesmen,
fifty yards from the Union Pacific tracks, I spent a long weekend
with Arthur, my mentor to be. In a voice ruined, he said,
by all-night draughts of whiskey and coffee, he praised
the nobility of his lemon and orange trees, the tang
of his loquats, the archaic power of his figs.
In a gambler's green visor and stiff Levis, he bowed
to his wounded tomatoes swelling into late summer.
Kneeling in the parched loam by the high fence
he bared the elusive strawberries, his blunt fingers
working the stiff leaves over and over. It was August.

He was almost happy.
                    Faithless, I had not found
the olive trees bursting on the hillsides west
of US 99. I knew only the bitter black fruit
that clings with all its life to the hard seed.
I had not wakened to mockers wrangling in my yard
at dawn in a riot of sexual splendor or heard
the sea roar at Bondy Bay, the long fingers
of ocean running underneath the house all night
to rinse off the pain of nightmare. I had not
seen my final child, though he was on the way.
I had not become a family of five nor opened
my arms to receive the black gifts of a mountain road,
of ground cinders, pebbles, rough grass.
                              At twice my age
Arthur, too, was faithless, or so he insisted
through the long sober evenings in Los Altos, once
crowded with the cries of coyotes. His face
darkened and his fists shook when he spoke
of Nothing, what he would become in that waiting blaze
of final cold, a whiteness like no other.
At 56, more scared of me than I of him,
his right forefinger raised to keep the beat,
he gravelled out his two great gifts of truth:
"I'd rather die than reread the last novels
of Henry James," and, "Philip, we must never lie
or we shall lose our souls." All one winter afternoon
he chanted in Breton French the coarse poems of Tristan Corbière,
his voice reaching into unforeseen sweetness, both hands
rising toward the ceiling, the tears held back so long
still held back, for he was dying and he was ready.

By April I had crossed the Pacheco Pass and found
roosting in the dark branches of the Joshua tree
the fabled magpie—"Had a long tongue and a long tail;
He could both talk and do." This is a holy land,
I thought. At a Sonoco station the attendant,
wiry and dour, said in perfect Okie, "Be careful, son,
a whole family was wiped out right here
just yesterday." At Berenda the fields flooded
for miles in every direction. Arthur's blank sky

stared down at an unruffled inland sea and threatened
to let go. On the way home I cut lilacs
from the divider strip of El Camino Real.
My wife was pregnant. All night we hugged
each other in our narrow bed as the rain
came on in sheets. A family of five, and all
of us were out of work. The dawn was silent.
The black roses, battered, unclenched, the burned petals
floated on the pond beside the playhouse.
Beneath the surface the tiny stunned pike circled
no prey we could see. That was not another life.
I was 29 now and faithless, not the father of the man
I am but the same man who all this day
sat in a still house watching the low clouds massing
in the west, the new winds coming on.
By late afternoon the kids are home from school,
clambering on my front porch, though day
after day I beg them not to. When I go
to the window they race off in mock horror,
daring me to follow. The huge crows that wake
me every morning settle back on the rain spout
next door to caw to the season. I could put them
all in a poem, title it "The Basket of Memory"
as though each image were an Easter egg waiting to hatch,
as though I understood the present and the past
or even why the 8 year old with a cap of blond hair
falling to her shoulders waves to me as she darts
between parked cars and cartwheels into the early dusk.

Sierra Kid

> "I've been where it hurts." the Kid

He becomes Sierra Kid

I passed Slimgullion, Morgan Mine,
Camp Seco, and the rotting Lode.
  Dark walls of sugar pine—,
  And where I left the road

  I left myself behind;
  Talked to no one, thought

Of nothing. When my luck ran out
Lived on berries, nuts, bleached grass.
  Driven by the wind
  Through great Sonora Pass,

  I found an Indian's teeth;
  Turned and climbed again
Without direction, compass, path,
Without a way of coming down,
  Until I stopped somewhere
  And gave the place a name.

  I called the forests mine;
  Whatever I could hear
I took to be a voice: a man
Was something I would never hear.

He faces his second winter in the Sierra

A hard brown bug, maybe a beetle,
Packing a ball of sparrow shit—
  What shall I call it?
Shit beetle? Why's it pushing here
At this great height in the thin air
  With its ridiculous waddle

Up the hard side of Hard Luck Hill?
And the furred thing that frightened me—
  Bobcat, coyote, wild dog—
Flat eyes in winter bush, stiff tail,
Holding his ground, a rotted log.
  Grass snakes that wouldn't die,

And night hawks hanging on the rim
Of what was mine. I know them now;
  They have absorbed a mind
Which must endure the freezing snow
They endure and, freezing, find
  A clear sustaining stream.

He learns to lose

  She was afraid
  Of everything,

The little Digger girl.
  Pah Utes had killed
  Her older brother
Who may have been her lover
  The way she cried
  Over his ring—

  The heavy brass
  On the heavy hand.
She carried it for weeks
  Clenched in her fist
  As if it might
Keep out the loneliness
  Or the plain fact
  That he was gone.

  When the first snows
  Began to fall
She stopped her crying, picked
  Berries, sweet grass,
  Mended her clothes
And sewed a patchwork shawl.
  We slept together
  But did not speak.

  It may have been
  The Pah Utes took
Her off, perhaps her kin.
  I came back
  To find her gone
With half the winter left
  To face alone—
  The slow gray dark

  Moving along
  The dark tipped grass
Between the numbed pines.
  Night after night
  For four long months
My face to her dark face
  We two had lain
  Till the first light.

Civilization comes to Sierra Kid

They levelled Tater Hill
  And I was sick.
First sun, and the chain saws
  Coming on; blue haze,
    Dull blue exhaust
Rising, dust rising, and the smell.

  Moving from their thatched huts
    The crazed wood rats
By the thousand; grouse, spotted quail
  Abandoning the hills.
    For the sparse trail
On which, exposed, I also packed.

  Six weeks. I went back down
    Through my own woods
Afraid of what I knew they'd done.
  There, there, an A&P,
    And not a tree
For miles, and mammoth hills of goods.

  Fat men in uniforms,
    Young men in aprons
With one face shouting, "He is mad!"
  I answered: "I am Lincoln,
    Aaron Burr,
The aging son of Appleseed.

  "I am American
    And I am cold."
But not a one would hear me out.
  Oh God, what have I seen
    That was not sold!
They shot an old man in the gut.

Mad, dying, Sierra Kid enters the capital

  What have I changed?
I unwound burdocks from my hair
    And scalded stains
    Of the black grape
And hid beneath long underwear

The yellowed tape.

Who will they find
In the dark woods of the dark mind
Now I have gone
Into the world?
Across the blazing civic lawn
A shadow's hurled

And I must follow.
Something slides beneath my vest
Like melted tallow,
Thick but thin,
Burning where it comes to rest
On what was skin.

Who will they find?
A man with no eyes in his head?
Or just a mind
Calm and alone?
Or just a mouth, silent, dead,
The lips half gone?

Will they presume
That someone once was half alive
And that the air
Was massive where
The sickening pyracanthas thrive
Staining his tomb?

I came to touch
The great heart of a dying state.
Here is the wound!
It makes no sound.
All that we learn we learn too late,
And it's not much.

I Caught a Glimpse

It happens when I've been driving
        for hours on two-lane roads winding

past orchards just after they've bloomed.

When I ask myself where I was when all
        this burst like the bounty of heaven, no
                answer comes back from the earth or heaven.

A hint of rain is in the air and the sky
        broods above a sudden stand of oak that
                rushes by. Between the trees coming

into the new green of their leaves light
        breaks for a second and within the light a path
                opens through the trees and the fields beyond.

Beyond, unseen, an ancient river runs
        high in its banks bringing the Sierras' gift
                back down to earth. The moment is so full

I have to close my eyes and slow the car.
        Should I go back the long, abandoned roads
                that lead me to this place and this moment

to find why I've become who I am
        and why that could matter. Slowly now
                I pass through a small town of scrubbed houses,

wide lawns, and empty streets. A rain has passed
        leaving little pools reflecting the sky
                that stares open-eyed at its own image.

If this were Sunday the bells would ring,
        if this were sixty years ago I
                would be a boy on foot no farther

than I am now with my eyes filled
        with so much seeing. I caught a glimpse,
                a road through the trees, a door

that opened a moment only to close.
        Twelve miles from Stockton. I could go west
                until I reached the sea or keep going

farther and farther into this valley
        past the truck stops and the ruined towns
                while the afternoon closes down around me.

The Sea We Read About

Now and then a lost sea gull flutters into
our valley, comes down in a burned cotton field
and simply gives up. Once I left my pickup
by the side of the road, dug a square grave
the size of a beer case, and dropped in the bird.
Quintero, the short, husky truck farmer
from Tranquility, stopped to call out. What was I
doing in late July under the noon sun
digging in someone else's field? I told him.
Slowly he unwound himself from the truck's cab,
took up his shovel, and trudged over to see
it was done right. After we tamped down the earth
we stood speechless in the middle of nothing
while a hot wind whispered through the miles of stalks
and Johnson grass. "Can you hear what it's saying?"
Quintero asked. For the first time I noticed his eyes
were green and one didn't move. "Been hearing it
all my life, 62 years," and head down under
the straw cowboy hat he turned to go, waving
a thick forearm at the sky. I should have asked.
I'd seen him often before, stooped in his field of melons,
pensive, still, and took him for part of the place,
one more doomed farmer. An hour later, nursing
a cold beer, I stood outside the 7-11
at the four corners listening, but the voices
inside kept breaking in, two young drivers
teasing the pregnant girl who worked the register,
her laughter egging them on. Suddenly the bearded,
shirtless one began to sing a Beatles' song,
"Why Don't We Do It in the Road," in such a pure voice
my whole world froze. Twenty-four years ago,
the war was ending, and though I wasn't young
I believed the land rose westward toward mountains
hidden in dust and smog and beyond the mountains
the sea spread out, limitless and changing
everything, and that I would get there some day.

LARRY LEVIS

© Kent Miles

Larry Levis was a native of California and was educated at California State University, Fresno; Syracuse University; and the University of Iowa. He published five books of poetry during his life, and a sixth posthumous book, *Elegy,* edited by Philip Levine. At the time of his death in May 1996, he was Professor of English at Virginia Commonwealth University, and he had taught previously at the University of Utah; University of Missouri; University of Iowa; California State University, Los Angeles; and in the Warren Wilson Creative Writing Program. His awards include the U.S. Award of The International Poetry Forum, a Lamont Prize, and selection for The National Poetry Series. He received fellowships from the NEA and the Guggenheim Foundation, and an individual artist's grant from the Virginia Commission for the Arts. In 1989 he was Senior Fulbright Fellow in Yugoslavia. His *Selected Poems,* edited by David St. John, is due from the University of Pittsburgh Press.

When I first came up with the idea for this project, Larry Levis was one of the first poets I contacted, one of the first who generously said he would contribute, one of the first I thought of for the absolutely unique view of California as he had it in his poetry, as well as for the overall brilliance of his work. As Philip Levine said in an interview I conducted for *Quarterly West* in 1997, "I think he was easily the best poet of his generation, at times I truly believe he was writing the best poems in the country." Larry died of cardiac arrest in May 1996, not yet fifty. Although for the last twenty years he lived at various points around the country, he always came back to California— mostly to Fresno, where he wrote his first poems, and to Selma, a small farming community outside of Fresno where he grew up and his family owned a ranch. Certainly the imagination, unique achievement, and profound humanity of Larry's poems do not need my comment. But a prose complement is one way this anthology gives us a little more of the life of poetry in California, and Larry was a spectacular writer of prose. Here are the last paragraphs he wrote about Philip Levine and his own young life as a poet.

Christopher Buckley

ould I have written poems in isolation? I doubt it. I grew up in a town
here, in the high school library, Yeats' *Collected Poems* was removed, cen-
red in fact, because two students had been found laughing out loud at 'Leda
and the Swan.' That left Eliot. For two years, largely in secret, I read and
reread Eliot, and I told no one of this. But finally one afternoon in journalism
class, while the teacher was out of the room, Zamora stretched out, lying over
three desk tops, and began yelling at the little evenly spaced holes in the ply-
board ceiling: 'O Stars, Oh Stars!' The others around us talked on in a mild
roar. Then Zamora turned to me and said: 'I saw that book you always got
with you. Once again, guy, I see through you like a just wiped windshield.'
There was this little pause, and then he said, 'What is it, you wanna be a
poet?' I said, 'Yeah. You think that's really stupid?' His smile had disap-
peared by the time he answered, 'No, it isn't stupid. It ain't stupid at all, but
I'd get out of town if I were you.'

"It was true. A town like that could fill a young man with such rage and
boredom that the bars of Saigon might twinkle like a brief paradise. You
could die in a town like that without lifting a finger.

"Whenever I try to imagine the life I might have had if I hadn't met
Levine, if he had never been my teacher, if we had not become friends and
exchanged poems and hundreds of letters over the past twenty-five years, I
can't imagine it. That is, nothing at all appears when I try to do this. No other
life of any kind appears. I cannot see myself walking down one of those
streets as a lawyer, or the boss of a packing shed, or even as the farmer my fa-
ther wished I would become. When I try to do this, no one's there; it seems
instead that I simply had never *been* at all. All there is on that street, the
leaves on the shade trees that line it curled and black and closeted against
noon heat, is a space where I am not."

from "Philip Levine," On the Poetry of Philip Levine: Stranger to
Nothing (University of Michigan Press, 1991)

Rhododendrons

Winter has moved off
somewhere, writing its journals
in ice.

But I am still afraid to move,
afraid to speak,
as if I lived in a house
wallpapered with the cries of birds
I cannot identify.

Beneath the trees
a young couple sits talking
about the afterlife,
where no one, I think, is
whittling toys for the stillborn.
I laugh,

but I don't know.
Maybe the whole world is absent minded
or floating. Maybe the new lovers undress
without wondering how
the snow grows over the Andes,
or how a horse cannot remember those
frozen in the sleigh behind it,
but keeps running until the lines tangle,
while the dead sit coolly beneath their pet stars..

As I write this,
some blown rhododendrons are nodding
in the first breezes. I want
to resemble them, and remember nothing,
the way a photograph of an excavation
cannot remember the sun.

The wind rises or stops
and it means nothing.

I want to be circular;
a pond or a column of smoke
revolving, slowly, its ashes.

I want to turn back and go up
to myself at age 20
and press five dollars into his hand
so he can sleep.
While he stands trembling on a street in Fresno,
suddenly one among many in the crowd
that strolls down Fulton Street,
among the stores that are closing,
and is never heard of again.

The Poet at Seventeen

My youth? I hear it mostly in the long, volleying
Echoes of billiards in the pool halls where
I spent it all, extravagantly, believing
My delicate touch on a cue would last for years.

Outside the vineyards vanished under rain,
And the trees held still or seemed to hold their breath
When the men I worked with, pruning orchards, sang
Their lost songs: *Amapola; La Paloma;*

Jalisco, No Te Rajes—the corny tunes
Their sons would just as soon forget, at recess,
Where they lounged apart in small groups of their own.
Still, even when they laughed, they laughed in Spanish.

I hated high school then, & on weekends drove
A tractor through the widowed fields. It was so boring
I memorized poems above the engine's monotone.
Sometimes whole days slipped past without my noticing,

And birds of all kinds flew in front of me then.
I learned to tell them apart by their empty squabblings,
The slightest change in plumage, or the inflection
Of a call. And why not admit it? I was happy

Then. I believed in no one. I had the kind
Of solitude the world usually allows
Only to kings & criminals who are extinct,
Who disdain this world, & who rot, corrupt & shallow

As fields I disced: I turned up the same gray
Earth for years. Still, the land made a glum raisin
Each autumn, & made that little hell of days—
The vines must have seemed like cages to the Mexicans

Who were paid seven cents a tray for the grapes
They picked. Inside the vines it was hot, & spiders
Strummed their emptiness. Black Widow, Daddy Longlegs.
The vine canes whipped our faces. None of us cared.

And the girls I tried to talk to after class
Sailed by, then each night lay enthroned in my bed,

With nothing on but the jewels of their embarrassment.
Eyes, lips, dreams. No one. The sky & the road.

A life like that? It seemed to go on forever—
Reading poems in school, then driving a stuttering tractor
Warm afternoons, then billiards on blue October
Nights. The thick stars. But mostly now I remember

The trees, wearing their mysterious yellow sullenness
Like party dresses. And parties I didn't attend.
And then the first ice hung like spider lattices
Or the embroideries of Great Aunt No One,

And then the first dark entering the trees—
And inside, the adults with their cocktails before dinner
The way they always seemed afraid of something,
And sat so rigidly, although the land was theirs.

Picking Grapes in an Abandoned Vineyard

Picking grapes alone in the late autumn sun—
A short, curved knife in my hand,
Its blade silver from so many sharpenings,
Its handle black,
I still have a scar where a friend
Sliced open my right index finger, once,
In a cutting shed—
The same kind of knife.
The grapes drop into the pan,
And the gnats swarm over them, as always.
Fifteen years ago,
I worked this row of vines beside a dozen
Families up from Mexico.
No one spoke English, or wanted to.
One woman, who made an omelet with a sheet of tin
And five, light blue quail eggs,
Had a voice full of dusk, and jail cells,
And bird calls. She spoke,
In Spanish, to no one, as they all did.
Their swearing was specific,

And polite.
I remember two of them clearly:
A man named Tea, six feet, nine inches tall
At the age of sixty-two,
Who wore white spats into downtown Fresno
Each Saturday night,
An alcoholic giant whom the women loved—
One chilled morning, they found him dead outside
The Rose Café…
And Angel Domínguez,
Who came to work for my grandfather in 1910,
And who saved for years to buy
Twenty acres of rotting, Thompson Seedless vines.
While the sun flared all one August,
He decided he was dying of a rare disease,
And spent his money and his last years
On specialists,
Who found nothing wrong.
Tea laughed, and, tipping back
A bottle of Muscatel, said: "Nothing's wrong.
You're just dying."
At seventeen, I discovered
Parlier, California, with its sad, topless bar,
And its one main street, and its opium.
I would stand still, and chalk my cue stick
In Johnny Palores' East Front Pool Hall, and watch
The room filling with tobacco smoke, as the sun set
Through one window.
Now all I hear are the vines rustling as I go
From one to the next,
The long canes holding up dry leaves, reddening,
So late in the year.
What the vines want must be this silence spreading
Over each town, over the dance halls and the dying parks,
And the police drowsing in their cruisers
Under the stars.
What the men who worked here wanted was
A drink strong enough
To let out what laughter they had.

I can still see the two of them:
Tea smiles and lets his yellow teeth shine—
While Angel, the serious one, for whom
Death was a rare disease,
Purses his lips, and looks down, as if
He is already mourning himself—
A soft, gray hat between his hands.
Today, in honor of them,
I press my thumb against the flat part of this blade,
And steady a bunch of red, Málaga grapes
With one hand,
The way they showed me, and cut—
And close my eyes to hear them laugh at me again,
And then, hearing nothing, no one,
Carry the grapes up into the solemn house,
Where I was born.

Winter Stars

My father once broke a man's hand
Over the exhaust pipe of a John Deere tractor. The man,
Rubén Vásquez, wanted to kill his own father
With a sharpened fruit knife, & he held
The curved tip of it, lightly, between his first
Two fingers, so it could slash
Horizontally, & with surprising grace,
Across a throat. It was like a glinting beak in a hand,
And, for a moment, the light held still
On those vines. When it was over,
My father simply went in & ate lunch, & then, as always,
Lay alone in the dark, listening to music.
He never mentioned it.

I never understood how anyone could risk his life,
Then listen to Vivaldi.

Sometimes, I go out into this yard at night,
And stare through the wet branches of an oak
In winter, & realize I am looking at the stars

Again. A thin haze of them, shining
And persisting.

It used to make me feel lighter, looking up at them.
In California, that light was closer.
In a California no one will ever see again,
My father is beginning to die. Something
Inside him is slowly taking back
Every word it ever gave him.
Now, if we try to talk, I watch my father
Search for a lost syllable as if it might
Solve everything, & though he can't remember, now,
The word for it, he is ashamed....
If you can think of the mind as a place continually
Visited, a whole city placed behind
The eyes, & shining, I can imagine, now, its end—
As when the lights go off, one by one,
In a hotel at night, until at last
All of the travelers will be asleep, or until
Even the thin glow from the lobby is a kind
Of sleep; & while the woman behind the desk
Is applying more lacquer to her nails,
You can almost believe that the elevator,
As it ascends, must open upon starlight.

I stand out on the street, & do not go in.
That was our agreement, at my birth.

And for years I believed
That what went unsaid between us became empty,
And pure, like starlight, & that it persisted.

I got it all wrong.
I wound up believing in words the way a scientist
Believes in carbon, after death.

Tonight, I'm talking to you, father, although
It is quiet here in the Midwest, where a small wind,
The size of a wrist, wakes the cold again—
Which may be all that's left of you & me.

When I left home at seventeen, I left for good.

That pale haze of stars goes on & on,
Like laughter that has found a final, silent shape
On a black sky. It means everything
It cannot say. Look, it's empty out there, & cold.
Cold enough to reconcile
Even a father, even a son.

Caravaggio: Swirl & Vortex

In the Borghese, Caravaggio, painter of boy whores, street punk,
    exile & murderer,
Left behind his own face in the decapitated, swollen, leaden-eyed
    head of Goliath,
And left the eyelids slightly open, & left on the face of David a
    look of pity

Mingling with disgust. A peach face; a death mask. If you look
    closely you can see
It is the same face, & the boy, murdering the man, is murdering his
    own boyhood,
His robe open & exposing a bare left shoulder. In 1603, it meant
    he was available,

For sale on the street where Ranuccio Tomassoni is falling, &
    Caravaggio,

Puzzled that a man would die so easily, turns & runs.

Wasn't it like this, after all? And this self-portrait, David holding
    him by a lock
Of hair? Couldn't it destroy time if he offered himself up like this,
    empurpled,
Bloated, the crime paid for in advance? To die before one dies, &
    keep painting?

This town, & that town, & exile? I stood there looking at it a
    long time.

A man whose only politics was rage. By 1970, tinted orchards &
    mass graves.

   •

The song that closed the Fillmore was "Johnny B. Goode," as
	Garcia played it,
Without regret, the doors closing forever & the whole Haight
	evacuated, as if
Waiting for the touch of the renovator, for the new boutiques that
	would open—

The patina of sunset glinting in the high, dark windows.

Once, I marched & linked arms with other exiles who wished to
	end a war, &…
Sometimes, walking in that crowd, I became the crowd, &, for that
	moment, it felt
Like entering the wide swirl & vortex of history. In the end,

Of course, you could either stay & get arrested, or else go home.

In the end, of course, the war finished without us in an empty row
	of horse stalls

Littered with clothing that had been confiscated.

	•

I had a friend in high school who looked like Caravaggio, or like
	Goliath
Especially when he woke at dawn on someone's couch. (In early
	summer,
In California, half the senior class would skinny-dip & drink after
	midnight
In the unfinished suburb bordering the town, because, in the
	demonstration models,
They filled the pools before the houses sold….Above us, the lush
	stars thickened.)
Two years later, thinking he heard someone call his name, he
	strolled three yards

Off a path & stepped on a land mine.

	•

Time's sovereign. It rides the backs of names cut into marble. And
	to get
Back, one must descend, as if into a mass grave. All along the
	memorial, small

Offerings, letters, a bottle of bourbon, photographs, a joint of
     marijuana slipped

Into a wedding ring. You see, you must descend; it is one of the
     styles
Of Hell. And it takes a while to find the name you might be
     looking for; it is
Meant to take a while. You can touch the names, if you want to.
     You can kiss them,

You can try to tease out some final meaning with your lips.

The boy who was standing next to me said simply: "You can
     cry....It's O.K., here."

                    •

"Whistlers," is what they called them. A doctor told me who'd
     worked the decks
Of a hospital ship anchored off Seoul. You could tell the ones who
     wouldn't last
By the sound, sometimes high-pitched as a coach's whistle, the
     wind made going

Through them. I didn't believe him at first, & so then he went into
     greater
Detail....Some evenings, after there had been heavy casualties &
     a brisk wind,
He'd stare off a moment & think of a farm in Nebraska, of the
     way wheat

Bent in the wind below a slight rise, & no one around for miles.
     All he wanted,

He told me, after working in such close quarters for twelve hours,
     for sixteen
Hours, was that sudden sensation of spaciousness—wind, & no
     one there.

My friend, Zamora, used to chug warm vodka from the bottle, then
     execute a perfect
Reverse one-&-a-half gainer from the high board into the water.
     Sometimes,
When I think of him, I get confused. Someone is calling to him,
     & then

I'm actually thinking of Caravaggio…in his painting. I want to
  go up to it

And close both the eyelids. They are still half open & it seems a.
  little obscene

To leave them like that.

Photograph: Migrant Worker, Parlier, California, 1967

I'm going to put Johnny Dominguez right here
In front of you on this page so that
You won't mistake him for something else,
An idea, for example, of how oppressed
He was, rising with his pan of Thompson Seedless
Grapes from a row of vines. The band
On his white straw hat darkened by sweat, is,
He would remind you, just a hatband.
His hatband. He would remind you of that.
As for the other use, this unforeseen
Labor you have subjected him to, the little
Snacks & white wine of the opening he must
Bear witness to, he would remind you
That he was not put on this earth
To be an example of something else,
Johnny Dominguez, he would hasten to
Remind you, in his chaste way of saying things,
Is not to be used as an example of anything
At all, not even, he would add after
A second or so, that greatest of all
Impossibilities, that unfinishable agenda
Of the stars, that fact, Johnny Dominguez.

SHIRLEY GEOK-LIN LIM

Shirley Geok-lin Lim was born in the historic British colony of Malacca, Malaysia. Arriving in Boston in 1969, she studied with J. V. Cunningham, to whom she dedicated her Commonwealth Prize-winning first book of poems, *Crossing the Peninsula* (Heinemann, 1980). Lim is currently Professor of English and Women's Studies at the University of California, Santa Barbara, and Chair of Women's Studies. Author of four books of poetry, three collections of stories, and two critical books, she received the American Book Award for her recent memoir, *Among the White Moon Faces* (Feminist Press, 1996). She has been the recipient of numerous other awards, including National Endowment for the Humanities Summer Awards and a Fulbright Distinguished Lecturer Award in 1996.

"California is NEW geography, new for the European immigrants that had been arriving there since the sixteenth century; new for a late arrival like me, coming in 1990 from pastoral upstate New York, from Brooklyn, and even earlier in 1969 from Malaysia, the southern-most tip of the Southeast Asian land mass, a time when most Americans thought of Southeast Asia as only the badlands and bar-rooms of Vietnam. But Santa Barbara is old with Chumash spirits, with the primeval whale routes from the North Pole to the breeding grounds of the Baja Peninsula. Its Pacific-scape is ancient, the same salt oceans of South Seas/Nanyang Islands which drew my Amoy ancestors from South China with visions of sugarcane fields, paddy terraces, and fat happy clouds. I see Pacific Asia out there on the horizon of the Santa Barbara Channel.

"Turning around 180 degrees, however, I see the Santa Ynez Mountains, the interior of continental America, filled with the bones and descendants of Indians, Spanish, Anglos, Germans, French, and yes, Asians. California is liminal; the shaking ground never lets you doubt that. My poems are full of quakes. They have hardly settled into a form before the new ones get shaken loose, tentative, unsettled. In California the only possible muse for me is Pablo Neruda, not because I share his poetics but because his poetry is full of the ancient cloudy visionary newness which broke the Americas apart."

In California with Neruda

I

Cockeyed Neruda dancing on a strobe
  of a thousand angels didn't ask
    about angels but for a drink of water.
Be my angel, my fat Chilean, stroke
  feathery breath, imploding pulse, wake me
    to the chaparral beneath the skin, the Pacific-
thundering surf inside my eyes. Oh come
to California and stand with me as earth
  coughs, rifts shimmer, adobe cathedrals cracking open
    roll like dice. Wise man of the Americas,
make a wise woman out of me. Seize
  my lines and do not let go, for death
    is not yet to be written in this new-found land,
foreclosing forms and poetry ended.

II

    When the grey watery air sifts through Santa Barbara
like flour in a pan, wholesome, light, changing element
to nutrient, and when between the swirling marine layers
the green ribs of palms sway, ticklish in early morning,
it is not yet three but already my angel is walking,
striking at old manzanita with his cane, his panama
hat cocked to his brow.
           Indoors the refrigerator clicks and groans,
an old lady mashing her cereal. He has no liking for crones,
departs through the colored glass door impatiently
(he is not deceived by decoration: a door is a door,
whether steel or glass). The street lamps pace him.
Bare bony structures with bright obscene noses,
they tell him about darkness visible, whose neighbors'
brown roses have shrunk into fall's clammy fists.

III

Not so fast, dear Pablo Neruda! The suburban tracts
sleep while you shuttle, but not the tossing khaki eucalyptus
or many-leafed olive trees guarding black messy feet.
The white undersides of rosemary flash by a pink wall,
oranges beckon like globed neons in run-down diners.

Lusty lavender spikes crust the tall bushes.
I pinch them, scented fingers; crumble them in my pocket,
sneezing, sinuses backed up, while you stride ahead
undisturbed by common colds, pollen, identities, all longings
of the middle-class and the female kind. Can you smell
the copper of menstrual overflows on my breath, and what
do you make of it in the murky California streetlight
before ambitious ignition keys jump-start the day?

      IV

Neruda, did you know history? Or did you live it,
    one day at a time, through the clichés of revolution
      and boring justifications? Crossing the green belt you glance
down at the creek, withered by August, its March
    impetuosity commemorated by upturned oaks
      and swathed sandy shoulders. Now its water
trickles a bathtub melody even a dog can step over
    with dry paws. These details do not detain you
      for poetry is larger than a September creek in suburbia.
You are determined to walk your nine miles,
    nine the shaman's number called up by association.
    "And that too is history," you murmur. "There is no poetry
but association, no history but poetry, which we swallow
with fresh eggs in the morning, one after the other."

      V

Nothing but contingency, a line of spermatozoa,
the body, the vulva, flexing to its heartbeat,
and words, a pure rhythm of naming one sensation
after another?
                  Is this why you get me up in the mornings,
angelic poet, to walk around and around?
Naming the traffic, the malls, the boys in their uniforms
    of defense and desire, women smoky with hurt
      making sandwiches for school lunches,
Indians chanting through pow-wows, Koreans hymning:
    the entire looping litany of the 49th parallel—
      blacks, whites, Jews, Latinos, Asians,
jamming Los Angeles and Disneyland, the continental
contingency of California breaking out
even as we hurry across driveways in the blink before sunrise.

Learning to Love America

because it has no pure products

because the Pacific Ocean sweeps along the coastline
because the water of the ocean is cold
and because land is better than ocean

because I say we rather than they

because I live in California
I have eaten fresh artichokes
and jacarandas bloom in April and May

because my senses have caught up with my body
my breath with the air it swallows
my hunger with my mouth

because I walk barefoot in my house

because I have nursed my son at my breast
because he is a strong American boy
because I have seen his eyes redden when he is asked who he is
because he answers I don't know

because to have a son is to have a country
because my son will bury me here
because countries are in our blood and we bleed them

because it is late and too late to change my mind
because it is time.

Monarchs Steering

Burnt sienna and sun they lie
on the sharp white petals submerged
in floral light. Arrived after three months
crossing from the bitter alcoholic milksaps
east to the Pacific where oranges brightly
palpitate to an orgasmic infusion.
One stops on an oleander leaf-tip,
another lifts off into warm oxygen,
and yet another luminescent pilot.

Two yards over a pair dallies.
Morning signals the passing Monarchs,
taking my eye, like silent flirts, like women,
after long journeying, taking to scent and heat.
I steer, to the years' indirection.

Riding into California

If you come to a land with no ancestors
to bless you, you have to be your own
ancestor. The veterans in the mobile home
park don't want to be there. It isn't easy.
Oil rigs litter the land like giant frozen birds.
Ghosts welcome us to a new life, and
an immigrant without home ghosts
cannot believe the land is real. So you're
grateful for familiarity, and Bruce Lee
becomes your hero. Coming into Fullerton,
everyone waiting at the station is white.
The good thing about being Chinese on Amtrack
is no one sits next to you. The bad thing is
you sit alone all the way to Irvine.

GLENNA LUSCHEI

Glenna Luschei's first book, *Carta al Norte* was published by Papel Sobrante, Medellin, Colombia in 1967. Her journal, *Café Solo* is now celebrating its thirtieth year. She has also served as Chair of COSMEP and has acted as literature panelist of the NEA. She is the author of a dozen books, chapbooks, and special editions, most recently *Back into My Body, Matriarch: Selected Poems 1968-1992,* and *Spirit of Place.* She has won the YM-YWHA Poetry Discovery Award and has been awarded

© Richard Morris

both the D. H. Lawrence and Wurlitzer fellowships in Taos, New Mexico, as well as a National Endowment writer's grant.

"I will never forget how astonished I was when I drove my family over the San Andreas Fault from Albuquerque to San Luis Obispo thirty years ago in August. The hills were tawny as a lion, the scrawny black oaks that dotted them stuck out angular legs like Kabuki dancers. Trucks whizzed by us on narrow Highway 41 piled high with onions like bald heads—queues sticking out from the scalp. How could I not be happy in a land that smelled like onions! I wasn't happy, though. It took a long time for me to learn the California scenery, language, and culture. California seemed amorphous. I didn't get it. The changes seemed imperceptible until six months after we arrived at the Golden Hills. They were now a luscious green.

"Whether I got California or not, it got me. The waterways traveled underground into my pores. I fell in love with California. I began to appreciate the seasons, especially as my new marriage to a lemon and avocado rancher flourished. There was a planting and a harvest here, as in my native Iowa where I detassled corn. Except here it grew on trees where the crop was even higher to pick. After these thirty years I feel that salt water flows in my veins. A legend prescribes that when you plant a palm tree, you ring a bag of salt around the roots. That's probably how they will bury me, too."

Arrangement

It's 110 in Atascadero
with oleander in full bloom
but poisonous.

How could I change the arrangement
of this bouquet?
It's perfect
but I can't find the theme.
The thistle is as lovely to remember
as the Chinese bell flower,
iris on Atascadero Lake.

When I bring together
silk & barbed wire
ferns curl about my fingers.
I haven't a green thumb.
I get by.

In Colombia
we gave away orchids
every day.
The boy who sold us cheese
round and moist as the Colombian sun
and wrapped in a banana leaf
asked me for flowers in a jar.
"I have to bury my brother,
drowned in the arroyo."

I like it here.
I belong.
I pass the snapdragons, stop
to give them water.

Here

Love's in the daily doings
the blister on the first roasting chili
the race to gather sheets
at the wick of lightning.

We fold the linen with lavender
and sage.

Love's the oar that draws us to the sea.

You propel me over quick

silver waves to San Luis Obispo,
through spidery hills of black oak,
call me home.

The mica I bring you
scatters in my pocket,
but the hunter's moon
tracks it to the tarmac.

Why scan the moon's two continents for love?

Our friends shout, "Look around!"

It's here beside us
on the dark side.

We fold the linen with lavender
and sage.

The Water Song

When you climb
Mount Tamalpais
and the squall you view at sea
beats you to your van,
sleet
hits the windshield
in badger prints.
You fall in love with water again.

You forgive the Berkeley fires.
that routed friends
from their homes,
the Yukon Express
that froze the groves.

When you catch a band
of mountain sheep
the rams kick and butt.
You know there will be lambs
in the spring.

When you hear the snowy tree
cricket sing the water song
you know the High Sierra flows
from another winter.

Water
in the Merced River
water over Nevada Falls
water over Vernal Falls.
In the ancient path of glaciers,
we praise the green hills.

The Pozo Basket

I wove this basket
from arrow grass
to cook
the fish that you would bring.

The other women knew
that you would not be back.

Wove it from tule
and bound it with pine gum;
other women knew
that you would not be back.

I lifted rocks from the fire
with oak sticks
and placed them in my basket
to cook the acorn mush
to cook the fish that you would bring.

I loved you
who took me lightly.

MORTON MARCUS

© Jana Marcus

Morton Marcus was born in New York City in 1936 and has lived in California since 1961. His work has appeared in such publications as *The Nation, Poetry, Poetry Northwest, The World, TriQuarterly,* and *Ploughshares,* and in more than seventy anthologies. He has published seven books of poems, as well as a novel and pieces for the theater. He recently retired from Cabrillo College in Aptos, where he taught literature and film for thirty years. He is a longtime host of a weekly poetry show on KUSP radio.

"Most of my poetry reflects my experiences in California, since I've spent more than half my life in the San Francisco Bay Area. Even my 'otherworldly' parables were inspired in good part by the environmental and social changes that have taken place around me, where hillsides and forests, seeming to vanish overnight, have been replaced by shopping malls; suburbs have slithered over the land in every direction; and animals and plants have become endangered species and, in some cases, have already disappeared. I've written about all these issues in one way or another, but essentially—and specifically—California has entered my work because of its location at the end of the continent. To me this geographic condition represents the end of the national impetus of westward expansion, as well as the physical goal of the American dream—however vague and confused that goal continues to be in the nation's collective psyche. For these reasons, California has provided me with a perspective from which to see my immediate environment and, simultaneously, to view the world. At times I imagine that just by living on the California coast I'm not only standing at the edge of the continent, but on the planet's eyelid, looking north, south, east, and west—acutely aware of my place between the bone pile of the earth beneath my feet and the cold, unyielding light of the stars above my head."

I Think of Those Mornings

I think of those mornings before dawn,
when it was still dark out and I'd drive
past the lighted windows of farmhouse kitchens:

first in a bus when I was ten, then on the way
to bootcamp when I was seventeen,
and now in my own car at forty-one.
There are windows still framed in my head:
the old woman in a shapeless pink dress
turning eggs or bacon in a pan;
two men I took to be bachelor brothers,
both over fifty, bald and belligerent,
seated across from each other, coffee cups
beneath their chins.

       Once, and once only,
a man and woman standing in the yellow light
holding each other by the elbows
with their fingertips.

       But mostly
it was the woman feeding others from a fry pan
held like a lowered hand mirror at her waist;
the old man in red-and-black checkered shirt
seated alone, elbows on the table,
head tilted to catch the light, holding
an envelope or a snapshot close to his eyes.

All those lives, those and many more,
glimpsed for a moment and then gone.
Iowa, Oregon, upper New York state.
The plowed fields, corn and wheat,
breathing in the dark, a damp mist
of loam and seed.

       Where was I headed
past those lives and never touching them,
leaving them in those farmhouses
where they rose each day before dawn
when it was still dark out, switched
the light on in the kitchen, heard
not the 5:45 L.A. bus
but a truck, was it?, or a heavy-engined car
going somewhere—to Stockton, maybe,
or Portland, Denver, Duluth—
as they pulled on boots,

set plates on the table, sighed,
and watched first light, a gray light,
swim up to the window and reveal
the plowed fields, corn and wheat,
where they had left them the night before.

Picnic on the Bay Bridge

driving across the Bay Bridge at 50 m.p.h.
my hands float from the steering wheel

my body expands suffused with light
and I flow through the windshield

hover before my speeding car
and watch myself driving with a silly grin

my wife is talking to the side of my head
my daughter grinding away in the coloring book

and only the baby sees that I'm gone
as she croons at my figure flying away

around me battalions of golden men
rise from their cars

and swim through the air
and women float out of their make-up

out of their clothes and shopping lists
children tumble and soar

all of us swoop through pouring down cold
and dance above the cars

some hold their groins others giggle
but only for a moment

and there are my wife and kids
in their golden creases of skin

they wait for me to breast stroke back
and then we wrestle and laugh

"did you bring the pickles and ham" I ask

"yes" says my wife and caresses my neck

"hey do you have any mustard over there"
asks a balding middle-aged man

we float him the jar and he
and a Mexican family swim over

tortillas and french bread
hams chorizos—and barbecued ribs

supplied by a school bus full of black kids
chanting verses from the Tao Teh Ching

under the guidance of an elderly Chinese
who conducts them in his rags of glowing skin

we eat we chant we dance and sing
while the toll gate shines far ahead

The Poem for Gonzales, California

for Tony Doyle, who told me Gonzales had been left off the California road map

Gonzales will always be
a cold, clear night
in early March, a place
on Highway 101
between Soledad and Salinas
where, returning late
from a trip to Santa Barbara,
I chose to pull off the road
and drive into a field,
exhausted, sick in soul,
halfway to divorce, and as sure
of my own death as I was
of the sour milk taste
coating the inside of my mouth.
When I switched off the engine
I heard the breathing
of my two small daughters
asleep in the back seat,
and knew that they would

continue on without me,
that the world would,
with no fanfare and less
concern.

A deep quiet
settled around the car.
The dark field encircled me.
The stars, a glittering panorama
through the windshield, ticked
across the sky. I was more alone
than I had ever been,
and didn't know
where that realization
would lead me.

Shut in that car—
an insect in his carapace
surrounded by the field
and the endless, inching
movement of the stars—
I listened to the breathing
from the back seat, knowing
that whatever I decided
would determine
the rest of my life.
Ten minutes later
I flipped on the ignition
and drove toward home.

This happened
in Gonzales, California,
a town that a friend now tells me
has been taken off the map.
It happened in a field
I could never find again
but have marked on my memory
as the place at my back
I start from and continue on.

Whales

Our future plunges with the whale:
chilled water weighs against our skulls,
flat forehead forces a passage
to that slow darkness miles below
where it swaggers into whale-shape—
that round unrolling from the end of darkness,
to the beginning of light.

We slide up through fathoms of his shadow,
butting the underside of water
until we break through the surface
and bask in the sun.

And when we roll in the swells
and release an easy breath,
his spout is a halo above our heads.

The Letter

I found the letter in a book I bought at an outdoor theatre turned flea market every weekend. It was June 1995 in a small town on the California coast.

The book was Tolstoy, *Anna Karenina,* and the letter was tucked between pages 434 and 435, where a delirious Levin, the day after he's proposed to Kitty, visits her parents' home. The letter—pinkish, sealed, not mailed, faintly redolent of talcum, like a pressed flower—was from a Sarah Harris, dated inside October, 1939.

Yes, I opened it and read how fine the trip was from Des Moines back to Cincinnati, suspecting nuances and unworded passages I had no way of understanding—or, more accurately, deciphering—to go along with what I took to be the mute appeal to Carl Bigelow, 913 McKinley Avenue, Des Moines, Iowa, in the final paragraph: "There didn't seem time for me to say all the things I needed to. Do you feel the same?"

The Tolstoy was a book club's bonus edition bound in grey leatherette. Had Sarah Harris purposely placed the letter between those pages depicting Levin and Kitty's jubilant betrothal? I had no way of knowing, and refused to suppose. However, I resealed the letter, affixed fresh stamps to the envelope, and sent it on.

JACK MARSHALL

Jack Marshall was born and raised in Brooklyn, New York. After high school, he worked in the New York garment center, and then as a seaman on a Norwegian freighter to Africa. He later moved with his family to San Francisco, where he worked as the manager of a clothing shop and as a longshoreman. After his first volume of poems, *The Darkest Continent,* (For Now Press) appeared in 1967, he was invited to teach at the University of Iowa Writers' Workshop for two years. His next book, *Bearings* (Harper & Row, 1970) was followed by *Bits of Thirst* (Blue Wind Press, 1976); *Arriving on the Playing Fields of Paradise* (Jazz Press, 1983), winner of the Bay Area Book Reviewers Award; *Arabian Nights* (Coffee House Press, 1986); *Sesame* (Coffee House Press, 1993), a finalist for National Book Critics Circle Award and winner of PEN West Award; and *Millennium Fever* (Coffee House Press, 1997).

©Naomi Schwartz

"For the past ten years I have lived on the coast in San Francisco, and my work has been infused, more by osmosis than by design, with that foggy, sea-drenched, bird-branched, sunset weather which, lived in for so long and naturally as breathing air, becomes inner weather, inhabiting us as much as we inhabit it: the open fluidity of western colors and textures, the moods of the Pacific Ocean, the habits of its many varied migratory birds, the cycle of the seasons."

Air Dagger

Sundown on the sand, and your shadow
    Tall as the 4-story condo across the highway....

Dipping, picking the wave's back-curling lip, spiraling
    Flocks of straw-billed terns

Dive at each other and—no two touching
    Wings—merge, touching

Down in a line, facing the lowering sun, the open
    Sea opening

All windows. Eyes looking out
    So intently forget

The face they're in, see
    Amid curls and scrolls of wood a powerful hand,

Pulsing in the undertow, draw back the bow.
    Now to go

Stretch out thin as gossamer thread held perilously
    Intact by nothing

More than a whim, as if random
    Mercy might release a little

Pure air, not chemical vapor propelled to high
    Heaven on octane fuel, taking

Our breath away. Taking
    Time out from the rush to the cliff-edge, that

One not fall
    From same, we're here

Slaking a thirst for the smallest
    Packet of energy making its way

Amid hostile moving metal, silver-
    Tongued like the shiny track

A finger leaves in velvet.
    And those who hunger, not linger, for

What remains will know their hearts
    Shared in the open…

To eat, to taste, to change
    The feel of time…the way the birds

Filter and fling
    The air through their hollow bones.

      The birds know. Follow the birds.

Wing and Prayer

Dear fellow infidel, let's pray
   That this daily poisoned rain pouring
Torrents of contaminant crude
   Does not become the norm from now on,

Or the nightmare dreamed I know now for sure
   Will be delivered. Earth's not cherry anymore, O-
Zone's broken hymen, eroded topsoil, rising waters, and forests
   Burnt faster than fired brain-cells, quicker

Than you can say "The self's cry
   In roasting meat tastes but cannot
Touch the source it eats," fire's
   The future. Prophets had foretold it, though

Prophets and the news they carry are always
   Too late. While the plane of fire more swiftly
Plays out what on the plane of earth takes
   Time, things have never been so

Hot as we are going to make them. Circling the center
   Close to all the extremities, there's something
Nuclear going on. With the compliments of
   What corporate birds of prey, casually polluting

Slaughterers, have the time-released, barely traceable air-
   Borne gas chambers been set
In motion? Who'll make a living
   Text out of the toxins? God must

Be real
   Pissed. Torched garden, infected fruit, dwindling
Herds running for their lives; sex never more
   Iffy, and loose

Sex definitely
   Out. In less than a lifetime, to see
Birth, and death, and the imminent unimaginable
   Death of birth, O endangered

Unborn
   Lovers of the golden-headed

Tamarin, wild mustang, Bengal tiger, snow leopard, bald eagle,
  Even the pea-brained dinosaurs lorded it

Over the mammals for 60 million years
  Until a hail of comets fused
Their molecules into fossil fuel, opening
  The way for us. Thank our lucky stars, indeed!

In a world where silk is
  Thread, web, and spider, too,
A door swings open
  On a life when the limbs in question feel

Underfoot the richness of
  Generations gone
As you pass them tumbling
  Down all the way, and light

From no solid source, illuminating no solid
  Body, presses for a little while the
Figure out of shape. It needs, like us,
  A wave

Of enchantment welling up from the lower levels
  To draw it out. Inexhaustible,
The combination of enchantments possible
  In the combination of one person

With another, offering looks that awaken, looks
  That can touch
You back. It takes
  Two to have one's

Heart
  Broken. Not I, but
Erik Satie has spoken
  Through the notes, echoing oceans

Apart between the hearts left
  Unbroken. And that's only the tip
Of the hunger there must be in paradise
  For its children to leap into hard,

Hard rest. They walk, bickering, out
　　Of the past into the distant
Present, on the street before the wind
　　Leaves for the other street

Corners of the world, undoing
　　What's been done by doing
What needs to be but won't be
　　Had. Now a lunging

Greyhound on the beach goes running down
　　Perfectly synchronized flocks of birds swooping
Offshore, that tremendous outstretched underbelly, outflung
　　Paws defying gravity, coming

As close to flying as we'll

　　　　get to heaven

JERRY MARTIEN

A fourth generation Californian, Jerry Martien is the author of *Shell Game: A True Account of Beads and Money in North America* (Mercury House), several chapbooks, and a collection of poems, *Pieces in Place* (Blackberry Books). He is a carpenter, community activist, and poet in the schools, and he also teaches at Humboldt State University.

© Sandi Potter Martien

"When I moved my mother from her native land, nearly a thousand miles north, to live with me in an old house on the dunes of Humboldt Bay, people would ask her where she'd come from. 'California,' she'd say. And they would look at me as if to ask: 'Where does she think she is?'

"Her father, Porfirio, was born near Mission Santa Clara—in a California that no longer exists. Although she changed name and identity, it is also where she was from, and because I'm her son, it is a native land I sometimes believe I remember. Another California has covered it over.

"The most dispossessed people talk incessantly of place. Often they use language to find themselves again. With poems they create another place—or discover in another landscape the land they remember. I live in exile from California and use these words to unearth my home."

•

"The poem arises from the ground of its making. By way of a human attention, deliberately placed there—held there, till it is shaped by the rule of that ground.

"The poem surrounds us. The poet loiters deliberately in the dooryard, maintaining cultural access to that nourishing circumstance. Speaks on behalf of the still-living, still-sacred grove, and labors to restore the springs to which we all go when thirsty.

"No 'poetry' then—only the poem we call *here*—*here* in the ground of our speaking. In place—in the discovery and acceptance of the living vernacular of locale. The spirit that moves our hearts and imagination, that finds expression in our water and air and food, that lives and speaks in the voice of river, ocean and forest, and in the incessant gossip of all beings. As it came to me, when I get out of the way, still talking to you here."

In Wild Iris Time

They grow on the sides of the mountain. As if the old days
were here again. Had never gone. As if nobody knew better
they appear on the sides of the mountain. Scattered
and in clusters they work their lives into a deep and
intricate beauty. A flower too delicate to be described.
You have to see them in the colors they wear. See them at home.
Where they stand on the sides of the mountain through wind and hail.
How they weather this precarious season. See how in past days
women pulled from the split leaf two long silky strings for
men to twist and knot into net and cordage, binding
tough as sinew, lasting as difficulty or pain. It was
something to do in the days it won't stop raining.
When everyone's ailing and even music and jokes won't
help and all things are crazed with change and increase but the
seed isn't in and the dry wood is gone and the ground is
too wet to dig and anyway it's about to rain again.
When there's no other string to twist. No knot left to tie.
At a time like this on this cut-over, abandoned, tilted land
like men and women in the rags they wear on the sides of the
mountain of heaven, they stand and sing welcome to a
season we didn't know we'd see each other in. They open—
the flower a promise: to bind then and now, heaven and here,
days like this, pain, beauty, and the days that remain.

Grizzly Mountain

Late 20th Century: Spring

We went on the trolley:
my mother & I took the trolley from
where we lived out on greenfield street into
downtown los angeles where you could
then walk from one store to another &
to get your size right the shoe store
had a machine that you stepped up a
step to get to & you put your feet in an
opening in the bottom of the machine I

tell you this is true I remember the
red trolley & how when you looked down
into or through the machine that was
inside the box your feet were in
you could see the bones of your feet they
were beautiful neon green which I guess is
the color x-rays are really I don't know
how those shoes fit or how I got home
or what my mother means when she says
california or what happened to the
trolley or the shoes or the machine but
everywhere in this green world my
feet take me now I see bones.

The Rocks Along the Coast

They were once like us, like we were.
      A part of the continent.
The ones close in get to keep their
      green, sometimes a tree, a few birds.
Farther out they wear away & at
      certain tides go under.

But in some opposite, equal justice
      at a point not too close in &
      not too far, to even the balance
They are added on:
      barnacles, limpets, blown sand
      maybe a seed.
Incremental droppings.

It could be the wearing down wins out
Leaving them stranded in their own
      by the main body's day-to-day
      breakdown and retreat.
Or they are thrust up and will remain
      by the sheer memory of the
      edge of the continent
Going over the edge of another continent.

It has to do with love and how love
      has everything and nothing
      to do with islands.
How it takes so much to be ocean
      so little to be rock.

There are no islands left along this coast.
All the rocks have names.

WILMA ELIZABETH MCDANIEL

Wilma Elizabeth McDaniel was born in Oklahoma in 1918. Called "the biscuits and gravy poet" by writer Eddie Lopez, she has lived in California's Central Valley since migrating there in 1936 with her Okie sharecropper family. Author and critic Cornelia Jessey praised her "dry and burning phraseology," while novelist James D. Houston described her writing as "absolutely unique and magical." Collections such as *Sister Vayda's Song* (1982), *A Primer for Buford* (1990), *The Girl from Buttonwillow* (1990), and *The Last Dust Storm* (1995) have garnered wide acclaim for the poet, who is arguably the finest writer to emerge from the Oklahoma Dust Bowl exodus.

© Gerry Pannell

"It is always awkward and quite unreal for me to attempt describing my life as a poet. I simply cannot remember when I was *not* one. It began as a very young child in rural Oklahoma and came with me to California in the Dust Bowl-Great Depression. I still live in the San Joaquin Valley, where much of my inspiration is derived. I continue to write almost daily, even though I am legally blind and stab my work out with marking pens."

A Realist of 1939–40

Eddie was a cute boy
and drove a snazzy
little roadster
what he saw in
our Cousin Cyanella
I never figured out
and his courtship
they only sat on the
running board of the car
and listened to his radio

he really loved the new
songs with Tony Martin
I remember the station
kept playing *South of the Border*
and then *I'll Never Smile Again*
with Frank Sinatra
Eddie would sway and
savor every note
Cyanella just shook her mane
of flaming auburn hair
and showed no emotion
this went on for hours one
Sunday afternoon
Uncle Doc passed through
the yard with the *Fresno Bee*
and glanced at the couple
The way things are goin'
across the water, he mumbled,
young fellers like Eddie better
get used to war, it's comin'

Asking Favors

Will one of you go
pretty please with
sugar on top
in my absence
a total stranger will do
salute the water tower
in my full name

Call out boldly
challenge that proud crow
who claims the grass
beneath it as its own
and I will be forever in
your gracious debt

Do rant and rave and
shake your fists at demon trucks
which shatter the quiet
of the Pancake House
As a further favor to me
let the iris blue of Sycamore Street
turn your head
as it turned mine years ago

Above all things just anyone
walk the rose fence foursquare
around Tulare District Cemetery
if the sky is clear east
of St. John's Church
yell my best regards to the Sierra

California Entertainment, 1936

No cotton picking that day
it poured rain the night
before
and washed out everything
but the tentpegs and Uncle Bart's
most precious dreams

They came out next morning
as bright as the valley sun
but the fields were soggy wet

No complaining from a man
with seven hungry children
he laughed and told little Clemmie
Boy, you and me is goin' up
among the swells on Sycamore
see how they live from outside

They crossed the railroad tracks
and stood beneath the Coca-Cola sign
beside Highway 99

never even got to Sycamore
instead they watched cars go by
for hours
counted seven license plates
they had never seen before

First Spring in California, 1936

The Okies wrapped their
cold dreams in army blankets
and patchwork quilts
and slept away the foggy
winter nights of 1935

From doorways of tents
and hasty shacks
now and then a boxcar
they watched for spring
as they would watch for
the Second Coming of Christ

And saw the Valley change
from skim milk blue
still needing sweaters
to palest green that filled
their eyes with hope

As they waited for odd jobs
the Valley burst forth
with one imperial color
poppies flung their gold
over acres of sand
like all the bankers in California
gone raving mad

Women wept in wonder
and hunted fruit jars to can
the precious flowers
in case next year
did not produce a bumper crop

My Room at Aunt Eura's, 1937

Working for school clothes
that Del Monte cannery summer
room and boarding
I slept in an iron bed with a faded
chenille spread
and saw sixteen years in a cracked
mirror
blistered cut and taped hands
dead tired feet
the bare walls welcomed me at night
breeze stirred the flimsy curtains
and brought the Man in the Moon
to my window
taunting me Borrow Jean Harlow's
evening gown
she will never miss it anyway
put on her slippers
come out and dance
I tossed
and turned to the wall where the
calendar hung
then fell asleep
and never heard the fishermen
come home from Pismo Beach

Ruby Red's Migrant Camp

The tin-roofed shacks
lived together with only
the width of a cockroach
separating them

and dearly loved their manager
with her flaming hair
and strangely gentle spirit

They wouldn't swear in her
presence or throw beer

bottles behind her back

Though she heard them
laughing and saw them
drinking every Saturday night

All vowed never to toss
a lighted cigarette at
Ruby's high-heeled feet

Fearing it would ignite
her hair and burn them out
of the sweetest life they
had ever known

JAMES MCMICHAEL

James McMichael was born in Pasadena. His books include *The Lover's Familiar, Four Good Things, Each in a Place Apart*, and *The World at Large: New and Selected Poems, 1971–1996*. He teaches at the University of California, Irvine.

"More generous than time, space extends toward me (and I think also you) its plural places. As any phrase does, a place has its separate and adjoining parts. I can outright *see* what these parts offer in the way of materials I call up in words, words that do less violence to these materials than the place-markers 'future,' 'present,' and 'past' do to time. Time I'm better off listening for, expecting not to have much luck."

from Each in a Place Apart

My parents had teased that if I ever
caught a fish I'd take it to bed. Warm lakes had
catfish. Trout were the fish I wanted. They were in the
mountains that abided out of view in almost every
Western I saw. In the benign ephemeral first frames with
boardwalks and tethered horses, frontages, a cloudless day,
kill was promised. More alluring were the extras.
They were harried sober people. The women had
children with them sometimes, and of the men,
any one might even then be on his way to rent a
pack train at the stables. This man had started planting
fingerlings in the high lakes six years before. They'd taken.
Having seen good brood stock there, he was heading
back to them now with his mules and tins and would
parcel them out. Until Mike Cady got his car
(he'd be buying it in June and then we'd go),
the *Inyo-Mono Fishing News* had pictures of big
rainbows and browns. They couldn't have been the last.

Above the canyons in the valleys that rose lake by lake,
there were others with the same pearl underbellies,
the same intransigent ways. Some shorelines dropping
headlong toward them through the top clear zones,
it was easy for me to translate into any equal
volume of water the air inside the tall green
handball court walls. Each was somewhere in a given cube.
The water touched their noses, it touched their sides. Hungry,
beautiful and secret, they held to the beryl half-light,
the sunken boulders opaline and faint. Mike and I had brought
sheepherders' bread and a can of black olives.
No one had been in there yet ahead of us over the snow.
Near the top, where the lake was, Mike said he was sick.
He got in his sleeping bag and didn't want to talk.
There was sun left only on the Inconsolables
and they were orange with it and riven, glacier-backed.
I fished a little in the outlet, which had thawed.
How deep the drifts would be at every saddle in the long
profile of the crest. Basins on the other side were
three days from any trailhead. Missing my dad,
I knew I should eat something, I knew I'd be awake all night.

from Four Good Things

                              A cat came
sleepily from a thick shrub and stopped and shook its head.
There was time between the bleatings of the horn to be
reminded and forget again the huckster and his fish
two streets away, then one, then out of hearing, gone,
the shadows of the fences less alert as the heat gave
way a little and the peas were shucked, all changes
watched for now as if one were confined and sitting up
in bed, alone, with nothing but the afternoon
outside along the ground toward the lilac and the
cactus in the foothills. The room didn't have that
loneliness of rooms she'd stopped to notice in her
haste to get her gloves or hat, rooms where she'd
asked herself how lonely it would be to have to
stay there for the afternoon and not go out.

She was reading about North Borneo, about a
concentration camp, the Japanese, their curious
honor and the cruelty that came from it. She hadn't
seen that in them, doubted it. She wondered what the
spareness of the things they'd lived with meant to
sailors on the carriers. The glare outside was
just what they would have stared through for their Zeros.
From the promenade, on each crossing, late,
later than this, she'd watched the clouds curve up in
tumbles that had brought no wind. Alone, it had been like
seeing a place for someone else whom one might never
tell about it, filled, as one was, with the colored
presence of what was there, with how it all spread
back and away and rounded, shone, went dim.
It filled one with the ease of trusting that the
other person too was in a place. Nor was it lonely
here. Her chair. The dressing table. Desk.
A blue slip cast ware and a single tile.
Light from beyond the hedges through the mica
panels in the shade, the lamp arresting it,
steadying for that last rush of sun that left her wanting
nothing more, not the lamp itself for reading nor the
food her mother brought, fresh vegetables and custard.
Elva. She was Elva. Under the one twilight,
the Esterbrooks' on Allen, Helen Thayer's, the tiny
cottage of the Kelsos' in the trees behind the
Elk's Club. Las Lunas, the McGowans'. Peg and Herb
Cheeseborough. The Hezleps. Orville. Allie Lou.
There were others who were more like family—Lucile,
Florence and Glen. Jimmie was at Lucile's.
Jim would be driving home from downtown past
Elysian Park and through the tunnels, past the glazed
deep pocket of the reservoir he might not see.
It was dim already in her bungalow at school,
the pasteboards in their slots, the sheets of rough
construction paper sorted by their shades and sizes.
Both rooms smelled like sweeping-compound, glues,
like the stark poster-paints in jars with white lids.
Occasionally, a car would turn from Madre onto Del Mar,
behind it and ahead along the streets

the separate conversations in the houses, trysts,
an evening with the radio. The sky was a pale wash.
It caught outside the windows all the late
small matters on the lawns, and lights inside were coming on
too soon.

Posited

      That as all parts of it
agree in their low resistance to flow,

so can it be agreed to call it water.
To say of water that it floods both
forward and back through places
difficult to place demands that the ensouled

themselves make places for their parts of speech,
the predicates arrayed in
front of or behind the stated subject—

water, in the case at hand. Water

attains to its names because it shows as one thing
speech is about.
It shows as water.
To say no
more than that about however broad a sea is

plural already,
it says there must be something

else somewhere,
some second thing at least, or why say
how the thing shows? Before it can be taken

as a thing, as sea,
there have to have been readied for it other
possible-if-then-denied pronouncements—land,
the sky. Possible that
somewhere in the midst of waters there could

be such things as might be walked on,

hornblende and
felsite, quartzite, remnant
raised beach platforms, shales,
a cliff-foot scree.

Until given back accountably as
extant and encountered,
nothing counts. Nothing counts until
by reason it is brought to stand still.
Country. That it stands over

against one stands to reason. Not without
reason is it said of country that it
counters one's feet. To count as

groundwork for a claim about the ground,

reason must equate with country.
To be claimed as that, as country,
sand blown inland from the dunes must
equal its having landed grain by grain.

All grains have their whereabouts.
From emplacements in their clumps of

marram grass and sedges, some will be
aloft again and lime-rich
grain by grain will land.

Country is its mix of goings-on.
For these to tally, befores from
afters must at every turn divide.
Before it turns,
a cartwheel has its place to start from. It

stands there in place. In place an
axle's width away, another

parallel wheel is standing.
Not for long.
After each wheel in concert leaves its
first place for a second,

it leaves again at once a third and more. No more nor

fewer are its places on the strand than it has
time for in its turning.
Imprinted
one at a time,
these places are the lines the cart

makes longer at each landward place.
Not late for what goes

on there as its heft at each next place bears
down onto the loams and breaks them,
the seaweed-laden

cart is in time. Time is the cart's

enclosure. There for the taking, time is
around the cart,
which takes it from inside. Around
stones in the dry-stone dyke are

times out of mind,
those times the stones' embeddings let them go.
The hill-grazings
also are in time, and the three cows.
The blacklands are in time with their

ridged and dressed short rows of barley.
As it does around

bursts that for the places burst upon
abandon where they were before,
time holds around

the moving and the resting things.

ROBERT MEZEY

Robert Mezey has taught at Fresno State, University of Utah, Franklin and Marshall, and since 1976, he has been a professor and poet-in-residence at Pomona College. His books of verse include *The Lovemaker, White Blossoms, The Mercy of Sorrow, A Book of Dying, The Door Standing Open: New & Selected Poems, Couplets, Small Song, Selected Translations*, and *Natural Selection*. His most recent book, *Evening Wind*, won a PEN prize as well as the Bassine Citation. His *Collected Poems* will be published by the University of Arkansas Press in 1999. He has edited *Poems From the Hebrew,* co-edited *Naked Poetry*, and with Donald Justice, edited *The Collected Poems of Henri Coulette*. His awards include the Robert Frost Prize, the Lamont Selection (for *The Lovemaker*), an award from the American Academy of Arts and Letters, a fellowship from the Ingram Merrill Foundation, one from the Guggenheim Foundation, and another from the NEA.

"There are many places in California that I love—Death Valley, Half Moon Bay, Mount Whitney—but the California that has figured in my poems (and gone deepest into my soul) is a dairy farm and a vineyard near Madera, and the foothills and mountains between Academy, and the middle fork of the San Joaquin in the High Sierra. A certain campsite in the wilderness, not far from Rattlesnake Lake, is more home to me than just about anywhere in the world, although it is now several years since my last trek there with Pete Everwine and Bill Broder, although it seems unlikely that I will ever be there again."

At the Point

Travelers long on the road
stop here for water and for the view.
Their children run
through the young and old pines,
splashing in the needles
or chasing the wild canaries, their

light cries
receding in the aisles of shade.

The light is so simple
and steady,
as if tiny beaks
had opened a vein of pure sunlight in the forest,
and the fathers and mothers
stand looking down,
their lives
jumping at the base of their throats
and little words
unspoken for twenty or thirty years
cling to their lips like droplets of water.

In the valley the taut fences
stretch pitilessly to the horizon
and all those who want to be someplace else
must follow them.
The hawks and owls crucified on the wire
have long since returned to their own country,
and the mouse trembles in ecstasy,
lost in the shadow of their wings.

Reaching the Horizon

Once it was enough simply
to be here. Neither to know
nor to be known, I crossed
in the full sight of everything
that stood dumbly in sunlight
or drank the standing water
when it was clear. I called them
by their names and they were what
I called them. In the low glare
of afternoon I advanced
upon my shadow, glancing
at the grass unoccupied,
into the wind and into
the light. What I did not know

passed shuddering toward me
over the bowed tips of the
grass and what I could not see
raced sunward away from me
like dust crystals or a wave
returning to its yellow source.

This morning the wet black eye
of a heifer darkens with the
passing seconds, holding my gaze.
It has grown cold. Flies
drop from the wall; guinea fowl
roost in the sycamore. Old
dog in the corner, the day
ripples into its fullness.
Surrounded by eyes and tongues,
I begin to feel the waste
of being human. The rose
of the sky darkens to a wound
and closes with one question
on its lips, and the million
stars rise up into the blackness
with theirs. If I spoke to this
formerly it was as one
speaks to a mirror or scummed
pond, not guessing how deep it is—
Now I see what has no name
or singularity and
can think of nothing to say.

Touch It

Out on the bare grey roads
I pass by vineyards withering toward winter,
cold magenta shapes and green fingers,
the leaves rippling in the early darkness.
Past the thinning orchard the fields
are on fire. A mountain of smoke
climbs the desolate wind, and at its roots
fire is eating dead grass with many small teeth.

When I get home, the evening sun
has narrowed to a filament. When it goes
and the dark falls like a hand on a tabletop,
I am told that what we love most is dying.
The coldness of it is even on this page
at the edge of your fingernail. Touch it.

Twilight Under Pine Ridge

Earth between two lights,
one just now draining away
from tiny trees on the western shoulder,
and one to come,
as the stars begin to open in the field of night.
On every slope great trees are flowering
in beautiful relation and yet
all solitary. In the early darkness
clear voices leave off
and fold inward toward sleep.
The grass
parts.
Lord God slides forward on his belly.

An Evening

The sun blazing slowly in its last hour

A horse motionless on a knoll
His long neck and mouth plunged toward the earth
His tail blowing in filaments of fire

Tuft of grass that bends its illuminated head over its own shadow
The grass sleepy after the long feast of light

And the new leafed figs dancing a little in the silence
Readying themselves for the night

An evening

Understood
By those who understand it not

CAROL MUSKE

Carol Muske teaches at the University of Southern California in the English Department. She is the author of six books of poetry and two novels, plus a collection of critical essays and reviews. She is also the recipient of many awards, including a John Simon Guggenheim Fellowship, a poetry fellowship from the NEA, and Ingram-Merrill Grant and di Castagnola Prize from the Poetry Society of America, as well as several Pushcart Prizes. She is a regular reviewer for the *New York Times Book Review* and lives in Los Angeles with her husband, the actor David Dukes, and her daughter, Annie Cameron.

Her most recent books are *An Octave Above Thunder: New and Selected Poems* (Penguin Books) and *Women and Poetry* (University of Michigan Press).

"I've lived in Los Angeles for fifteen years now—two years longer than I lived in New York City. I have to admit that I've never felt completely at home in California—with the exception of the time I lived in San Francisco and Mill Valley when I was in graduate school. But Los Angeles is the very essence of transience with its freeways and earthquakes. Though my daughter (now fifteen) was born here and I've lived in the same house since 1984, I still think of myself as a kind of visitor here. I think this 'visitor' quality shows up in my poems. The landscape—the desert, the ocean, the canyons—never fail to surprise me and move me, yet leave me with a sense of profound uneasiness. 'Field Trip' and 'The Fault' (which was written after coming out here from NYC to teach for a quarter at U.C. Irvine in 1978) and 'Little LA Villanelle' all address this uneasiness. The desert is traditionally a place for the soul to wander, encounter temptation, suffer trials. I've had a very good life here—I have good friends, and I love teaching at USC—and my actor-husband plugs us in to the Industry world every now and then. Nevertheless, I know that the desert is just there, beneath us—I feel its presence all the time. A kind of 'Ozymandius' syndrome.

"What I thank Los Angeles for is the gift of isolation (available anytime one doesn't feel like driving somewhere!)—which has allowed me to work in peace when I want to. I've gotten so much more work done here than I ever did in NYC. Many writers here squawk about there being 'no community' in L.A.—but that suits me just fine. I think we have all the community we can stand in our lives—we need to be alone, to think, to recollect emotion in tranquillity. Los Angeles has allowed me to do this."

Coming Over Coldwater

I drive fast, uphill
& static picks what the radio plays
to pieces. The palms are idle, spotlit,
above the occasional court a late wind pays

their crowns. On shifting lots
to the canyon top, houses built on chance
zigzag like lines of coke on a mirror.
One too close to the other and no insurance

for big sliders. Still, something
permanent waits here to reclaim itself:
solar panels hoard the sun, under a redwood,
a woman at her kiln stares at the fiery shelf.

It's no safe harbor. What is?
When it blows, the Santa Ana blows
right down to the brick, but like
the green spike of mint or marjoram

faded into a stew, there's a hint
of original taste here. The scent
of what these slowly falling neighbors
cook in one pot, but apart, meditates

in the air, sort of Moroccan.
In the dead eye of the brights, I spot
red tiles, a way of life. I like it.
Offstage, Mother Pacific turns up

her thousand winged collars.
Further out, is a Zen ring
of islands, air-brushed, fanned up
like sand from a wind machine, where wing

over wing, the land lets go. I
wouldn't call it exile at all. Are you
coming home to Christ? the sign asks,
and I think of the thirty-two

years it took him to work up
an appetite for human company.

When he cried *Sitio*, I thirst,
someone offered him hyssop

on the cross. His tongue
a black dart, he turned and spoke
kindly to the person next to him.
He was happy then, promising heaven

to a thief, drinking in the earth
himself, still, its streams
and green canyon pools. *I thirst.*
Out on Coldwater, I hit low beams.

Field Trip

Downtown, on the precinct wall,
hang the maps of Gang Territories,
blocks belonging to the red Bloods
or blue Crips. Colored glass hatpins

prick out drive-by death sites—
as the twenty-five five-year-olds
pass by. They hold each other's hands
behind their tour guide, a distracted

man, a sergeant, speaking so far over
their heads, the words snap free
of syntactical gravity: *perpetrator,*
ballistic. The kids freeze in place,

made alert by pure lack of comprehension.
Then, like the dread Med fly, they specialize:
touching fingerprint pads and then their faces,
observing the coffee machine (the plastic cup

that falls and fills in place), the laser printer
burning in the outlines of the Most Wanted
beneath a poster of a skeleton shooting up.
It's not so much that they are literal minds

as minds literally figurative: they inquire
after the skeleton's health. To them a thing

well imagined is as real as what's out the window:
that famous city, city of fame, all trash and high

cheekbones, making itself up with the dreamy paints
of a First Stage Alert. The sergeant can't help
drawing a chalk tree on the blackboard. He wants
them to see that Justice is a metaphor, real as you

and me. Where each branch splits from the trunk,
he draws zeros and says they're fruit, fills each
with a word: arrest, identification, detention,
till sun blinds the slate. Not far away, through

double-thick glass, a young man slumps
on a steel bench mouthing things, a clerk
tallies up personal effects. Now he comes
to the gangs, how they own certain colors

of the prism, indigo, red—he doesn't tell
how they spray-paint neon FUCKS over
the commissioned murals. The kids listen
to the story of the unwitting woman

gunned down for wearing, into the war zone,
a sunset-colored dress. She was mistaken
for herself: someone in red.
She made herself famous, the way people

do here, but unconsciously—becoming
some terrible perfection of style,
(bordering as it does, on threat.)
The sergeant lifts his ceramic mug,

etched with twin, intertwining hearts,
smiling like a member of a tribe. Later,
on the schoolroom floor, the kids
stretch out, drawing houses with chimneys,

big-headed humans grinning and waving
in lurid, non-toxic crayon. Here is
a policeman, here a crook. Here's a picture
of where I live, my street, my red dress.

                    Our planet, moon. Our sun.

Last Take

I watch them killing my husband.
    Trained assassins, pumping round after
round from behind a camouflage truck:
    they crouch toward his crippled form.

Under the white floodlights,
    blood jets sputter from his chest,
his head's thrown back. He shouts out a name, sliding down
    the white walls against the damp flag of his shadow.

A little guillotine shuts. Hands sponge the wall.
    He stands, alive again, so there's no
reason to fear this rehearsed fall, his captured cry,
    the badly cast revolution that asked his life.

The damask roses painted on the folding parlor screens
    of the phony embassy are real in a way, but the walls
are fake, and fake, too, the passion of these two naked human bodies
    embracing on the Aubusson: nevertheless, they obsess

the eye like any caress. Off-camera, the actor stroking his stubble
    of beard, the actress's hands on her own small breasts.
Presented with the mirror of our sentiments, it seems
    possible to believe that we love the world, ourselves—

Waiting in the wings like extras, full of desire
    projected away from us. These sky-high fingers
of light imply, offhand, all night, we stand in for God
    who is nothing to fear. He gets up and falls down again

in slow motion. A boom swings into the frame,
    then out. Loaded dice are shaken onto green felt before
the trembling hands of the unwitting victims. A roulette
    wheel turns: the red, the black, chemin de fer.

The train crosses the border: inside, rows of people jammed
    together, watch, weep. The real
sky behind the starry backdrop fills with stars. The lovers kiss.
    I want to ask How much? How much do we love each

other? But the director in his cherry-picker signals another take:
    The sky grows light. It's late.

The Fault

I

At dawn, falling asleep on the freeway,
I watch the sun come up in purgatory
and pray with the radio: *Save us.*
Past nuclear reactors, the blind remainders

of the brain: *Save us.* L.A. to Newport,
the eye becomes its own compass: due south
is the globe's curve, not Hell, though
the earth lowers and extends: one enormous runway
into the mouth of the diamond mine. The aerial

tows a light, the hood lamps pick a hitchhiker,
offramp. The searchlights tangle in ice plant, climbing the exit
wall. The burning eyelids of the savior move
on a marquee. . . . The News reports it's snowing again

Back East, though I can't imagine that kind of white.
The day I learned to swim, there were no clouds,
just the dissolving monument of sand and I sank
without sound, where the reef dropped like a fault

in the earth and perched a long time on the gravestones
before surfacing. Then I swam, that simple ambivalent
stroke beginners use, with no faith in the body's buoyancy,
no faith in the oldest fault,
the parched intelligence of tide.

II

What is the name of that flower?

The wind sidesteps itself
in the courtyard
where the lame learn the waltz of the crutch.
Bougainvillea. Mimosa.

I have use for the gratuitous;
spurs dragging in dust,
a turn in death's rented tux.
This could be a hospital in paradise—

nothing shines all night like these bedside iris,

nothing shines like the feet of the dying.
I swear I have roots somewhere.
I've learned to stand perfectly still
and fill the flower with my anxieties.
Narcissus. Forsythia.

I've learned to applaud the dervish palms,
the deaf. This may not be summer,
but the wind's in the cyclamen.
Imagine a word that specific.

Imagine a skidmark, a dazzling limp
across the continent between our hearts.
There are purple flowers
along this road
and the earth laid out on its altar
has no last words for us.

It's light again
and again I sign love,
my imaginary name.

Irvine, California
Winter 1978

MARISELA NORTE

Marisela Norte's work has been featured in *ELLE, Interview, The Los Angeles Times Sunday Magazine, L.A. Weekly, La Opinion, Rolling Stone, FACE, Wire and Buzz Magazine.* In 1990, she recorded "Norte/ word," a bilingual spoken word collection of stories and poems, which received critical acclaim. She has performed at the Poetry Circus in Taos, New Mexico, The Mark Taper Forum in  "Diva L.A.," the Los Angeles Theater Center, and at local high schools in Los Angeles, where she conducts poetry workshops for students.

"I was born in 1955 and raised in East Los Angeles. 'Educated' through the Los Angeles City School System, I grew up in a 'Spanish only' household thanks to my Chihuahua-born father and Veracruz-born mother. English was learned via the small black and white television and on the big screen at the neighborhood theaters in East L.A. My childhood had a running commentary in English and Spanish, thanks to my parents. I graduated from high school in 1973 and attended Cal State Los Angeles as an English major. In 1978 I abandoned my formal education after an English professor returned a paper I wrote, asking what was I doing in his class and if I was 'illiterate.' It was about this time that I rediscovered public transportation and downtown Los Angeles, taking refuge inside such childhood haunts as Clifton's Cafeteria on 7th and Broadway, Grand Central Market, the counter at J.J. Newberry, and the tea room in Bullock's department store, where I began to write.

"In 1980 I answered a small ad in the *Los Angeles Reader* for a 'Latino Writers Workshop' that met in a storefront on Spring Street in downtown Los Angeles. It was there that I met with writers such as Helena Maria Viramontes, Victor Valle, Manazar Gamboa, Mary Helen Ponce, Luis Rodriguez, and Naomi Quinones. The workshop was one of the most positive experiences I had, as I was able to emerge from my 'literary closet' and read my work to other Chicano/a writers.

"In 1985 I began doing solo spoken word performance with percussion accompaniment by Willie Loya and Darrell Aguilera. My work was performed at The Women's Building, LACE, Club Lingerie, SPARC, The Variety Arts Theater, the Museum of Contemporary Art, and the U.C. campuses. I worked different venues, sharing the stage with Wanda Coleman, Exene Cervenka, Dave Alvin, Eloise Klein Healy, Harry Northup, Joel Lipman, and Henry Rollins, among others."

Angel

1

A stray bullet
lodged between
my fears
between fingers
that stick
leaves broken
'English Only'
on already
red shoes

Monday morning
Lunes Lunes
Los Angeles
La 98
La FM
La Latina
work week begins

Drive-by
shooting victim
on Wilshire Boulevard
will not
"…report to the unemployment line…"

A struggle
to keep my place
among the original
displaced person
odd woman out
damsel in this dress

I slight man's voices
on the street
those that cling
to the bottom
of already red shoes

men's voices
that land
too close

when they spit
as they cross
themselves

men's voices,
that will never have
anything new
to say to me

Tired talk radio
blasting proposals
in one ear
"Can a violent relationship be turned around?"
"Can a dead man still be turned on?"

Bad TV Infomercial
late at night
Brenda Vaccarro squeals
"Oooh! Light his fire!"
Offering salvation
to marriages that sag
like old mattresses
propped up
on their bellies
left lying
against telephone poles
in other people's neighborhoods
where a child prays
for a good night's sleep
and buries
his fists
deep
into
black wires

2
Lunes Lunes
Los Angeles
Ciudad Lunatica

Where a woman is raped
murdered

thrown into the trash
where she will land
on soft pink pillows
of disposable HUGGIES
"Especially for Girls!"

Where Police will tie
a big plastic yellow ribbon
around the City dumpster
in a mock show of support
for the female troops
who must face their attackers
daily
on the way to work
or
in our dreams

They called her
"Suspected Prostitute"
NHI
No Human Involved
and left her body
inside
as they wheeled her down
an alley
for closer inspection
further investigation

Homeless man
on Flower
remains invisible
Big Spender
ignores
Orange Vendor

A 24 carat Jesus
swings
on a lonely trapeeze
in the window
of a Discount Jewelers

I think about
the Cha Cha girl

left crying
at the bar
think about
how pretty
his wife
really is
think about
El Guapo y su Abuelo
wonder out loud
which eye
the girls
fall for
first

La Vaga
she sips
a bloody Valentine
Girlfriend
gives me
some advice
tells me
how I
should get serious
once and for all
and just write a book
and call it: NO SEX AND THE SINGLE GIRL

3
A stray bullet
lodged between
my fears
between memory
against desire
leaves past and present
on already
red shoes

Women behind bars
at the 24 hour
Daddy's Donuts

Deaf mute angels
throwing hand signs
in the dark

A friendly sign
that offers
"Buches Al Gusto" and
"Flautas Estilo Juan Gabriel"
with a smile
and a twist

Homeless man
on Flower
sings
impromptu blues
for a cup of coffee
and remains invisible
I give him half
my sandwich
wrapped in
a poem
and he
calls me
"Angel"

Peeping Tom Tom Girl

I am a Peeping Tom Girl, and from my seat on the downtown bus, I
have been driven through, been witness to, invaded by las vidas de ellas.
I've made myself up to be the girl who sits in the back with the black
mask over her eyes, the high school doll too anxious to experiment, la
muchachita stuffed into the pink lampshade dress who listens as her
parents argue through different neighborhoods. She shuts her eyes and
tries to memorize the menus on the chalkboards outside.

And then there is this woman…the widow with the gladiolus who
never misses a day of forgiveness, who gladly lays her flowers down this
woman—la viuda. Y la otra? Esa? She just sits and sits and counts todos
los días en Ingles y en Español. La mandaron al Diablo con su bolsa del

mandado. Mujer de papel-corazon de carton. She sleeps in doorways, Hefty bag wardrobe, broken tiara and too much rouge.

Uno dos tres cuatro four hundred and twenty nine trece cero cero cero X2…She is the Countess, Nuestra Señora, la Reina Perdida que cayo en Los.

And then there is Silent who taught a friend of mine how to flick her cigarettes out of a car window and be so baaad in the process. Silent, who spends a lot of time in the Welfare office now, filling out those pink and blue forms. Can't find a baby-sitter, a good man, a job? She smiles, blowing the smoke out of her nose and sending the butt of her Marlboro out of the office window and on to the Boulevard. She rides those buses that I do, balancing boxes of Pampers marked half price and pulling two kids, a pink one and a blue one behind her on a string.

"Just pull my little string and I'll do anything… I'm your Puppet…" 15 years ago Robert gave her that 45. They used to ride the Kern bus home and make out in the driveway until they thought their lips would fall off, but they didn't. Puppet…passion…Pampers…what were those words in the middle?

And then there is Rosemary, who is still in Junior College and can't decide between a career in Real Estate or dancing. She hangs out at the local hangouts, fluttering her long lashes and flashing her long legs at some men's eyes and sometimes older men buy her drinks and make vague promises.

"I'll take good care of you"
"I'll drive you straight home"
"Let me take care of that car payment"
"I want to take you out to dinner"

And almost always they are old enough to be her Father or long-lost Uncle. Silver-haired, loose tongued, quick handed, nit-witted men, dangling electroplated lollipops in front of her eyes. And Rosemary says, "Sure, why not? I want someone to take care of me, someone who'll make me his forever Mija, pay my bills, take me dancing, send me day-old roses…I don't care." Her friend Rosary thinks she's crazy and doesn't mind telling her so. They've been friends now for about ten years. Been through absent menstrual cycles, low-paying jobs, conceited men they both thought they'd never be able to live without. And everyone used to get them confused until Rosemary made the distinction in everyone's yearbook. In red ink right below her hollow smile she scribbled: *"Rosary beads/Rosemary bleeds"*

Bells ring. It is my cue to start walking and I make all the cracks in the sidewalk. Like a lost tourist, I curse the crowds and can't help wondering why so many of us are getting pregnant, getting grey hair or being lied to. I see the girls, las chicks. I follow them around, become them for the afternoon. The light goes red as two Doñas discuss lipstick.

"Fíjate que lo compre a medio precio!"
"No!"
"Sí y es de Revlon!"

Downtown Los. When I am alone, dark eyed men speak to me in languages I don't understand. A standing distraction—the blank man in the Brooks Brothers suit. He smells like leather bound books. Our heads turn, it is a short ceremony. We spend long summers back East, raising baby alligators. To him I am a "beautiful terrorist" and unsuccessful advance. Glancing avenues as lights go on and off inside me— inside me it is all white heat sometimes and the dark eyes are persistent-insisting.

I flirt back, shrug my shoulders, I should be barefoot on some Italian coast, steamy, smoldering, a burning girl, red toe nails, a devilish laugh, my long hair, dark skin, his soul tangled in mine. Suddenly, I am beautiful—too beautiful for my own good. But this dream dies fast as I am pushed away by an angry woman carrying too many packages and an unwanted child in her swollen belly.

Suddenly I am back…sick, weak, I haven't written in days. Guilt-ridden, not half a woman. I want out of my own skin, I can't stand the stupid image, the imperfect body, the pink sponge rollers.

Never been to Europe only half a million films…
"Uno dos tres cuatro four hundred trece trece cero cero cero X2 X2 X2 U2?"
"May I take you out to dinner?…cloth napkins."
"Ay Dios, ruega por nosotros, ruega por nos, por Los."
Entonces le daremos fin a esta pesadilla donde muchos solamente somos actores sin papeles.

DAVID OLIVEIRA

David Oliveira was born in
Hanford and raised in Armona,
thirty-five miles south of Fresno in
California's great Central Valley.
He studied poetry with Philip
Levine at Fresno State University,
in a class that included Bruce
Boston, Larry Levis, and Greg
Pape. His work has been pub-
lished in numerous journals, in-
cluding *Americas Review, Art/Life,
Café Solo, The Evergreen
Chronicles,* and *Poetry
International,* and in the anthology,
A Near Country (Solo Press, 1999).
He is the publisher of Mille Grazie

© Steve Aguilar

Press, the creator of *Poet Cards* (trading cards featuring poets), and co-editor
of *Solo,* a national journal of poetry. He lives in Santa Barbara.

"Growing up in the San Joaquin Valley, the world seems flat and boundless.
Even the towns are built flat, hardly a building ever taller than the trees. Only
rarely, at sunset or in the crisp, clean air following a winter rain, is one re-
minded of the real physical boundaries that insulate this geography: the
grandeur of the Sierra on one side, and the ancient rolls of the coast range on
the other. The mountains are distant and sheltering, and the life in between,
if not changeless, is steady and predictable. Unlike other parts of California
where seasons pass almost imperceptibly, here they are distinct: summer al-
ways hot, winter fog always cold and unbreachable, spring always bursting
with the pink and white blossoms of fruit trees. It is this sense of constancy in
a defined and reasonable world that is the source of the fundamental opti-
mism at the core of my writing, and I believe, the work of most poets from
the Valley. Living in this landscape is not easier, nor easier to comprehend,
than anywhere else. The land has been abused by corporate and political in-
terests for decades, just as each successive wave of immigrants has been ex-
ploited and vilified. So, in this regard, the Valley is like most places. Yet,
surrounded by a vast horizon and the evidence that anything can grow here,
we make a truce with the land, an acceptance, which is not surrender. Life, if
not good, is not bad; and the scent of corn and grapes in the long, warm, twi-
lights of summer proves that there is a future and it may be better—which is
also the message of poetry."

A Little Travel Story

Though it is not cold,
the man puts on his business coat
so that motorists, using this remote highway
to return from their weekend at the beach,
might recognize his walking
as the temporary inconvenience
of one who had not planned to walk.
But because it is also dark now,
his smile appears in the headlights too late
to change anyone's hurry.
It would be simple, at this point,
to turn your attention
to the hard facts in the lives
of the Mexican farm worker and his pregnant wife,
who are the ones who stop for the stranded driver,
who, in a language he does not understand,
invite him to ride to a telephone
in the back of an old gray truck
with the company of two children.
But this is, finally, not the story of a poor family
who could not think of other than helping,
nor is it a story to show the generosity
of the hapless walker
whose gratitude buys a month's groceries,
nor is it the story of his car
that, for reasons it keeps to itself,
quits fourteen miles from the nearest phone.
This, you will be surprised to learn,
is the old story of the moon
which no one sees rise behind them
in the June night, one day away
from being full above all their fortunes.
When the moon is a ripe apricot,
its glistening sugar easy
to pick off the kiss of a lover,
who thinks the sweetness will last
for just the moment they are tasting?
Even if you stand beside the road

and watch the moon grow small,
aging to white in the span of one night,
you will not understand anymore than you do now
about the roundness that rolls each moment away
from this life you love so much.
It is only this little thing the story wants to tell.
The travelers find their way home.
The moon goes to sleep on the other side of the world.

Paso Robles, San Luis Obispo, San Luis Obispo

All our lives we've been told how things work.
Yet we persist in believing we barely age,
until some warm afternoon, we catch, by surprise,
a reflection in a store window,

hardly recognizing who we have become.
We take our turn at this, as if following
one another up a mountain without a clear trail,
our steps heavy from the need we carry

to be somewhere else,
some place we have never been,
and will not know when we arrive.
I think of a child's game played in the car

with my brothers and sisters as Dad drives
to the coast on Highway 41. Beverly
reads aloud a road sign, *Paso Robles 45 miles,*
and a hubcap falls off. At the next sign,

it's my turn. I say *Paso Robles,* then before
anything bad happens, Robert starts repeating
the line below, *San Luis Obispo, San Luis Obispo,*
and the hubcaps stay on. Never again

will any of us say *Paso Robles* without
adding two charms of *San Luis Obispo;*
towns we drive through on the way
to somewhere else, linked

in a small arsenal of protections
with Latin spells from mass.
We take it as our mission to say
the dangerous words at odd moments,

quickly adding the incantation that saves
someone from bad luck, a preemptive strike
to rid the world of another reason for sadness,
to let us be happy more often than we are.

The way a photograph of a picnic,
kept for years on the dresser, loses
subtle grays in the lawn, and the spread
of the blanket fades into dim folds

of someone's dress until only dark lines
marking the kindness of a smile, or
shadows proving the curve of an eye,
rise from yellowing distance into a face

beautiful beyond the burden of detail;
so small moments of glad luck
stand out in the picture I have become.
In the picture I dream of becoming,

on a beach, the smallest grain of sand visible
between my toes, watching the expanse of ocean
turn to the enormity of sky, there isn't
enough room for all the brown flights of sparrows

I want to remember. I want so much.
Desire hangs from my cheeks in the morning,
pulls with the weight of years; speaks my name
in the music of coffee, the traffic of work;

whispers at me in public places to let my eyes
call to passing faces which don't stop.
Today want follows me as I'm driving
along those same highways of childhood.

Each road sign now points to a place
where I'm missing a friend; and
I want to be like these hills, which are just hills,
skins of straw blades mining August light

for their splendor—no thoughts of travelers
or the roads where every turn is a sadness for someone.
I say I want to go first, but in truth,
I don't want any of us to go at all.

Foolish wants of a person no smarter than myself.
Like magic words, the few tricks I've learned
that charm the universe to my side
to keep pain at bay, only work when they work,

and there remain unavoidable moments
in the elegance of days passing between
light and dark, when hurt is all I can do.

San Joaquin

for Larry Levis

The red that iron becomes when held
in fire long enough to brand
the backs of cows explains this place.

See it again as the color of dusk
after the glow from the hot valley air
lingers into the time allotted to stars.
See it in the blush on ripe fruit
and in the sunburned faces
of those who pick the fruit.

Know this color by its smell,
and when these landscapes are concealed
under a vast gray sea of fog,
the scent will not let you be fooled
into thinking red has deserted you.
As much as you can bear will leave,
but the flow of trucks,
in their red river of tail lights
taking so much out of this valley
to empty into the great ocean of want,
does not abandon you.

You abandon them all.

One day, sitting in the kitchen of the house
where you were raised, you will hear,
as though for the first time,
the steady song of traffic
from the highway which passes through
a hundred similar towns, indistinguishable
but for their names painted on water towers,
and you will tell the man and woman
sitting across the table, that a stillness
has left you, that you have chosen
the life of poetry and so will wander the earth
in the shame of questions without answers.
Then because none of you truly understands
what more to say, nothing more is said.

●

You have often heard it, and from no one famous,
that a person carries the place where they are born
within them; it is your good luck
to always be in a place where things grow.
Today a question takes you
to a small dark room where you wait alone
by the window for the last drop of rain,
and because you are impatient,
you suspect the answer is not in waiting,
but in how waiting is endured.
By evening, your sufferance grows into serenity
shaped in someone else's nakedness—and if desire
seems a barren answer, at least, it is familiar.

●

It is the last time you are sipping
coffee in the Piazza di Spagna.
A tourist, you are tired of watching tourists
and look down the legs
of the table to where bits of red
have fallen away in the weather
to reveal a layer of white underneath.
In the patches of paint you see
the piebald backs of cows,
the way they lined up once in a pasture

on a path of their own making, indifferent
to the child trying to hurry them along.
Perhaps the child is you, and perhaps,
if you look up quickly, it is autumn again
and the piazza disappears into
the old vineyard behind the pasture,
the grapes long since dried into raisins
and sent to where people eat raisins,
the leaves, on which you have written down
all the lies you know, turning to rust.

Summer

When I think of the house
it's always summer and I'm running

to the front yard from across the street,
each foot touching the searing tar, softened

in the midday heat, just long enough
to send the other foot to its next landing,

hotter than the last—and why
I moved so far from the shade, or why,

since it's the same race to either side,
I come back, gets lost in

the tangled waves of air over
the fiery road, and on the dry grass

which only seems cool because
it isn't melting and is all I want.

C. MIKAL ONESS

C. Mikal Oness' work has appeared in several literary magazines across the country, including *The Iowa Review, Shenandoah, The Colorado Review,* and *Solo.* He is the author of *Husks* (Brandenburg Press) and *Melancholy & Apology* (Aureole Press). He teaches creative writing and the art of the book at the University of Wisconsin-LaCrosse, where he edits and operates Sutton Hoo Press, a literary fine press that publishes limited edition handmade books of contemporary poetry and prose.

© Carole Patterson

"One clear lesson to be learned about poetry from the California landscape is that one need not be overtly political in poems. Anyone with a conscience who looks at the California landscape can see, especially with regard to its delicate chaparral, that man's touch on the environment, like the more severe impervious layers in the south of the state, are a terrific blight. Though the touch may be lighter as we retreat to the diminishing rural and natural areas, the foiled search for solace and reprieve from mismanagement and idiotic engineering makes it as disheartening.

"I have been transplanted several times throughout my childhood and adult life on account of family discord and divorce, and later for a graduate education in writing, literature, and fine press printing and publishing, but it was my origins and several returns to living on the ethereal border between Southern and Central California that taught me the emotional and spiritual value of landscape and place for making poems. In that region I was always looking for a way to retreat into the remarkable natural setting that is so undervalued and so wonderfully dry. The smell on my hands—or the memory of it—from a day of bouldering around the sandstone crags in the foothills behind Santa Barbara always brings me to a kind of godly peace—a dry shell of perspiration on my skin in the evening as I leaned back on solid handholds going up a crack, it was as if I leaned over the entire Pacific. I learned in California that climbing doesn't work for the soul if you think you are 'conquering' nature, but if you are in a rhythm with that nature, then the artform expands your senses to unreal perceptual limits."

August 1990

I sit too still and think about five years
ago in Santa Barbara. My niece
to do her first ballet, and that day Don

and I arrange for brunch at the Upham Inn
before I go to see Kell dance; I dream
the night before of bringing her a rose.
And it seems now as if brunch were a dream—
a fourteen dollar plate of shrimp and ham,
champagne from ten to twelve, and staggering
to my car. What did we talk about? Our jobs?
I loved Don's Nietschzean plume of a moustache,
his balding head, his years above my own.
I loved his craft—rail caps he made on the boat
gleamed with my varnishings each day; they were
his lips glinting with scotch; they were my lips.
I only remember this: a sharp right turn;
in retrospect, a dreadful look of horror
on a woman's face; then time goes past; I wake
to a loud slide, a crash of glass; my dash
board spins; I fall against the roof, the road
through the open window; I pull myself
out of my car, I think; I walk myself
past Donny, past a full crowd looking on.
I was, I say. I drove. It was me driving.
Yes, yes, yes, yes. I understand. I'm fine.
And powerless—that's what it is you know—
on the curb pulling my ripped shirt over
my head, refusing help from the paramedics—
I am refusing help for the last time.
Because years later walking down the street,
or sitting on my bed at night, it comes
to me that I have done this, and someone
is dead, and that a mother must still weep
just north of here; I can begin to hear
her now. I can begin just now.

Climbing

I

I woke as mist licked the pavement,
as slow drops sponged into bare wood
like pain. Soon, a tempermental rain

on porch steps will rob the dust
of its contemplations, pulling it
from its nest between grains of light.

                    Just so,

the manzanita is comfortable
here, timeless as the blackbirds
yet more alone—hardened and red,
as if rage gleamed skyward on its limbs.

        II

Tunneling through chapparal
my flesh scores like the hide
of a fox, my bones knock
soundlessly on sandstone
tumbled and receding
to slag into the blue
between pinnacles.

                    And still,

swallows bank inches
from my throat
on long passages
between clouds. I hear
them sigh when they feel
my breath, and twitch
in their course as if to sail
clean from the body, translating
without attrition, to air.

        III

Boundary for the red-shouldered hawk
is not sky, or beyond. And the field mouse,
to be pinched lifeless between his chest
and starbursts of morning dew,
is no more innocent than the wind
snapping down splay reeds.

                    Regardless,

with only trimmed wings and vision
the hawk is easy at that place
we merely hinge upon at death.

Of All There Is

I returned to the church
of my childhood near the house
I was born in to see what
it was I had believed. I once chipped
gray paint from my porch steps
while goats and peacocks loafed
on hardpan that occasionally,
in spring, blushed into lawn.
A small boy, I would coat my face
with chocolate in the lazy spins
of the tractor tire hung
from the chestnut tree.
But I cannot remember Sundays...

Today, when I walked
to the back by the creek
and turned a flat stone, I still
found worms and frosted
shards of blue glass.
I still found salamanders,
the tender wound that is their skin
far too vulnerable for a boy's hands,
for the reflective confusion
of their coffee-can prisons,
for even the small stones
set near them for company.
I held a spotted one
gently for almost an hour,
and it shook. I shook.

I shook for it in my hand
then got into my blue Dodge Dart
and headed for home. I picked up
a hitchhiker who bought us
tall cans of beer and stayed on
as far as Atascadero. I listened
to him talk of cathedrals he had seen
in Montreal, and tapestries in France.
"For me," he said, "the backlit halos on angels

seem nothing more than wisdom,
or their souls, eclipsed. Of all there is,
that much, at least,
I understand."
                    We drove
even when the sun had colored
like the embers on our cigarettes,
and when the grapevines,
crucified along the Estrella
were only fragmentary
against the glow.

Pulling in the Nets

Lake Cachuma, California

The wheat cock up their shoulders and turn away
                                from a confidential breeze.
But along the roadside they might bend low in their stalks,
                                face down in straightjackets.
It's hard to duck the sickle with such delicate spines.

I saw a whitish bird buckle
across the window of a motor home.
                        One quick pop of the neck
and flutter-whirl of chest down
                        to dislodge its soul—
heavy beyond the millions of insects
flaked from the grill.

            •

Fettered saplings around the tract homes of Camarillo
yield up their thin boughs, shake them in the wind
as if in hope of retreat
                    down through their lashings
where spring, though blue across the plains,
                                stays somnolent
in the cracks of white dirt
                    which zag the flowerbed.

In Santa Barbara there's not much difference.
Tense layers of jacaranda buds
                              snap under cyclists
and give their small sighs back to the wasp
                              and the hornet...

Here, in the muddy reservoir
                              spiked with ghost limbs
the spillway is clogged
                              with autumn's net—
the buoys float unattended
                              with the dingy foam.

        •

I'm guilty of the silk dust of butterfly wings
                              resilient on my fingers
Legs spasmed and tucked hopelessly.
                              If it was penance,
it was an awful one, but even the monarch
with its high-ranking brassard
                              takes to the wind like litter.
No one suffers for that...

I can't be blamed. I'm like a pull of fur
on barbed wire rocking gently in this breeze,
wanting nothing more
                              than to float to the grass.
Truth is a salt block which seems to melt itself back.
I am a small tongue
                              which no longer gives
to the spongy tricks of the peach.

If I had the choice,
                and I do,
the pomegranate would be my bucolic
                              with its tiny poems of blood
to gash my chin and spill over my wrist,
staining me beyond the seine of this life—
the pith shredded and sluiced away.

ROBERT PETERSON

Robert Peterson was born in Denver, Colorado, in 1924. He grew up in San Francisco, where his parents owned a hotel. During World War II, he served in as a medic in the 86th Infantry Division. He has one daughter, Laurel Glenn, and currently lives in Fairfax with his dear companion, Joan Kloehn. His most recent book is *All the Time in the World* (Hanging Loose, 1996).

© Arleen Goodwin

"For much of the time in early years, I lived in parochial Bay Area boarding schools (three, altogether) of different denominations. Homesick in all of them. 'Another word for lack of faith,' said the nuns. I now know, of course, that this was mostly loneliness. Anyway, for me, emotions associated with home have always been at about the same level as the riddle of the meaning of time.

"Signifying an obsession—for as long as I can remember—with this capricious concept ('the abiding place of the affections'—Webster), the title of my first book (1962) was *Home for the Night*. My first real home (in my case, a gift, as I believe any true home must be) was room 208, with daily maid service and a view of downtown, in the Fielding Hotel. But soon enough, in the service of imagination and curiosity—and because my parents were well liked—the entire building at 386 Geary Street became my domicile. Before I was twelve, then, I had not only a happy fire-and-earth-quakeproof home but the opportunity for frequent discussions of this good fortune and the meaning of life with a capable, adult staff.

"At the same time, reading Eugene O'Neill and Somerset Maugham, I was dreaming of other, more exotic homes—on ships, or in Tahiti or Pago Pago. Later, via chance, necessity, love, doubt, or merely sloth, for varying periods of time I've lived on beaches, under bridges, in canoes, foxholes, co-ops, and the occasional chairs of psychiatrists. As poet Kenneth Hanson says with great, calm wisdom, 'Any place can be Ohio, if you choose carefully.'"

Brief History of the City

"A huge brightly lit ship emerges from the harbor," says K.
Several times a year, we ask to hear the whole story again.

Smiling as always, Dr. B picks up his opium pipe, hand-carved in

Pasadena.
But this yob never had the nerve to smoke it.

Slowly, somewhere, we see sheer black nylons on heavenly legs.
It looks like the first time. Hope to god she knows what she's doing.

While the bridges went up, we let the dogs run, & made conversation.
Yes, the bridges opened. Gradually, other things we anticipated
        did or didn't happen.

"Reality is a crutch." Who wants to bet that's Chinese, or Danish?
Listen, man, that's enough. Get out, & take your viola da gamba
        with you.

Autumn

Pickpocket leaves/the wind
in its borrowed overcoat…

Two crows
like black eyebrows

On the stubborn face
Of a sky

Now and Then

Now and then I find myself
in that part of the city
where I used to live
when I was young.

So many things have happened since I left.
So much changed.
And the few people I still know
don't recognize me.

I look up at the window that used to be mine
in days when my father owned the hotel.
And remember, before going on

How as a widower he played poker with Hughey and Sven,
knew the Mayor, and insisted that someday
I'd be President of the Association.

San Quentin 1968

That's the prison
And yeah, this is Tuesday.
By this time mañana
Aaron should be home & dry.*

He'll be strapped in that weird chair
shortly before 11.
Cyanide will drop, you'll hear a faint clink
& the doc, around 11: 10, will nod & say, 'O.K., that's it.'

Birds. Whiskey. Apples. Love. Air.
Later in life—tomorrow perhaps—
some of the things we'll think of.
Yeah, that's the joint, & Aaron's number's up.
And tonight, if he asks
double chocolate malt, carton of Camels
& a little jazz
We, the People, treat.

*Aaron Mitchell. Until 1992, the last man to be legally executed in California.

September 5

In Shanty Malone's, hot night one day after
Farewell Testimonial Old Pard Ballou

gazing wall on wall heroes' chronic
photographs not close enough to ponder

all them unique inscriptions, thinking
financial affairs—Boxer bitch to & fro

desperado among customers, sniffing
the soles of my native feet, displaying

sterling silver tag reading Providence, R.I.
but no promise of reward, three sailors

reverent before picture, "Opening Day
Coast League Seattle 1937," two gents

sizing up on gin, antagonistic to Opera
vast remainder of the population

of the City out of its head elliptic
under a dandy moon this Friday

beginning Fall San Francisco 1950

ADRIENNE RICH

Adrienne Rich is the author of more than sixteen volumes of poetry and four prose works. She has received many awards and prizes, including a MacArthur Fellowship in 1994 and the Academy of American Poets, Dorothea Tanning Prize in 1996. Her newest book, *Midnight Salvage*, was released by W.W. Norton in 1999.

"I came from the Northeast to live in California in 1984. Where I came soon revealed itself as an enormous unfamiliar country whose history, geography, ethnicities, economics, weather, the very directions 'east' and 'west,' meant something else. California was a new language, a new landscape, 'rain' and 'distance' required new definitions. The Loma Prieta earthquake brought it home to me and me to it: the unsealing of freeways and mountainsides sealed me to citizenship of neighborhood, town, county, state of natural wealth, disaster and beauty, state of possession and oppression, state of human extremity and human remorselessness. Above all, here on this profound, menaced sheet of water and light, Monterey Bay, hourly remaking itself, revising its questions, at the edge of the enormous fields.

"Much of my poetry since 1984 has been an attempt to locate myself here, to record how my own questions have been changing in a particular light and region, where language itself is a contested field. It seems to me that this has inevitably entered my poetics."

from An Atlas of the Difficult World

I

A dark woman, head bent, listening for something
—a woman's voice, a man's voice or
voice of the freeway, night after night, metal streaming downcoast
past eucalyptus, cypress, agribusiness empires
THE SALAD BOWL OF THE WORLD, gurr of small planes
dusting the strawberries, each berry picked by a hand
in close communion, strawberry blood on the wrist,

Malathion in the throat, communion,
the hospital at the edge of the fields,
prematures slipping from unsafe wombs,
the labor and delivery nurse on her break watching
planes dusting rows of pickers.
Elsewhere declarations are made: at the sink
rinsing strawberries flocked and gleaming, fresh from market
one says: "On the pond this evening is a light
finer than my mother's handkerchief
received from her mother, hemmed and initialled
by the nuns in Belgium."
One says: "I can lie for hours
reading and listening to music. But sleep comes hard.
I'd rather lie awake and read."   One writes:
"Mosquitoes pour through the cracks
in this cabin's walls, the road
in winter is often impassable,
I live here so I don't have to go out and act,
I'm trying to hold onto my life, it feels like nothing."
One says: "I never knew from one day to the next
where it was coming from: I had to make my life happen
from day to day.   Every day an emergency.
Now I have a house, a job from year to year.
What does that make me?"
In the writing workshop a young man's tears
wet the frugal beard he's grown to go with his poems
hoping they have redemption stored
in their lines, maybe will get him home free.   In the classroom
eight-year-old faces are grey.   The teacher knows which children
have not broken fast that day,
remembers the Black Panthers spooning cereal.

•

I don't want to hear how he beat her after the earthquake,
tore up her writing, threw the kerosene
lantern into her face waiting
like an unbearable mirror of his own.   I don't
want to hear how she finally ran from the trailer
how he tore the keys from her hands, jumped into the truck
and backed it into her.   I don't want to think

how her guesses betrayed her—that he meant well, that she
was really the stronger and ought not to leave him
to his own apparent devastation.   I don't want to know
wreckage, dreck and waste, but these are the materials
and so are the slow lift of the moon's belly
over wreckage, dreck, and waste, wild treefrogs calling in
another season, light and music still pouring over
our fissured, cracked terrain.

•

Within two miles of the Pacific rounding
this long bay, sheening the light for miles
inland, floating its fog through redwood rifts and over
strawberry and artichoke fields, its bottomless mind
returning always to the same rocks, the same cliffs, with
ever-changing words, always the same language
—this is where I live now.   If you had known me
once, you'd still know me now though in a different
light and life.   This is no place you ever knew me.

But it would not surprise you
to find me here, walking in fog, the sweep of the great ocean
eluding me, even the curve of the bay, because as always
I fix on the land.   I am stuck to earth.   What I love here
is old ranches, leaning seaward, lowroofed spreads between rocks
small canyons running through pitched hillsides
liveoaks twisted on steepness, the eucalyptus avenue leading
to the wrecked homestead, the fogwreathed heavy-chested cattle
on their blond hills.   I drive inland over roads
closed in wet weather, past shacks hunched in the canyons
roads that crawl down into darkness and wind into light
where trucks have crashed and riders of horses tangled
to death with lowstruck boughs.   These are not the roads
you knew me by.   But the woman driving, walking, watching
for life and death, is the same.

X

Soledad. = f. Solitude, loneliness, homesickness; lonely retreat.
Winter sun in the rosetrees.
An old Mexican with a white moustache prunes them back,
                    spraying

the cut branches with dormant oil.   The old paper-bag-brown
         adobe walls
stretch apart from the rebuilt mission, in their own time.   It is
         lonely here
in the curve of the road winding through vast brown fields
         machine-engraved in furrows
of relentless precision.   In the small chapel
Nuestra Señora de la Soledad dwells in her shallow arch
painted on either side with columns.   She is in black lace crisp
         as cinders
from head to foot.   Alone, solitary, homesick
in her lonely retreat.   Outside black olives fall and smash
littering and staining the beaten path.   The gravestones of the
         padres
are weights pressing down on the Indian artisans.   It is the sixth
         day of another war.

     •

Across the freeway stands another structure
from the other side of the mirror   *it destroys*
the logical processes of the mind, a man's thoughts
become completely disorganized, madness streaming from every throat
frustrated sounds from the bars, metallic sounds from the walls
the steel trays, iron beds bolted to the wall, the smells, the human waste.
To determine how men will behave once they enter prison
it is of first importance to know that prison.   (From the freeway
gun-turrets planted like water-towers in another garden, out-
         buildings spaced in winter sun
and the concrete mass beyond: who now writes letters deep in-
         side that cave?)

If my instructor tells me that the world and its affairs
are run as well as they possibly can be, that I am governed
by wise and judicious men, that I am free and should be happy,
and if when I leave the instructor's presence and encounter
the exact opposite, if I actually sense or see confusion, war,
recession, depression, death and decay, is it not reasonable
that I should become perplexed?

                From eighteen to twenty-eight
                of his years

a young man schools himself, argues,
debates, trains, lectures to himself,
teaches himself Swahili, Spanish, learns
five new words of English every day,
chainsmokes, reads, writes letters.
In this college of force he wrestles bitterness,
self-hatred, sexual anger, cures his own nature.
Seven of these years in solitary.   Soledad.

But the significant feature of the desperate man reveals itself
when he meets other desperate men, directly or vicariously;
and he experiences his first kindness, someone to strain with him,
to strain to see him as he strains to see himself,
someone to understand, someone to accept the regard,
the love, that desperation forces into hiding.
Those feelings that find no expression in desperate times
store themselves up in great abundance, ripen, strengthen,
and strain the walls of their repository to the utmost;
where the kindred spirit touches this wall it crumbles—
no one responds to kindness, no one is more sensitive to it
than the desperate man.

XI

One night on Monterey Bay the death-freeze of the century:
a precise, detached calliper-grip holds the stars and the quarter-
            moon
in arrest: the hardiest plants crouch shrunken, a "killing frost"
on bougainvillea, Pride of Madeira, roseate black-purple succu-
            lents bowed
juices sucked awry in one orgy of freezing
slumped on their stems like old faces evicted from cheap hotels
—into the streets of the universe, now!

Earthquake and drought followed by freezing followed by war.
Flags are blossoming now where little else is blossoming
and I am bent on fathoming what it means to love my country.
The history of this earth and the bones within it?
Soils and cities, promises made and mocked, plowed contours of
            shame and of hope?
Loyalties, symbols, murmurs extinguished and echoing?
Grids of states stretching westward, underground waters?

Minerals, traces, rumors I am made from, morsel, minuscule
         fibre, one woman
like and unlike so many, fooled as to her destiny, the scope of
         her task?
One citizen like and unlike so many, touched and untouched in
         passing
—each of us now a driven grain, a nucleus, a city in crisis
some busy constructing enclosures, bunkers, to escape the com-
         mon fate
some trying to revive dead statues to lead us, breathing their
         breath against marble lips
some who try to teach the moment, some who preach the
         moment
some who aggrandize, some who diminish themselves in the face
         of half-grasped events
—power and powerlessness run amuck, a tape reeling backward
         in jeering, screeching syllables—
some for whom war is new, others for whom it merely continues
         the old paroxysms of time
some marching for peace who for twenty years did not march for
         justice
some for whom peace is a white man's word and a white man's
         privilege
some who have learned to handle and contemplate the shapes of
         powerlessness and power
as the nurse learns hip and thigh and weight of the body he has
         to lift and sponge, day upon day
as she blows with her every skill on the spirit's embers still burn-
         ing by their own laws in the bed of death.
A patriot is not a weapon.   A patriot is one who wrestles for the
         soul of her country
as she wrestles for her own being, for the soul of his country
(gazing through the great circle at Window Rock into the sheen
         of the Viet Nam Wall)
as he wrestles for his own being.   A patriot is a citizen trying to
         wake
from the burnt-out dream of innocence, the nightmare
of the white general and the Black general posed in their
         camouflage,

to remember her true country, remember his suffering land:
        remember
that blessing and cursing are born as twins and separated at birth
        to meet again in mourning
that the internal emigrant is the most homesick of all women and
        of all men
that every flag that flies today is a cry of pain.
        Where are we moored?
        What are the bindings?
        What behooves us?

SOJOURNER KINCAID ROLLE

Sojourner Kincaid Rolle came to California in 1978 to attend graduate school in Berkeley. Her work has appeared in several chapbooks: *Murmurings of an Open Heart; Our Strength Will Grow; The Mellow Yellow Global Umbrella; A Hand Reached Out; Between Us*; and *Let the Butterflies Continue* (with Armando Vallejo). She has also been published in the *California Quarterly, Coffee Press, Squaw Review, Café Solo,* in the anthology, *Earthwords,* and in the on-line magazines *ArtDirect, Afrigeneas* and *Caspita for Kids.* For seven years, she produced and hosted a cable television show, "Outrageous Women." Since 1993, she has hosted "Poets Night," a monthly reading series featuring local and regional poets. In 1997, she debuted a website called "PoetsNet" on the RAIN Network. She currently lives in Santa Barbara, where she leads poetry and prose writing workshops.

© Rod Rolle

"I was born in Marion, North Carolina. Now I am a Californian. Every time I travel a curling, curving road, or see a green cast lake, I am mentally transported to the Blue Ridge Mountains. Lilac jacaranda trees populate the streets of Santa Barbara much like mimosa trees with their delicate pink blossoms lined the backyard at my childhood home. Snatches of poems from my youth sing in the background—*My heart leaps up when I behold a rainbow in the sky; I think that I shall never see a poem lovely as a tree; Two roads diverged in a yellow wood....*These rainbows, these trees, these roads have been experienced by other eyes, other hearts, other feet. Yet, my soul wants to share its own sacred explosion—to report its own heart's palpitations—to take all roads—and wander off on seldom-trodden paths. Each excursion is a poem.

"I love the wild places. I could poke for hours at the edges of an unkept field—trying to see who has chosen to live there. I thrill at the sight of a little white butterfly searching out the last blooms of a season. My heart leaps when I behold the unbordered ocean or spy a red-tailed hawk circling above. My notebooks are brimming with observations of and musings on the natural world. I want to write as the grunion run across the beach on a summer night and to have my pen drip the first blush of dawn. I seek the quiet places—unruffled silence and solitude—free for the taking. I want to write a thousand odes to trees. I agree with those who call California a state of mind—a state so vast I, too, can call it HOME."

Hands in the Motion of Prayer

Mottled hands cupped deep
like the pouch of a brown pelican
reach for the bounty of the sea
while crows claw crabs
from web-footed gulls and
soar to perches once claimed
by cooing birds

Hands softened by surf and sand shimmer
like suave salmon flashing a satin coat
stroke the battering waves
cradle the hammered ears of passing argonauts
consorts with dolphin and otter
in full view of predators
inviting their touch

Gnarled and pebbled hands
like the barnacled backs of fabled turtles
groveling among the agate and cobalt
Finger-thin pincers mince lifeless
shells and held fast debris
curling into the sworled chambers
teasing out the left behind

Hilled stands of western hemlock
high above the rugged coast
Blunt fingered limbs forming stately portals
house the gentle prayers of crust creatures
soft winds swaying
slowly swirling ribbons twirling
blowing murmured aspirations

Toward the sky

The Birds' Refuge

It was solitary and serene
Wild and unordered
Somebody else's domain

The Canada geese were always friendly
approaching cars in large gaggles
accepting from human hands

Sparrows dotted the wet earth
Pigeons strolled freely
Kildeer hopped beneath the tangled brush

Eggs were layed and hatched in the tall wheat grass
California scrub oak full with acorn
Calling blue jay and red-headed woodpeckers

One could kneel at water's edge
and commune with the cormorant

It was once that way

The Blue Rock

This blue stone
once lay like any other pebble
on a rock-infested beach.
Now it warms my palm.
a tiny remembrance
of a day by the sea
and my small vow.

This rock
once lay in the shadow of Diablo
near groves
where sojourning monarchs suckle
near roads
where guardians of the earth stood
and were arrested.

I lie in the same loam
wallowing among the blue rocks
awaiting the gritty water
the sacred cleansing
sanding my body
smoothing my spirit
preparing for my watch.

keeping watch

i. north

i sit at the foot of snow-capped mountains
i listen to sounds older than my heart
beats on a hollowed drum squeals of a grey whale
i admire the gilded scales of long fishes
we are survivors

ii. east

i wear pearls and silk
my hands hold threads gathered from the spectrum
i weave my own diaphanous shroud
butterflies light on my shoulder
i move among the birds of paradise
my heart open

iii. south

i rock in a hand-me-down chair
keeping time with a paper fan
humming bye and bye
wearing my mother's mother's shawl
petunias blossom in a window box
a bubbling cobbler cools on the sill
i soak my feet in warm rain water
alone but not lonely

iv. west

winds storm across my breast
outside my door
desert flowers tend themselves
dust devils dance in the july heat
from chiseled sand and sacred clay
my fingers mold a vessel for the water's journey
i chew soft a brush made of yucca
i paint legends of the earth on its body
i tend the fire in which it hardens
i no longer hunger for love

DIXIE SALAZAR

© Don Weed

Dixie Salazar is a visual artist, poet, and novelist who lives in Fresno. She has worked as an art therapist, courtroom artist, poetry teacher at Corcoran State Prison, and art teacher at Chowchilla Women's Prison. Currently, she teaches writing at California State University, Fresno and parenting at the Fresno County Jail. In 1986 she received an M.F.A. from Columbia University in New York and served as assistant editor at *Parnassus: Poetry in Review*. She has a chapbook, *Hotel Fresno* (Blue Moon Press, 1988); a novel, *Limbo* (White Pine Press, 1995); and a book of poems, *Reincarnation of the Commonplace* (Salmon Run Press, 1998).

"Even Fresno natives take part in Fresno bashing at times, but I, along with many other Fresnans, had to discover its attractions by leaving. It wasn't until I spent two years living in New York that I realized that, unbeknown to me, a subtle and alarming osmosis had taken place and I had become a Fresnan. It was alarming because I had planned to try and move somewhere nicer after graduate school and there I was missing Fresno fog, freeways, and funky thrift stores. There was much to love in New York (when I wasn't battling it), but it was as if aliens had planted a microchip inside me, and now I actually preferred grape vineyards and cultural impoverishment.

"It's easy to love Barcelona or Berkeley, but to love Fresno takes a keener eye, to see beyond the Golden Arches and giant Long John Silver's anchor hooked into the pastel conversion layered skyline. Loving Fresno is much like the process one goes through learning to love (accept) one's nose, or hips, or chronic skin condition. It takes a certain maturity and almost zen-like enlightenment to embrace a landscape that boasts one of the longest stretches of fast food restaurants in the world. But it is precisely this 'commonplace…that can be endowed with immense, even startling power' according to Ray Carver, and it is that possiblility (so abundant in Fresno) that intrigues me and, I hope, filters into my writing.

"Fresno has been accused of lacking identity, partly because of its enormous diversity, and perhaps this touches some chord within myself, since I suspect that the struggle for identity definition (being half Anglo and half Hispanic) fuels most of my writing and visual artwork:

"At the Fresno DMV, a Hmong clerk explains the new smog requirement to a stately black woman in a wool suit with a silver fox fur.

"I catch the Vietnamese man who has just cleaned our carpet ogling the Victoria's Secret catalogue that drops through the mail slot.

"Later I sit in the yard, grapefruit thunking yellow globes at my feet, a neighbor's *chorizo* and *canciones* circling the wisteria arbor, the first stanza of a poem growing on the page where Davy Crockett meets Coronado. I cross my feet in the lotus position and wait."

Cricket at Central California Women's Facility

Can you hear it
trilling between
Kotex boxes
and blue toilet
water in a cold,
cement corner?
A song, dragged up
from the bed of
a river or
a tin cup of rain,
song of old shine
luck, and hard time
born of a sweet
and dirty friction—
pebbles, grains of
salt, ashes, mice
droppings, cake, spit,
and random dots
rubbed between wings
of innocence.
Bend down now and
lift it into
a paper cup,
a wet song tossed
back to the wind,
a curse, a prayer,
a tiny voice
croaking out one
last reprieve for us all.

E is in Heaven

for Ernesto Trejo (1950–1991)

E is in heaven
dancing with the moths
dreaming again while
fully awake
of a wide Fresno yard
familiar as a small
white worm asleep in
the heart of a rose.
The romantic anarchist
perpetually in love,
the overdrawn economist—
he maps a fortune in
tomorrow's dust.
The starry-eyed arsonist
setting beautiful fires
pauses for one last snapshot
in the garden
he only knows from the window
and stoops over carrots, soft
hands posed on the hoe.

When rain falls
like a memory of music
or breathing in sleep,
E is sitting still,
refusing to enter
or escape, refusing
to bow or applaud,
wanting to hold what
keeps slipping away,
the light, the sparrow,
speckled shadows flapping
from the sycamore
where he would perch
a while longer as
the evening goes, holding
the last note of a
fading tune we would

refuse to relinquish
if there was any way
on earth.

Hotel Fresno

On Belmont, low riders
give the finger to King Muffler,
the moon, whatever moves in the dark.
Headed for The Flamingo,
La Nueva Tapatia, Moon Dog Inn,
they wait for the light to change
on a street of no change.

In a room, shaded
by dark feathered birds,
the old man waits,
a room that holds its breath
behind the window fan
scissoring air.
With a sweaty finger,

he dials time slowly.
Time is busy,
and so he waits.
He waits at the Hotel Fresno
for the lady with the alligator purse
and foreign accent to collect,
for the man with the cigar-shaped scar.

On the corner of Inyo and Y
a young man waits,
neon slipping down his brow
to where his shades cast back
the Walk—Don't Walk
of a red dissolving hand
like the lost guide of Yaki winds.

But he doesn't cross
as if frozen between centuries,
waiting for a different light.

At Mayfair, the all night clerk
rings the cigarettes by,
seeing lights of El Dorados,
The Big Spin, and Dollar Machines.

A teenager takes her Salems and change,
steps outside to the curb
where she cocks her hip and thumb,
waits for a ride to anywhere
away from these people
wearing loneliness
like old bathrobes pulled close.

On Motel Drive,
shadows jump from box cars
into cinders and bottle caps,
wait for the freight's long vowel
to shudder away
so they can cross the singing ties,
find some way to crack the frozen

core of this winter night.
She has always been in line
even as she waited to be born
while her mother waited
in line after line, as she waits
now for her number
that is never called,

one leg-bound baby,
another low riding her hip.
All day asleep in the park
to the click of checkers,
all night, rocking
in time to the rain.
He has stopped waiting now,

nothing to wait for here
where the leaves don't fall,
and the constellations petrify,
where only watermarks bloom
on the wall, and the mirror

reflects the moon, hooked
around a rusted rosette.

Meteor Showers—Yosemite

If, when a blind moth
eclipses the moon
outside of time
you can't see wishes
re-lit from the tail ends
of old wishes—
look up from a bed
of eyeless needles
to the owl's cry
vaporized
into a streak
of light, a spark
stirred from the hot bed
of smoky stars
little deaths
you must be ready for
with all your eyes.

Moulton Transformations

*after Lorentz Transformations: A set of equations that transforms one
observer's frame of reference into that of another's.*

"If the universe has a heartbeat, its rate depends upon the hearer." *Gary Zukav*

(for Chuck Moulton 1936–1995)

If it's Tuesday
on the corner of Olive and Wishon
and the sun has polarized its light
on Ophelia, Queen of the garbage bins
asleep behind the Golden Chinese Restaurant
her belly full of vanilla ice cream and chicken wings

and if the I Ching
of a shopping cart rattles

the alley behind the Brass Unicorn
where morning glories choke the flywheel
of a Plymouth Galaxy now in its fifth incarnation
as a museum of sycamore sun prints and musical belt buckles

and if a black lab
who answers to Shadow
limps up from the Limbo world
of Old Saint Nick and kiss this
where some scientifically inexplicable
phenomenon has refracted the silver sphere

of the Tower Theater
through the cracked prism
of a Yamaha windshield, rainbowing
a river that floods from Olive and 99
all the way to the Sierra Nevadas and beyond
and if that yellow tiger kitty pees on a grimy fortune

that says your t.v. set
will be trouble free for the next
ten years…then maybe it's possible
to sing or breathe backwards, back to the moon
in a pool of spilled beer outside the Wild Blue
where Roy Bailey sweeps up the belly dancer's lost coins

and crushed joints
of the night before…and if
belief in solar explosions and
the fortuitous convergence of stars will do it
then perhaps the phone will ring once more and release
that old familiar, telepathic, horological, isochromatic,

irrevocable isosceles
growl that announces the spot
on the calendar marked by Schrödinger's cat
in a room moving beyond the boundaries of common sense
the Eternity of an hour on another ordinary First Tuesday
of course dependent on the relative velocity of the observer.

DENNIS SALEH

Dennis Saleh is the author of five books of poetry. His most recent book, *This Is Not Surrealism,* won the first chapbook competition from Willamette River Books. A new collection of his poems, *Rhymses' Book,* will be published by Quicksilver in 1999. His poetry, prose, and artwork appear widely in such magazines as *Art/Life, Artword Quarterly, Happy, Pacific Coast Journal, Pannus Index,* and *Pearl.*

© Fish

"California, last gasp of a continental land mass, last lunging grasp of manifest destiny. America once seemed the future of the world, and California the future of America; too many times, all Americans seemed to want to come here, address of hope, where anyone could start over. Inevitably, the Golden State became the end of too many rainbows.

"People outlasted their dreams and wore out promise. What comes true, becomes old. The air darkens, perhaps irredeemably; the water muddies. Prosperity founders, concentrated in too few pockets. The Red Line is torn up to make room for cars and freeways and gas stations; Walt Disney chats on the phone with J. Edgar Hoover. Anything's next. In California, even the future grows old.

"What's left is always the sea. Repose of horizons. Bed of light. The sun follows its dream down to its watery end. At the beach, ceaseless conclusion. Each wave throws itself futilely down. Yet, still, permanence. The sea has never stopped, and the land has never gone away. Paradox, but more than an idea. Here, in California, you can stand at the edge of contradiction and look at it.

"Egyptians thought that in the West, where the sun went, was the next life; the dead were called 'Westerners.' Did they know something we don't? Where's home, where you've been, or where you're going? Which is more timeless, the future, or permanence? Whatever, the seashore shrugs. Here, time and existence can make a motto. *Etcetera ad infinitum.*"

Summer

The sun has rung
the bell

of a grape
into a raisin

a wadded
leather clapper

left from
something grand

Darkened
housefronts

glow a
soft blue-white

from a box
of the future

It's the
Fifties

Summer
of the century

The night
will be warm

until
morning

No moments
are like this

anymore
you can say of

June July
August

December Nap

The cat rubs his body
on the floor
and makes electricity

The little snaps
flick off his body
in a line

and I trace
a Z of static
with my finger

in the smudged air
of hours
in the room

Where the sea is grey
minutes come in
off of it

and slide up the hill
with no sound
like the waves

Each wave says again
nothing
to say

The sea will always
go on like this
wearing itself out

like an endless month
tidying its hem
preparing

It will be in church
when the year
is swallowed and gone

All day the moon
is in the sky
customary fragile

like balsa
a coal
in the ceremony of sky

It sees all the way
into January
in its vigil

but looks faint
constellation of one
The Sleepwalker

A gull drops to where
a jellyfish smiles

on the beach

a faint scarf a silver trail
dissolving
leading to nothing

like the afternoon
leading to sleep
at the year's end

I take my shadow
by the hand
time to rest

Crabs

The crabs lie to themselves.
In a shadow pointing in from the rocks
across low, scrubby grass
they click quietly.
The vacant heat is gone,
water slaps in the growing dark.
Soon the crabs stir, sliding down unhurt.
They skitter down the rocks then hold still,
like broken paper plates or crushed bags.
The dark fine line reaching away frightens them,
the sand shines beneath them.
At the water's edge they start
at water and sand washing past.
Moving up and down the beach
their shadows spindle across weeds and glass,
through patches of light beneath rotting wood.
When they are as far as they ever go they stop,
near the water,
waving and clicking out past themselves.

Beach, Later

The moon makes a sign. Another wave comes in.
A wind drops shadows on the sand, tatters,

like insects come to rest, or single, stiffened hands.
The white expanse shines in place, stretched
between edges lost in distant black night.

The last gulls lifted into the air hours ago,
and the last cars pulled away, all more or less silent
with the passage of light. The gulls pointed out to sea,
and the cars drove in lines, remembering
the light but never reaching it.

At four o'clock you could see a Texaco tanker,
but it slipped away. A strip of sea combs in place,
the bruised net slackens with the tide.
Where a few, colored sparks blink is the horizon,
and then even the sea is gone.

The moon lights what it can, hints of things.
A piece of styrofoam sticks up, or a scrap of wax-bag
on a shelf of waste wood, evidence from the day.
Then hands pick over the little stories, the crabs,
like little statues of memory, looking while they can.

The moon falls, hours wash up with the sea.
The low waves flicker and roll onto rock ledges,
the last candles of movement go out up and down the beach,
the last stars swing further back into sky.
Clouds heave down and join the roots of water.

A steady deep grey rocks in the sea,
the thoughts of darkness are its own.
The strip of land comes to the sea and lies beside it.
It is a hole even the sun is swallowed into.
It is where everything is kept.

Sentry

Moon.

Another hour has come through the opening,
pass out its little light,
some for all.

LUIS OMAR SALINAS

Luis Omar Salinas is an important American poet and is one of the most acclaimed Chicano poets writing today. He has received the Stanley Kunitz Award from Columbia University, a General Electric Foundation Award, and in 1987 was invited to read at the Library of Congress. He has published seven collections of poetry, beginning with *Crazy Gypsy* in 1970. His most recent books are *The Sadness of Days: Selected and New Poems* (1987) and *Sometimes Mysteriously* (1997), which won the Salmon Run Press National Prize for poetry. He lives in Sanger, California.

© Luis Orozco

"I came to Fresno in 1948 as a child. In 1968 I began attending Fresno State under the tutelage of Phillip Levine and Robert Mezey. Fellow students— D. Rail, C. Moulton, J. Veinberg, G. Soto, L. Levis, C. Hanzlicek—influenced me. Synonymous with Fresno: Peter Everwine, William Saroyan, and Chicanos—their presence was as powerful as the almond orchards and strawberry fields.

"Yes, Fresno is in the center of the great San Joaquin Valley, which is crisscrossed with rivers that push to the Pacific through a checkerboard of fruit trees and vineyards. Imagine, take a short drive and fish for trout in melted snow. And all around, the farm workers who stoop all day dropping grapes on paper trays in a valley of wealth where only a few are the selfish and the rich take it all.

"The poem 'My Fifty-Plus Years...' reflects on the unflinching labor of these workers, predominately Mexicans, who seem to reap little financial reward on earth. In my poem for Larry Levis, I wanted to honor his mysteriousness, darkness, loneliness, the ominousness of his death—like a ship in the night. 'Sometimes Mysteriously' is one of my favorite poems. The poem reminded me of St. Francis's prayer recited at an AA meeting I attended last year:

> God grant me
> the serenity to accept the things I cannot change,
> the courage to change the things I can,
> and the wisdom to know the difference."

For Larry Levis in Memory

In your mystery,
you sleep—
your eyes, your hands
Captain of your ship.

The deck a mute place
for silences,
a small place for your
loneliness.

A Selma farmer, a poet
gone east.
How poetic your lives,
and how unpoetic
your death, friend.

The fog and the gray
waters so deep,
I wonder what harbor
your eyes see now,
now that you've traveled
so far.

Middle Age

I converse with my uncle
here, where the day begins
early like a hen in the cold
seeking higher ground.
My dreams come here
like a beaten toenail.
And I feel as if
I've been incarcerated
for the better part of my life.

I raise my beer to my uncle
toasting him on his third marriage.
He tells me, "No man need be alone

especially with October
in the trees, fruit ripening
and the abundance of sunlight."
I am caught speechless.
I have no wisdom
to speak of—unlike
my father who ages gracefully.

My uncle says, *"Espera la*
suerte, wait for luck,
and do what you can with it."

I leave his house
and step outside
to the fresh smell
of autumn
walking through the thinning
olive groves—
the sky fearful,
half empty of birds.

My Fifty-Plus Years Celebrate Spring

On the road, the mountains
in the distance are at rest
in a wild blue silence.
On the sides of the highway
the grape orchards unfurl
deep and green again
like a pregnant woman
gathering strength
for the time to come.
And with the passing
of each season
human life knows little
change. Forty years
in this valley.
the wind, the sun
building its altars
of salt, the rain that

holds nothing back,
and with the crop
at its peak
packing houses burn
into morning,
their many diligent
Mexican workers stacking up
the trays and hard hours
that equal their living.

I've heard it said
hard work ennobles
the spirit—
If that is the case,
the road to heaven
must be crowded
beyond belief.

Nights in Fresno

It is pleasant in October
where the nights lie lovely
driving away the valley heat.
This evening, I drive
through the sad part of town
and see the streets
huddled in the shadows—
I stop the car and walk.
I catch the murmur or breathing
and long silences
and drink from a bottle
of wine, passing slow as a cloud among
faces Van Gogh would have been
familiar with,
faces that wake
to the same dismantled vision.
Hands shaking
with the cold milieu of twigs,
itching their bones.

I say a prayer
and I'm off
to a warm kitchen
and hot coffee,
an air of solitude
growing around me
ripe with darkness.

Sea Song

The moon is singing eloquently,
this night of rancheras.
I swim in the moonlight
to the soliloquy
of seagulls, and the night air
has the fragrance of a young woman
who has bathed in rose petals
and is singing to no one.
Love is here like a mermaid
and I'm as lonely as a fish
in an aquarium.
But memory keeps me smiling,
and hope dances on the seashore
like a schoolgirl skipping rope.
Summer's end carries its promise,
and I'm off to life,
angel-faced,
a little burdened
by my freedom.

Sometimes Mysteriously

Sometimes in the evening when love
tunes its harp and the crickets
celebrate life, I am like a troubadour
in search of friends, loved ones,
anyone who will share with me

a bit of conversation. My loneliness
arrives ghostlike and pretentious,
it seeks my soul, it is ravenous
and hurting. I admire my father
who always has advice in these matters,
but a game of chess won't do, or
the frivolity of religion.
I want to find a solution, so I
write letters, poems, and sometimes
I touch solitude on the shoulder
and surrender to a great tranquility.
I understand I need courage
and sometimes, mysteriously,
I feel whole.

SHEROD SANTOS

Sherod Santos is the author of three collections of poetry, most recently *The City of Women* (W.W. Norton, 1992). A fourth collection, *The Pilot Star Elegies,* is due out in 1999. He teaches at the University of Missouri, Columbia.

© Rob Hill

"After years of a rather nomadic life in the Air Force, my family finally settled, in 1965, in a hillside house just a mile or so from that wide, horseshoe-inlet where the Carmel River empties into the sea. Normally the river runs dry by late spring, and it's an easy thirty minute walk through ice-plant and sea grass to follow the embankment down the northern side, to traverse the gaping mouth of the river and arrive at the tip of Carmel Point, whose crescent beach runs just below the house that Robinson Jeffers, the quintessential California poet, had built from stones he'd hauled up out of the sea.

"My father, whose family goes back three generations to the hop fields of Mendocino County, had remembered Carmel as one of those utopian artist communities that appear in California from time to time. My mother is a painter who was raised in the south, and I suspect my father had that in mind—Carmel's family of artisans, its incomparable stretch of seacoast— when he took us there to settle. I was fifteen when we arrived, and, having spent most of my life either on or around military bases, Carmel felt rather alien to me—cultivated and rich and societal. And given how much its character had changed since that formative community of artists, my parents must've found it odd as well. I hadn't known about Jeffers then (in fact, the first 'local writer' I'd read with interest was Henry Miller, who lived only half an hour away), and poetry was something I'd only approached reluctantly. But I soon came to hear about the Jeffers house—the stone embodiment of the Jeffers myth—and the name had begun to form itself as a remotely beckoning island in the mind.

"No doubt, it was during that period that certain key if unconscious decisions were made about the shape my future life would take, and I suspect that Jeffers's looming presence played a meaningful part in those decisions. To paraphrase Patrick Kavanagh, a boy once fiddled around with verses and discovered they were his life. Still, it wasn't until a year or so later, when I'd enrolled at the nearby junior college, that I began in earnest and on my own to read through Jeffers's poems. At the very same time I began to scribble down those first terribly heartfelt utterances I blushingly referred to as 'verses.'

"But despite the no-doubt burning passions with which I invested those pages, I suspect my enthusiasm had less to do with the *poems* I was writing than with the *poet* I was reading, and with the *place* in which I was reading him. For now, these many years later, I realize that what I needed at the time was not a poet who would mirror my own mind (for at that age I could hardly pretend to possess one), but *make real* for me a notion of sensibility durable enough—as durable as stone—to sustain the buffetings of my own wildly undirected yearnings. And Jeffers was nothing if not durable.

"For that reason more than any other, I believe my early infatuation with him—and my immersion in the rock-ribbed landscape from which the body of his poems was born—was extremely lucky for me. Lucky because it turned my attention away from the insular fascinations of literary affairs, and turned it back to phenomenal things, to what one of his poems has called 'this wild swan of a world,' the raw physical reality around us. And from that lesson came another: what's required of us, as Jeffers explained it in a letter to a friend, is 'to fall in love outward without hating inward,' the most difficult of all the lessons in the arts."

Jeffers Country

The town the wealthy come to, not overly
concerned with how the clerks and waiters
here drive cars expensive as their own—
a *fin de siècle* Marxist dream it's great to kill

a weekend in. Bay leaves season the air
along Ocean Avenue, which dips down
to the beach, that cypress-lined, granite-faced
allegory he worried into something more

inhuman than a paradise of sticks and stones.
A doubled bell-tone echoes off the Carmelite
mission's stuccoed walls, and now
the bride and bridegroom, pausing a moment

in the portico, will feel their backlit shadows
dwell in the house of a Lord grown congenial.
He imagined the strophe and antistrophe,
the steelhead nosing at the riverbank,

the banked warheads nosing underground,
but here the Empire's less like Shiva
than the motel's picture postcard,
where a gelid harvest moon looms above

Point Lobos, as though a great dog,
startled from sleep, had opened its eye.
And, he wondered, we wonder why
treetops and people are so shaken.

Midsummer

Late in the day, the sun-
Enameled wavelets softening,
The heat dying slowly
Along the motel's beach-side

Redwood deck, and you step bare-
Armed and lipsticked out
Among the potted
Fuchsia's breakneck flowers

Sculling on the breeze,
And watch, a moment,
As the pelicans out beyond
The breakers tack up

Over the swells, then
Drop down pick-
Axe hard
Like a sudden outburst

In the quiet air. And I
Am reminded then of
Propertius'
Furious, flax-haired Cynthia

Driving down the Tiber
Behind her white,
Clipped cobs, the woman
In whom, as in some shadowy

Door, he'd found love's
Dark other left
Loitering, pungent-sweet,
Unbuttoned a little

And slick with desire,
With eyes like black florets
At the center
Of a ruff. We stood

Eye-level with the white-
Wash as it lunged
And reddened up
The pebbled sand, earth-

Drawn, pined-for, all strain
And freshening, and, not
About to set things right
Or wrong, we held

Our peace, and before too long
It was twilight still
Winnowing the shore
Of our sure, small heat.

Near the Desert Test Sites

(Palm Desert, California)
for Logan and Renée Jenkins

Unlike almost everything
Else just surviving here
In summer, poison flowers
Flourish in this sweltering
Heat, tangling like blown
Litter in fences around
The trailer parks and motel
Pools, and turning the islands
Pinkish-white between
Divided lanes of freeway,
Where all day long against
The burnished hubbub of U-
Haul trucks and automobiles,
Off-the-road vehicles and
Campers, the oleander shakes
Its brightly polished pocket-

Knives, as at the motorcade
Of some ambassador hurrying
Through a village of the poor.
And every day by late after-
Noon the overwatered lawns
Around the shopping mail
Still burn off brown, their
Pampered opulence upbraided
By the palms' insomniac
Vision of one ineffable apoc-
Alyptic noon. But the smell
Is somehow sweeter than
That makes you think, a dry
Lemon-sweetness, as if some-
Where nearby wild verbena
Has been forced to leaf
By a match held up to each
Bud—and the silo-skyscraper
Holiday Inn at the famous
Resort "Where the Horizon
Ends" could almost be that
Match the way the heat
Sloughs off it like after-
Burn. And yet, because
Of the way the sun in-
Tensifies everything, one
Always has the feeling there
Is much less here than meets
The eye: the halcyon blink
Of a shard of glass, a Lear-
Jet wafted into vapor out
On the tarmac's run, the way
Common quartzstone gives
Off heat which seems to come
From inside itself, and not,
In fact, from that more-
Than-imaginably-nuclear sun
Which every morning starts
Up so illusionless, and every
Evening slow-dissolves

On the blue and otherwise
Planetary hills, like a Valium
Breaking up on the tongue.

On the Last Day of the World

As usual, the guard who worked
the night shift at the boardwalk

returned home tired to his bed.
The sky began to whiten:

a window opened, and pigeons
were playing in the waterfounts.

There were fishermen smoking
on the docks, and someone

was already swimming when the sun
finally rose, and a few

passersby paused to watch that
gradual expansion of light along

the shoreline—it was more
as if someone had tilted the sea

toward the sun. The bakery
shutters were thrown open early

on the promenade, and at first
signs of heat the elderly

gathered, sipping their ices,
in the water-colored shade

of the palmleaves. And then
the bathers, with their bright

suits and baskets, began
to come out from the striped

tents and take their places
in the sand. And close

their eyes against the sun.
And softly, as though not

to disturb the afternoon, softly,
a radio love-song drifted out

through the air...so that
the guard turned over, once,

in sleep, and the sea gulls
made blue rings in the sky.

What else was there then, but
the music, and the warm sand?

Tahoe Nocturne

Do you have the Poems of Han-shan in your house?
Han-shan asks at the end of his poem. Cold mountain.
Ice-flowers on the windowpane. Exhausted from sledding
all afternoon, the boys have dragged their sleeping bags out
in front of the fire, Lynne under blankets beside them.
Having earlier drawn the shortest length of broomstraw,
I've been sitting up reading by lantern light
these words that no one will believe. Now, past midnight,
rising to bank up hardwood for that slow burn through
till morning, and I suddenly recall my childhood wish
to live invisibly, to close my eyes and not be seen.
A fear of death? I think perhaps the opposite: a desire
to escape the life of facts. A thousand, ten thousand miles...
Do you recognize me, air, where once I wandered?

DENNIS SCHMITZ

Dennis Schmitz has published several books of poetry, including *We Weep for Our Strangeness, Goodwill, Inc., String, Singing, Eden,* and *About Night: Selected and New Poems.* He is the recipient of the Discovery Award, grants from the NEA, a Guggenheim Fellowship, the di Castagnola Award (Poetry Society of America—best book-in-progress), and the Shelley Memorial Award.

"In particular, I enjoy writing the *orientation* part of a poem, in which I locate (or relocate, if the poem has a literal place in mind) myself in order to speak. How not to be a spiritual tourist? My Eden may be California's north coast—Point Reyes and north—the fogged-over cliff areas, a ragged surf, sand strips, many birds. But to be an Eden, it has to be lost eventually, just as a country-western cynic says that by definition all love is unrequited.

"So I stay a citizen of the Central Valley—rice fields so big that they're sown by airplanes, big-business nut and fruit orchards interrupted by strip malls and freeways, Bermuda grass. Maybe someday I can talk about them. Until then, I go refugee, I go small. Backyard nature: the surprised opossum scavenging fallen oranges and yard-fruit, the outlaw but accomodated animal life, bird-dropped-seed volunteer brush and trees. For a while, the Sacramento Delta was my alternate Eden; the backwaters were the Mississippi River of my boyhood. I turned myself out of that Eden. Here I am—between places, a Californian."

Abbott's Lagoon

The storm's still everywhere I step,
affectionate like a lover who touches you

with pliers, at the periphery
of the ego little wavelets like blisters.

The lagoon's surface is folded
in labial wind-stirrings; a few birds twitch

in & out of the water onto the sand
that's the color of a rainblasted trenchcoat.

Then, at the edge of the ocean,
I study three minutes (I time myself

to know when to wade in) the loose
mound in the backwash that's flexing

& bobbing in the ocean's insomnia.
Is it the suicide you always promise in the storm

against yourself, or just more kelp
torqued around its own embrace, loving

any sort of afterlife, self-tangled like all
of us, oozing the bottom's root-grease

into the water around it? Glad to be puzzled,
I step back, turn from all the evidence

& trot into another morning's work-out.

Carmel

Vulgar paw-prints on the BMW
trivialize the threat, but the car's siren,

still in pique, pursues
a tired raccoon. A few valleys east,

Calif recites lightning over Sierra
foothills to curse the cheap

tract houses, but here animals still argue
the wilderness these raked white beaches

& millionaire "cottages" pretend.
Robinson Jeffers built rage first

then poems from the fog-scuffed rocks he bore
grunting up from this same beach

to make a tower he could be tall in.
We stoop to enter Jeffers' world;

his wife would rap the low ceiling between them
when his pacing overhead stopped & the poem

might've squeezed in the whole Big Sur coast.
Miles south & a real wilderness away, Hearst bought

a vision too big for himself—the shiploads
of statuary parodied in CITIZEN KANE,

the private zoo—only a tourist arrow knows
its way through his castle's cluttered acres.

In Carmel, Loretta & I go out the gate
Jeffers used—now designer homes crowd it.

The BMW is local, the raccoon bred
to add to the car's relevance.

Prosperity is only a small god,
but you pray to it—just in case.

Monstrous Pictures of Whales

—the skeleton of a whale on the beach
near the mouth of a small river—

"…the mere skeleton of the whale bears the same relation to
the fully-vested and padded animal as the insect does to the
chrysalis that so roundly envelops it."   Melville

1
        habits:
false. shoals.
& our hearts float

in the precious
oil. deep
in our heads the quiescent

        we were
before our illness:
mammals. ambergris

vestigial penis

perhaps
you & I identify

the long withdrawal: when
      the soft
edges wash & the stones

come clean

2

a jeep was stopped

inside
the skull. white

cormorants wobbled
their great

wings shaken
empty:

between the
ribs, turned sharply

into the windshield

3

with this map

I have left my house
with this skin wavering

over its own blue paths
the river
below is a direct turning
from the dryness
the mountains that nest

in the brown
forests, burns, sinks,
subtle switchbacks that go

nowhere. once
everyone went by boat.
Foster's, Finger Gap.
heat

lightning chokes the
passes. the blood
descends

describing the possible
journeys. to this shore
the river comes
for the sake of the flesh

we follow it

    4

a) one may drown in a windowpane

b) we may be seen floating white
   & wrinkled in our own eye

    5

        in the center

the self turns
within currents the other

turns. try
to come back to the smallest
pool first. find straws
feeding

        till they
sink in rain-
pools. perhaps the river

failing
here. the whale half-
fish crushing

        the crowns of dune-
grass & the restless

bones at last
dig through fat & foreign
stones, flash

white out of the surfeit

MAURINA SHERMAN

Maurina Sherman was born and raised in Ventura, California. Her earliest memories are those of lemon blossoms, eucalyptus, sand crabs, earthquakes, and wildfires. Always a coastal dweller, Maurina was educated in Santa Barbara and San Diego, and is now a science writer and editor in La Jolla. Her chapbook, *Heaven's Road,* is from Woodhouse Press (1993). Maurina's poems have previously appeared in *The Bloomsbury Review, A Critique of America, The Pacific Review, Quarterly West,* and *South Florida Poetry Review.*

"The way I see it, California is so much a part of the fiber of my being that I really can't separate it from other influences on my writing. My fortune has been that I have always lived in landscapes that have, quite simply, offered up poems. The stunning coastline, foothills, and mountain passes of Santa Barbara gave me my first poems. As I pushed south to San Diego, the poems laced together abundant natural images with the sweet music of California place names—*Camino Cielo, Matilija, San Buenaventura.*

"Despite what eastern detractors might claim, this golden state does have seasons, and weather, and soul. One just needs to pay a bit of attention to the details. It may often be seventy-five degrees and clear here in Southern California, but each November when the Santa Ana is blowing in from the east, there's a light and an edge to the sky that is uniquely our own. And it reminds us who we are, and where we are, and how we got here. And it gives us poetry."

Towards Sunset at Camino Cielo

A warm day for November, and we
stand above the cut of the ravine,
the green wake of brush slicing through
the amber delays of autumn. The sun
drops slowly behind us and slides
its dark fingers over dried twists

of sage, toyon, and manzanita—shadows
of rotted stumps, fence posts gape
like missing teeth and one of those
air-grey posts leaps suddenly as you
raise your arm and wave at the silence.
You want nothing more than to know
where we stand in this thin evening tide
ebbing toward the canyon floor.

Like dark water, the shadows lengthen
and we know that if we could
we'd circle high above this gorge
and dive down straight into
the quiet, open eye of the mind
with the studied aim of a red-shouldered hawk
seeking its space upon the earth,
taking with us this sliding shale,
these scrub oaks with branches gnarled
like babies' fists at birth,
these outcroppings of Matilija sandstone
formed when even the ocean was uncertain,
and so leave nothing for the spring
but the blue-white bloom of ceanothus
and a blood-red smear of light
on the hard chaparral of heaven's road.

Blackberries

for Drew

Already at a thousand feet,
I leave the shade of cottonwoods
and head towards the river.
Today it is wide,
its bed an easy riprap
for the slip of current
and those few remnants
of alder or sycamore.
And though it is July and warm,
the slow moving water,

colder in places, quickens
my pace to the other bank...

And it's not the bay laurel
that has me thinking of you,
or the big leaf maple whose
leaves drift to the forest floor
like thick books put down,
but these blackberry vines—
their green and bitter fruit
that will not ripen
this dry summer long.

If you were here I know
you would want to pick them all,
save them from this hard place,
this chaparral where no rain
will come to soak their roots,
where they will never grow
sweet with juice.
You would pick them all
until your shirt—full like a basket
heavy with damp clothes—
sat in the crook of your arm
the way you hold a child—then you'd
carry them home, put them
on the windowsill and tell me
that after two days of afternoon sun
we'll eat their fresh light like kings...

A week later I'd rinse the last bowl
of hard, sour buds down the sink and
remember an evening last winter
when you rocked your second child
from a bad dream,
holding her against your chest
like that armful of berries,
placing her finally on quilts
to blossom in moonlight.

San Buenaventura

Sunday, and the thin lull of evening
light lingers into eight o'clock.
The amber glow of streetlights hums
the frantic-winged beat of moths
and I am back on El Dorado Street.
It is 1969 and the fresh spine
of sidewalk connects fifteen houses
that are a four year-old's whole world.
I sit on the front lawn and hear
my father's litany as he finishes
the yard work.
                 Oxalis, dichondra, Snairol…

My mother wears shorts and sandals
and sits near me. We eat tacos wrapped
in orange paper that is see-through
when the grease soaks in.
She drinks a Pepsi from the bottle
and I wish I were a grown-up
so I, too, could clutch a taco in one hand
while lifting a slender glass bottle in the other.
But growing up seems a lifetime away—
or perhaps never—as my own hands
barely encircle my dinner
and I can't let go, even to wipe
the grease from my chin.

This Body

This body at night is the sound of the swaying creak of trees as they sink
      their roots to the river bank.
This body is wide as the autumn sky in one breath, and narrow, still, to
      slip from earth for a moment to fold outward into bloom.
This body is everything I am and if I sit with it long enough, it loves
      everything I love.

This body is all I have to walk through snowfall or swim in the sea.
This body carries me through summer and when it becomes dry and sharp

as sagebrush it will lie on cobbles in the river and dip its mouth to drink.
This body lifts me to the joy of garlic and savory—will take in olives and
    basil, black plums and papaya.

This body brings me to you and longs for you as it longs for water and salt
    and all that surely still is the sea.
This body will stretch its arms to hold another body or a stone and all that
    is the earth.
This body unfolds from me when the sky is black or bleeding in the light
    of stars or the moon and sinks into me again at dawn.
This body nods to me as I pass through it, returning from sleep.

MAURYA SIMON

Maurya Simon is the author of four volumes of poetry, most recently, *The Golden Labyrinth* (University of Missouri Press, 1995). Her fifth book, *WEAVERS,* based on a series of paintings by Los Angeles artist Baila Goldenthal, is forthcoming from Blackbird Press in 1999. She is the recipient of an NEA Grant in poetry for 1999. She teaches creative writing at the University of California, Riverside and lives in the Angeles National Forest.

"I moved to California as an infant and have lived most of my life here since. California's heady, stimulating, wildly varied landscapes have located and dislocated much of my thinking and my writing. Even when I travel to the farthest, most exotic reaches of the earth, I feel intensely homesick for California and for its austere or lush landscapes.

"Indeed, I feel doubly blessed to have lived in two dramatically antithetical places: in Hermosa Beach, with its languid, spindrift-laden days, and, for the past fifteen years, in the San Gabriel Mountains, surrounded by rugged granite peaks and subalpine forest wilderness. What appeals to me about this state is that every reach of the imagination seems realized, materialized in some natural landscape within its borders—vast deserts, quiet valleys and chaparrals, great lake beds turned to salty or grassy plains, monumental canyons, giant redwood forests, colossal mountain ranges, volcanic craters, and the placid or thunderous shores along the Pacific Coast.

"In terms of my writing, you can take the woman out of her landscape, but you can't remove the landscape from the woman: they're inseparable and indefatigably intertwined. Our geographical exterior world molds and re-forms our interior geography in ways that are both subtle and profound. So, even though you may recognize native plants and locales in my poems, there are often deeper strata, containing finer cells of import and allusion, beneath the words and images themselves. I'm talking about the *ethos* of this place, of California—a quality that critic Roger Fry defined as 'that which the works of art of a period exhale.' But I'm also thinking of the characteristic *spirit* of California, something that's wholly illusive and impossible to articulate, something as incandescent and ungraspable as the seasonal marine layer, as seductive as the scent of eucalyptus, as perplexing as the sound of a raven's clicks and caws, as strange as Christmas in Palm Springs, as bewildering as earthquakes, and as improbable as a thousand lavender jacaranda in bloom all at once."

Boy Crazy

I used to watch the roses loosen
their pink wigs as I clocked the rain.
One-two, one-two, the drops plunked
the petals down into the gutter.
Drenched, I strolled my way into town
hoping to meet the boy I shuddered
to think of, the boy with hair black
as patent leather, the boy with the sneer
that dangled like a cigaret from his lips.
I was feverish with innocence, my skin
aglow, my shadow almost voluptuous.
Past the blue houses and an old Volvo
backfiring from an alley, past
The Lighthouse where once Dizzy Gillespie
had blown me a kiss when I was twelve,
past the Mermaid Restaurant where I first
saw my father flirt with a fierce waitress,
I finally made my way to the pier.
Only one fisherman crouched near a pail
of squid, and his hair was yellow.
The sound of rain was swallowed by waves
pounding the shore with white fists.
Over Catalina half a rainbow perched
like a tweezed eyebrow raised in surprise.
I kept track of how late he was,
while clouds paired up on the horizon,
and the minutes fell away like bits
of torn paper into the surf. But,
he came, after all. Dizzy, elated,
faint with restraint, I played it cool.
Kiss me, kiss me, he whispered, sneering
his powerful sneer as he bent over me,
his thin hands cupping the two blades
of my shoulders. Hot ice was what I felt—
a melting and stiffening, a strange tug
in my thighs, blood rushing everywhere.
He had to go home at last, and so did I.
But I stayed and swayed on the pier

to watch the wing-rowing pelicans pause
in mid-air before they released themselves
from their bodies' bows, and dove
into the amethyst waters below.

Keeping Track

That's what I was doing on a Wednesday morning,
while out on Falls Road, slugging my slow way
through a foot of sodden snow, and suddenly
exalted by a trail the dog and I had sighted:
deep pug marks whose petalled toes were blurred
by thick winter fur, and which raced before us
in bounding gaps, straight lines, staggered pairs.
I knew something was up when Sam's coat rose
stiffly off his back; his ears, nostrils flaring.
A mountain lion had prefaced us only hours earlier,
had climbed past the same outcroppings of granite,
had paused, like us, on edges of icy precipices,
to stare far below to the ski lift parking lot,
where blocks of color aligned themselves together,
and where bite-sized skiers lined up like beetles.
We followed the puma's prints for more than a mile,
and so bent was I to my trail that I wholly forgot
to be mindful of other pleasures, other dangers:
for suddenly, above us, the mountainside we hugged
bellowed, buckled, loosened a thousand tons of snow
that roared down upon us a white, cataclysmic fury—
we ran, and ran and ran—then stopped to cringe
behind a boat-shaped boulder that, like a huge wall,
broke the raging avalanche into twin Amazons of death.
Like two twigs trapped in the calm, unseeing eye
of a tornado, we stood transfixed as the mountain
shuddered free its oceanic cargo, its cosmic freight,
the noise so deafening it drowned out the dog's howl.
My hand still holds that awful sound in its bones:
my hand's trembling even now; it is writing down
this poem, so that all of me flinches to remember

what I nearly surrendered one day in early March,
when I lost track of the wildness of the world.

The Dolphin

Just off the Santa Monica Pier,
a dolphin swam in tight circles
for hours, having lost its power
to echolocate a wiser course.

No matter that photographers,
marine biologists, and reporters
with their mini-cams and prayers
tried to will it from its torment:

the dolphin churned and turned
with dizzy ardor, as if devotion
to repetition could set it straight,
could help it navigate to freedom.

Was it toxins spewed in the ocean
that sent its brain to spinning,
or do dolphins, just like humans,
go off the deep end, either with

or without reason? Exhausted,
finally, the dolphin drowned.
On t.v. it looked as still as time.
But it keeps circling in my mind.

The Sea Sprite, Hermosa Beach

How many empty hotel rooms
await the souls who'll bed down in them
lightly as grey rain settling into spindrift.
And how many coiled springs will compress,
quivering, under the weightless weight of sighs,
under each sad light circling itself
like a tired dog preparing to sleep.

Those rooms hover in the airy corridors
of mind, unstirred forever, though tampered
habitually into tidiness by migrant maids—
exotic birds poorly camouflaged by severe shades.
Those rooms' womanly shadows size up
the flotillaed walls with measureless gazes,
then those shadows fade, too.

Only one room for rent beckons to me,
to the world in me that blindly enters rooms;
it calls to me like death's dream of life.
Can you remember when you didn't want to sleep,
back when childhood was a spiraling stair in space
you climbed and climbed, getting everywhere at once?
Its top landing is that room,

all awash with the ocean's saline touch,
where the curtains breathe deeply in and out,
chanting some daily mantra for forgetfulness.
Its floor is frothed with summer clouds;
its windows open and close like God's eyelids.
Take me there now, so we may pull the green sheets
over us quietly, feeling at home, at last.

GARY SNYDER

Gary Snyder is a cultural, national, and, for California, a regional—or bioregional—treasure. For more than thirty years his poetry and life have worked to praise and preserve the earth.

© Nathan Sivins

He has published sixteen books of poetry and prose. *Turtle Island* won the Pulitzer Prize for poetry in 1975. *No Nature,* a volume of selected poems, was a finalist for the National Book Award in 1992. He has been a Guggenheim Fellow and is a member of the American Academy of Arts and Letters and the American Academy of Arts and Sciences. As Professor of English on the faculty of the University of California, Davis, he has been instrumental in starting the Nature and Culture Program. Since 1970, he has lived with his family in the watershed of the South Yuba River in the foothills of the Sierra Nevada in northern California. His most recent book of poems is *Mountains and Rivers Without End.*

Above Pate Valley

We finished clearing the last
Section of trail by noon,
High on the ridge-side
Two thousand feet above the creek
Reached the pass, went on
Beyond the white pine groves,
Granite shoulders, to a small
Green meadow watered by the snow,
Edged with Aspen—sun
Straight high and blazing
But the air was cool.
Ate a cold fried trout in the
Trembling shadows. I spied
A glitter, and found a flake
Black volcanic glass—obsidian—

By a flower. Hands and knees
Pushing the Bear grass, thousands
Of arrowhead leavings over a
Hundred yards. Not one good
Head, just razor flakes
On a hill snowed all but summer,
A land of fat summer deer,
They came to camp. On their
Own trails. I followed my own
Trail here. Picked up the cold-drill,
Pick, singlejack, and sack
Of dynamite.
Ten thousand years.

This Poem Is for Deer (Hunting 8)

"I dance on all the mountains
On five mountains, I have a dancing place
When they shoot at me I run
To my five mountains"

Missed a last shot
At the Buck, in twilight
So we came back sliding
On dry needles through cold pines.
Scared out a cottontail
Whipped up the winchester
Shot off its head.
The white body rolls and twitches
In the dark ravine
As we run down the hill to the car.
                      deer foot down scree

Deer on the autumn mountain
Howling like a wise man
Stiff springy jumps down the snowfields
Head held back, forefeet out,
Balls tight in a tough hair sack
Keeping the human soul from care
                on the autumn mountain

Standing in late sun, ear-flick
Tail-flick, gold mist of flies
Whirling from nostril to eyes.

      •

Home by night
              drunken eye
Still picks out Taurus
Low, and growing high:
              four-point buck
Dancing in the headlights
              on the lonely road
A mile past the mill-pond,
With the car stopped, shot
That wild silly blinded creature down.

Pull out the hot guts
              with hard bare hands
While night-frost chills the tongue
              and eye
The cold horn-bones.
The hunter's belt
              just below the sky
Warm blood in the car trunk.
Deer-smell,
              the limp tongue.

      •

Deer don't want to die for me.
              I'll drink sea-water
Sleep on beach pebbles in the rain
Until the deer come down to die
              in pity for my pain.

Night Herons

Night herons nest in the cypress
by the San Francisco
stationary boilers
with the high smoke stack

at the edge of the waters:
a steam turbine pump
to drive salt water
into the city's veins
mains
if the earth ever
quakes. and the power fails.
and water
to fight fire, runs
loose on the streets
with no pressure.

At the wire gate tilted slightly out
the part-wolf dog
would go in, to follow
if his human buddy lay on his side
and squirmed up first.

An abandoned, decaying, army.
a rotten rusty island prison
surrounded by lights of whirling
fluttering god-like birds
who truth
has never forgot.

I walk with my wife's sister
past the frozen bait;
with a long-bearded architect,
my dear brother,
and silent friend, whose
mustache curves wetly into his mouth
and he sometimes bites it.

the dog knows no laws and is strictly,
illegal. His neck arches and ears prick out
to catch mice in the tundra.
a black high school boy
drinking coffee at a fake green stand
tries to be friends with the dog,
and it works.

How could the
night herons ever come back?

to this noisy place on the bay.
like me.
the joy of all the beings
is in being
older and tougher and eaten
up.
in the tubes and lanes of things
in the sewers of bliss and judgment,
in the glorious cleansing
treatment
plants.

We pick our way
through the edge of the city
early
subtly spreading changing sky;

ever-fresh and lovely dawn.

Why Log Truck Drivers Rise Earlier Than Students of Zen

In the high seat, before-dawn dark,
Polished hubs gleam
And the shiny diesel stack
Warms and flutters
Up the Tyler Road grade
To the logging on Poorman creek.
Thirty miles of dust.

There is no other life.

GARY SOTO

Gary Soto is the author of eight books of poetry and is one of the most acclaimed poets of his generation. Among other awards, he has received a Guggenheim Fellowship, an Academy of American Poets Award, The Discovery-The Nation Prize, and *POETRY's* Bess Hokin Prize. His *Selected Poems* was a finalist for the 1995 National Book Award in poetry. He lives in Berkeley with his wife, Carolyn, and daughter, Mariko.

"I conjure up inside my head an image of our old street, one that was torn down in the name of urban renewal at the beginning of the 1960s. It was, as some might imagine, a blighted area: junkyard to the left of us, a pickle factory across the street, broom factory and warehouse of books and magazines down the alley, the almighty Sun-Maid Raisin refinery in the distance, and weed-choked vacant lots. Braly Street was an area that was almost all Mexican. This was south Fresno, where there were plans to bulldoze our barrio and make room for an industrial park. Nothing of the sort was constructed, and the good people of Fresno remember this. To this day there are empty lots, weeds and rubble, and the meandering of stray cats. This place, this emptiness, and these few totems of the past haunt me and have shaped my work and its sense of loss.

"These pictures muster up memory, imagination, and the willingness to care for the smallest of objects. It's not unusual for me to close my eyes for a moment or two, to see people and things in their place, from my father, dead now, and an uncle, also dead, to our dusty-white house, the bean plants, the almond tree where I hung ridiculously by an army belt, the fishless pond, my uncle back from Korea sleeping in the sun porch. Nothing much happened. No one pushed ahead, no one got rich. Everyone leaned their sadness on fences, sat in twos and threes on porches, or, if you were younger, bobbed on car fenders. We all faced the street, that river of black asphalt, and kept our eyes busy on every car that passed. I spent my first six years running like a chicken from one dirt yard to another, and I can't think of a more curious or unadorned childhood. It's these images that I take to the page, whether the subject is that street or another street and time. It's these first images, these first losses when our street was leveled to the height of yellow weeds, that perhaps made me a writer."

The Elements of San Joaquin

for César Chávez

Field

The wind sprays pale dirt into my mouth
The small, almost invisible scars
On my hands.

The pores in my throat and elbows
Have taken in a seed of dirt of their own.

After a day in the grape fields near Rolinda
A fine silt, washed by sweat,
Has settled into the lines
On my wrists and palms.

Already I am becoming the valley,
A soil that sprouts nothing.
For any of us.

Wind

A dry wind over the valley
Peeled mountains, grain by grain,
To small slopes, loose dirt
Where red ants tunnel.

The wind strokes
The skulls and spines of cattle
To white dust, to nothing,

Covers the spiked tracks of beetles,
Of tumbleweed, of sparrows
That pecked the ground for insects.

Evenings, when I am in the yard weeding,
The wind picks up the breath of my armpits

Like dust, swirls it
Miles away

And drops it
On the ear of a rabid dog,
And I take on another life.

Wind

When you got up this morning the sun
Blazed an hour in the sky,

A lizard hid
Under the curled leaves of manzanita
And winked its dark lids.

Later, the sky grayed,
And the cold wind you breathed
Was moving under your skin and already far
From the small hives of your lungs.

Stars

At dusk the first stars appear.
Not one eager finger points toward them.
A little later the stars spread with the night
And an orange moon rises
To lead them, like a shepherd, toward dawn.

Sun

In June the sun is a bonnet of light
Coming up,
Little by little,
From behind a skyline of pine.

The pastures sway with fiddle-neck,
Tassels of foxtail.

At Piedra
A couple fish on the river's edge,
Their shadows deep against the water.
Above, in the stubbled slopes,
Cows climb down
As the heat rises
In a mist of blond locusts,
Returning to the valley.

Rain

When autumn rains flatten sycamore leaves,
The tiny volcanos of dirt
Ants raised around their holes,
I should be out of work.

My silverware and stack of plates will go unused
Like the old, my two good slacks
Will smother under a growth of lint
And smell of the old dust
That rises
When the closet door opens or closes.

The skin of my belly will tighten like a belt
And there will be no reason for pockets.

Harvest

East of the sun's slant, in the vineyard that never failed,
A wind crossed my face, moving the dust
And a portion of my voice a step closer to a new year.

The sky went black in the ninth hour of rolling trays,
And in the distance ropes of rain dropped to pull me
From the thick harvest that was not mine.

Fog

If you go to your window
You will notice a fog drifting in.

The sun is no stronger than a flashlight.
Not all the sweaters
Hung in closets all summer

Could soak up this mist. The fog:
A mouth nibbling everything to its origin,
Pomegranate trees, stolen bicycles,

The string of lights at a used-car lot,
A Pontiac with scorched valves.

In Fresno the fog is passing
The young thief prying a window screen,
Graying my hair that falls
And goes unfound, my fingerprints
Slowly growing a fur of dust—

One hundred years from now
There should be no reason to believe
I lived.

Daybreak

In this moment when the light starts up
In the east and rubs
The horizon until it catches fire,

We enter the fields to hoe,
Row after row, among the small flags of onion,
Waving off the dragonflies
That ladder the air.

And tears the onions raise
Do not begin in your eyes but in ours,
In the salt blown
From one blister into another;

They begin in knowing
You will never waken to bear
The hour timed to a heart beat,
The wind pressing us closer to the ground.

When the season ends,
And the onions are unplugged from their sleep,
We won't forget what you failed to see,
And nothing will heal
Under the rain's broken fingers.

Braly Street

Every summer
The asphalt softens
Giving under the edge
Of boot heels and the trucks
That caught radiators
Of butterflies,
Bottle caps and glass
Of the forties and fifties
Hold their breath
Under the black earth
Of asphalt and are silent
Like the dead whose mouths

Have eaten dirt and bermuda.
Every summer I come
To this street
Where I discovered ants bit,
Matches flare,
And pinto beans unraveled
Into plants; discovered
Aspirin will not cure a dog
Whose fur twitches.

It's sixteen years
Since our house
Was bulldozed and my father
Stunned into a coma...
Where it was,
An oasis of chickweed
And foxtails.
Where the almond tree stood
There are wine bottles
Whose history
Is a liver. The long caravan
Of my uncle's footprints
Has been paved
With dirt. Where my father
Cemented a pond
There is a cavern of red ants
Living on the seeds
The wind brings
And cats that come here
To die among
The browning sage.

It's sixteen years
Since bottle collectors
Shoveled around
The foundation
And the almond tree
Opened its last fruit
To the summer.

The houses are gone,

The Molinas, Morenos,
The Japanese families
Are gone, the Okies gone
Who moved out at night
Under a canopy of
Moving stars.

In '57 I sat
On the porch, salting
Slugs that came out
After the rain,
While inside my uncle
Weakened with cancer
And the blurred vision
Of his hands
Darkening to earth.
In '58 I knelt
Before my father
Whose spine was pulled loose.
Before his face still
Growing a chin of hair,
Before the procession
Of stitches behind
His neck, I knelt
And did not understand.

Braly Street is now
Tin ventilators
On the warehouses, turning
Our sweat
Toward the yellowing sky;
Acetylene welders
Beading manifolds,
Stinging the half-globes
Of retinas. When I come
To where our house was,
I come to weeds
And a sewer line tied off
Like an umbilical cord;
To the chinaberry
Not pulled down

And to its rings
My father and uncle
Would equal, if alive.

Street

para Ernesto Trejo

What I want to remember is a street,
A wide street,

And that it is cold:
A small fire in the gutter, cats running
From under a truck, their tails up
Like antennas. A short woman
With a short cane, tapping
Her way
Past the tracks.
                    Farther away,
An abandoned hotel
Whose plumbing is the sound
Of ocean. In one room,
A jacket forever without a shadow
And cold as the darkness it lies in.

Above, an angle of birds
Going south. Above the birds,
Clouds with their palms open and moving
Toward the Sierras.

Dusk: the first headlights come on,
And a Filipino stands
Under a neon, turning a coin
In his pocket.

Blanco

My sister comes, quietly,
Stepping where I step,
The street numb from the fog.

We are explorers.
                    In our yard
With a flashlight on
And eclipsed by the cold,
We know the sun is lost to this,
The woodpecker to its whittle,
The worm to its stitch
That closed our father's grave.

And ear pressed to the ground,
My sister speaks of
Ants nibbling the pods unstrung
From eucalyptus,
Roots cradling the skull's smile.

Hands curled into binoculars,
I focus on
What is suddenly a house wrapped
In incense. Inside,
Our father at a table
Listening to us move
As the earth moves.

I spit into my sister's palms,
Rubbing them brown with the dirt
Pinched from our lives.
I point *over there,*

And linking her small hands
Into a telescope,
She centers on the white
He could step from, his voice clear
And burning a hole
Where this sky is once more…

The Effects of Abstract Art

Charlie, our one hope, called the cucos from Braly Street
To line up. Since half had been in road camp,
Shackled and such, they followed his orders
And had their faces drawn in charcoal.

These thugs went away smiling at their portraits,
And Charlie, too, went away—
Three months later he was in Paris,
Fresno still stamped on his furrowed brow
And dripping farm water behind his ears.
He walked on snow,
And ate bread and cheese. He drank coffee
At outdoor cafes, an accordian of homesickness
Living in his chest. Girls helped,
And a vin ordinaire dark as the Middle Ages.
He studied the art of the time.
The river cracked its dull mirror of ice,
And suddenly in a heatless room
He was going abstract, the chairs no longer chairs
But buckled wood and juts of timber.
He painted a Nazi with a boot for a head
And a cathedral leaning in an atomic wind.

The river thawed from hot human tears.
The fish drank that brew and hopped onto dinner plates,
This according to Charlie's suddenly cubist art.
Back in Fresno, he showed the cucos
His new art, the crooked lines, the negative space,
And every face beautifully out of whack.
The cucos couldn't figure,
Charlie's drawing so good just months before
And now the eyes of farmers dripping like eggs.
Was he now a wino? A myopic young man?
Had existentialism weakened his blood?
My uncle looked over Charlie's fingers—
Poor guy, no telling when a train ran them over.

ROBERTA SPEAR

Roberta Spear lives in Fresno with her husband and two children. She grew up in nearby Hanford and received a B.A. and M.A. from California State University, Fresno. Her three books of poetry are *Silks* (1980), published as part of the National Poetry Series; *Taking to Water,* which won the 1985 Literary Award from PEN, Los Angeles Center; and *The Pilgrim Among Us* (1992). She has also won the Jams D. Phelan Award in Poetry and is the recipient of writing grants from the NEH, the John Simon Guggenheim Foundation, and the Ingram Merrill Foundation.

"My grandparents moved to the San Joaquin Valley not long after the turn of the century. From that time until the 1970s, the Valley consisted of small farm towns separated from each other by vast stretches of cultivated land. When I left home in the 1960s to go away to college, I didn't expect to return. I hated the blistering heat in the summer, the fog in the winter, the lack of culture, and the absence of geography. I wanted to live in beautiful places. And, for a brief while, I did—Santa Barbara and Laguna Beach, San Francisco, New England, and, later, North Carolina. However, I eventually returned to Fresno to study poetry. I also returned to the orchards and vineyards, to the home of field workers, Portuguese dairy farmers, and my old Armenian neighbors, to the Fresno poets and the poets of Spain, to Levine and Everwine and a group of talented young writers all celebrating the place I had once mocked. Levine championed everything from the valley dust to the factory worker; Miguel Hernandez wrote of love from his infested Spanish prison cell; and William Saroyan had crafted a charming story of a bicycle ride from Fresno to Hanford, my home town. I discovered that I had a long way to go.

"Over the last thirty years, I have come to learn that two essential components of this celebratory tradition in poetry are passion and careful observation. While I was never lacking in the first, the second was a task made all the more difficult by living in a place that often seemed desolate and impoverished. Difficult, but not impossible. Even now, if you drive east a few miles into the countryside or the nearby foothills, the fields of yellow grass with their outcroppings of rock and skeletal oaks are still reminiscent in their rugged beauty of parts of southern Europe. The three poems here address a landscape and people that I have taken for granted most of my life and, at times, consciously turned away from. I am very moved that my friends in this book have had the tenacity to stick it out here for more than three decades and to make, as Hernandez once did, such exquisite 'lullabies for the onion.'"

A Nest for Everyone

The possum with four crazed paws
and a mouthful of broken teeth
is too old to brave the highway
again for a chase that blurs
into flight. The cold morning sun
grazes the husks of November,
the shoulders of workers crouched
between vines. They lower
their knives, the bronzed
leaves fall to the mud, and
the fluttering stops for a moment.
Then a wave of crows ascends
from a furrow, each bearing in
its beak a token of the season—
a flailing worm, a wisp of straw,
the strip of an old sleeve
that once bound an arm or
a shattered brow and still has
the fiery stain to show for it.

Last night, this side of a steamy,
blackened window, my children
wanted to believe that there
must be a nest for everyone.
As my son struck a match, the soft
wick of the candle flared into
a prayer for our survival.
It is the dead of winter and
vines are fluted with darkness,
wired to wooden stakes. It will
take all eight candles to cast
the light of their small faces
on the glass. And many more

than that to warm all the cupped
hands waiting not far beyond.

This month, the man who holds
the deed to this gnarly orchard and
that parcel of sleeping grass
is moving slower. Hours pass,
the rows of numbers won't bear fruit.
He leans back on his chair and
stares up at the empty sky of
his kitchen ceiling. Whatever
fluttered into the fields will
go back the way it came:
birds, leaves, the endless
bleating of the neighbor's bull,
even the workers themselves
quickly dividing limb from sky,
and the stars that will rise soon
over this valley. They will all
go back to the schemes of earth
and air, like those wild nests
left vacant in winter, embracing
the light, letting some of it go.

Good Men

The slow, blue shadows of the olive groves
follow the workers back into town.
Like patches, the shadows cling
to the sweaty folds of their shirts
and trousers. But the men imagine
something else has weighed them down,
like hunger or the day's heat
or a weariness so deep that
even love could never reach them.

Yet the sashes of darkness curl in
the dust around each trunk.
They are as blue as the shadows
under the eyes of a woman

whose picture lies crumpled on
the floor of the garage where
the men sleep: elbow to thigh,
toe to skull, they seldom
roll into dream or dare to
think of delicate nails
dragging their inky stain across
the shoulder of moonlight.

When I've seen them at dusk,
tracing the threads of gravel in
their last, few steps
down the alley, hunched over,
their swollen knuckles
shoved into pockets, I've wanted to
call to them to forget the olive,
the sagging plum, the worm nestling on
the balconies of rotted bark,
and stand up straight.

But their boss has already told them
what good men they are—
Preciliano, Jorge, and Cantu
with a few black nuggets
rolled up in his cuff.
The boss's wife appears with
piles of tortillas that will soak up
the day's shadows and banish
their hunger. And tomorrow,
these *good men* will go out once more
to kneel under the branches and
pry off fruit whose firm,
bitter flesh never falls
willingly into the palm.

River Song

It is the sun's doing
when the walls of ice break
from their blue shadows.

Ravines uncoil, pools
glittering open their dark eyes.
The bare essentials rise
to the surface—mica,
seed, bone. The marmot
babbles to the cool
heart of stone, his song
trickling downward.

And it is the moon's work
when, on a night in
late April, water comes
to the valley floor.
It threads itself through
the Laton weir, the litter
of gravel and moss
and budding muscats. A black
froth clings to the lip of
each pump, and stars
wash over the fields.

Sullied, reeling,
the river returns to
its empty bed. It has
swallowed whole shelves
of sand and bark,
gulped down slurred oaths,
broken glass, abandoned
car parts and, where
a herd has crossed upstream,
a cloud of dung and
a dragonfly perched on
its last free ride.

Now we may gather.
In willow coves, roots
suck thin air and boys
cut the current with sticks
and burned shoulders.
Freed by wind, scraps of
cottonwood ride the slow,

glossy surface. We kneel
in the rusted shallows
at the water's edge beside
workers washing off at sundown.

Everywhere, tracks left
by others—hoof, heel print,
mollusk and craw, whole
bodies pressed into silt
now blackened and glazed
like an ancient text.
And everywhere above,
in their own noisy river,
crows blessing these
remnants, this water that will
vanish before it is saved.

DAVID ST. JOHN

David St. John's most recent collections are *The Red Leaves of Night* (HarperCollins) and *In the Pines: Lost Poems, 1972–1997* (White Pine Press). He teaches at the University of Southern California.

"The idea of California exists for me not simply as an idea of home and homecoming, of solace and consolation, but also as a truly powerful paradisiacal notion as well. For the boy I was—growing up in the San Joaquin Valley, in Fresno—the shores of California, the beaches from San Diego to Big Sur to Mendocino, awaited me as places of profound relief and release. The Sierra Nevada were a constant looming presence in my imagination, a refuge that always hung at the edge of dailiness. During the almost twenty years that I was living in the Midwest or on the East Coast, I would often marvel at my good fortune of having been born in California. Now, for the past twelve years I have been able to walk in just a few minutes time to the western edge of this country, to the beaches of Venice and Santa Monica.

"What could be more glorious?"

from Of the Remembered

I

I will tell you. Maybe
You're leaning in the open
Doorway of some Irish bar,
Watching a single tug
Edge a little clumsily into its
Slip, in a Baltimore twilight;
Maybe we're driving the bluffs
Of New Mexico one Sunday morning,
Or maybe the coffee's just
Starting to boil
In the bare kitchen of your rickety
House by the Pacific, as every

Circular pulse of the lighthouse
Slices the dawn fog. Maybe,
At midnight, high on the catwalk
Of the abandoned cannery, we'll
Watch the bent
Ghost drag his skiff onto the shore,
Turning its keel to face the partial
Moon. Maybe it's this drifting in time
You'll no longer imagine, or the body
Of my voice that you hate. Tell me—
Because you remember a woman calling
Out in our sleep? Because nothing's
Left, if
We're alone? *Tell me.* I will tell you.

II

I grew up in California,
Where everyone stood a little closer
To the sun. In the San Joaquin
Valley, where I lived, the orchards
And vineyards ran from the Coast Range
To the Sierra foothills;
Those low barracks in the fields went
Politely ignored until the harvest;
Those months of winter fog,
Just the simple revenge of every swamp
Drained off for farm land. Summers,
To escape, I drove to the mountains
Or west to the Pacific, where the beaches
Sprouted heavy eggs of tar as
The off-shore wells
Broke down. In spring, the Sierra streams
Flushed and cleared with melting snows;
I'd sit by a falls, picking watercress.
Once, I watched a dazed squirrel
Drop from a high pine onto a rock
Below. At the tree's base
I dug a shallow bowl in the dirt,
And wrapped the squirrel's split face
In the thick robe of its tail. Late

That summer, I walked
Blue Canyon with a friend, along the trail
His great-grandfather had first broken.
We sat on the slanted porch
Of the loggers' company mess hall; inside,
Cast-iron stoves with grills as wide
As beds, still greased like obsidian. My
Friend whistled an old square-dance reel,
Stomping his boots on the broken boards,
To keep time. A year ago, one afternoon
In Big Sur, I was telling this same story
To my son as we knelt at a cliff's lip
Watching the waves ravel over the rocks.
He stopped me short, pointing to a crescent
Cove where a piece of swollen driftwood
Listed in the tides. I cleared the focus
Of the binoculars onto the coarse fur
Of a seal, its corpse. Even
I tire of emblems. One night, lost
In the typical smoke and liquor
Haze of a club in Montreal, I listened as
The awkward quartet lapsed and soared close
To dawn. Nobody cared if the sax missed
Its cue from the bass,
Or if the brushes shrugged off the drums,
About those bridges the piano player found
And lost. Yet, as I imagined the words
I might hang to the melody, the sax player
Stood and held a single low note
Over the dim room. The piano player stopped,
The drummer. Then slowly the sax began again,
In that breath caught by the entire bar,
Another tune none of us could name.

III

> Why, it must be close by him, at that moment, his old home that he
> had hurriedly forsaken and never sought again, that day when
> he first found the river.   *Kenneth Grahame, The Wind in the Willows*

I had walked out into the meadow
Of words, utterly lost. I can remember

My mother and father waving from the towers.
A few blackberry hedges forked here
And there, dividing the meadow into its maze;
The stiff green walls printed
With buckshot, rat droppings, owl garbage—
Berries, any stain on my fingers. Yet,
I'd never imagined the succulent tongues
Others' dreams could offer. That day, such
An elegant script drew its cirrus on the sky.
I know if the child runs from every meadow,
These weirs and copses, he comes only
To the backwaters flooding the tall, erect grasses;
A surface breaking with the letters of a law....
So, it is this animal sense of belonging
Which lifts your face into the folded blessings
Of the air, into this night blanketing every crib
Of cornstalks by the coiled highways. Though
We too can rise like woodsmoke
From a thin chimney in the pines, as each of our
Lost books kindles the ravings of that fire
Which bakes those dozens of chattering blackbirds
Into one very sweet and remarkable pie.

IV

I first slept along this estuary years
Ago, where the Navarro fans into the Pacific;
I was married, twenty. A few days before,
Driving out of the mountains above
Santa Cruz, I stopped at a country store
Along the way. Outside, the newsrack:
Cambodia, Kent. I drove north until I came
To this wide scallop of sand and driftwood;
I wanted to stand by the flat waves. In our
Truck, parked in a cliff hollow of pine,
My wife was singing our son to sleep
As the spray whipped up across the night,
Covering me. I've read in books
How a person might one day splinter into slivers
Or spines of light, but I only remember falling
Unconscious on the white sand. And it makes little

Sense, the noise I heard in the distance
As I came slowly back to myself, maybe just blood
Circling in my ears, or the scrub of the cliff
Set humming by the rising storm, or else
An iron dulcimer
Struck somewhere out beyond the sea. Now, this
Morning, walking again these banks of the Navarro
Towards the Pacific shore, the beach seems so calm,
So undramatic: only the limp kelp, a few driftwood
Limbs, the sand. As I walk beside the water,
I've kicked up out of nowhere
Half an old pair of dice—the wobbly Captain
Rattling the bones in his pocket, chancing it all
On the horizon. Yet this single die is so
Small, so beaten by the waves, sand, and coral
Its holes seem carved at random, its edges
Almost round. I know just where I'll use this ivory
Knuckle: I'll slip it into a game of liar's dice
As I lift the felt cup off the polished counter
In front of the solitary bartender. Then, I'll tell
This story, though the chances are
It's nothing he'd really listen to, let alone believe.

IX

Twin memory, we all seek it
As some God seeks us, though we
Await a softer, more temporal
Lover. That family
We carry across our shoulders,
The coat dedicated to the unending
Winter, advises us on each mistake.
Snow covers the leaves, shadows die
Into a mutual orbit, myths burn
In their seasonal constancy, Tonight,
I remember a story I once read
Of a hero who, to begin his quest,
Must sail across the sky
To its other shore, where his father
Waits, ages dead, to teach him those
Secrets which unlock evil, pointing out

Every road radiating from our star.
Norse? Hindu? Neither, I think.
I've only taken pieces of several
To make one story I love, one chord
I hear most. My friends know it,
In those words for their dead fathers,
That long approach. One summer, as my
Own father's heart rose like a hummingbird
Into his throat,
I wanted to speak *then,* not in any
Postscript of prayers, how I'd hold his head
In my arms. Now, as the snows still brush
The trees of Baltimore, I know my father
And his curious heart are walking again
In the California sunlight, not yet knowing
This melody is his. If I drove for six
Days west, I might ask him, on that other
Shore, for those answers I'm not certain
I wish to know. Chalice of mountains,
Valley of figs and grapes, where he lives.
And though I travel randomly now, at great
Distances, perhaps those spaces we cannot
See across are less dark
Framed by the two bodies we still carry,
Each for the other. And though my own son
Knows memory pales only slightly any day
Apart, if we stand together
As my graceful father walks the steep path
Along the limestone wall at this garden's end,
Perhaps we'll both see, as I still wish to see,
If, as the stone door closes, faith follows.

JOSEPH STROUD

© Linda Fox

Joseph Stroud was born in Glendale, California, in 1943. He is the author of three books of poetry: *In the Sleep of Rivers* (Capra Press, 1974), *Signatures* (BOA Editions, 1982), and *Below Cold Mountain* (Copper Canyon Press, 1998).

"I'm a native son, and except for travels and brief residences in Greece and Spain, have lived in California all my life, for the past thirty years in Santa Cruz (and for the past four years dividing time between Santa Cruz and a cabin in Shay Creek on the east side of the Sierra). The California landscape is etched in me deeply and permanently and has shaped my interior life in a way not unlike the glacial carving of granite in the mountains of the high country not far from Shay Creek."

Grandfather

Now I see you
In a small California town
Asleep under fig trees, the black fruit
Swollen and ripe. Your shadow seems
To deepen on the morning grass as peppertrees
Scatter their leaves like rain.
Or seeds.

I remember a summer morning
We sat on your porch, the warped boards
Pocked with holes and nails. The fields
Freshly cut. The pond rimmed with willows
And magnolias. You tried to tell me
Why my brown bitch had eaten her young.
It was a morning of bees.
I saw the light sing on their wings,
A mellow gold quaking into music.

You must have heard too
For when I turned you had fallen into a dream,
Your throat humming with veins.

Then I heard that other music. The cicadas.
The green frogs. My bones
Drained like the sap of trees
As I dreamed myself into the heart of the pond.
I forgot everything I ever learned.
Except your voice. Down there.
Singing of home, death, a blossoming tree.

Homage: Summer/Winter, Shay Creek

In the Shining

I've got my chair and a good book and I'm sitting
out behind the cabin in a shaft of sunlight, reading.
A couple of Steller's jays who might be my friends
perch themselves on branches in the ponderosa
and sugar pine. They can't read the book I've got
but they can read me, and they watch very carefully
for that moment when my hand reaches in
to my pocket and pulls out some crusts of bread
which I toss out over the forest floor and the jays
spring off the limbs and streak down in a blue blaze,
scoop the crusts and are back in the limbs again
chortling. This is the way of my life these days—
lazing, serene, but not so indolent, not so torpid
that I won't get up now and then, grab my chair,
and move to another spot, over there by the cedar,
to that new place shining now in the sun.

Manna

Everywhere, *everywhere,* snow sifting down,
a world becoming white, no more sounds,
no longer possible to find the heart of the day,
the sun is gone, the sky is nowhere, and of all

I wanted in life—so be it—whatever it is
that brought me here, chance, fortune, whatever
blessing each flake of snow is the hint of, I am
grateful, I bear witness, I hold out my arms,
palms up, I know it is impossible to hold
for long what we love of the world, but look
at me, is it foolish, shameful, arrogant to say this,
see how the snow drifts down, look how happy
I am.

Oh Yes

Oh no—
now we're in for it, everything's slamming shut,
closing shop, the leaves on the cottonwood are crying
fuck it and letting go in the wind, the cold
is coming, winter storms are massing at sea,
morning ice on the deck and the dog skids off
in a blur of legs, then it rains and rains and rains,
and the plague is upon us, strange fevers and aches,
the body spelling it out, impossible to ignore,
you're in a machine consuming itself,
and this morning walking out, you look up
at the persimmon tree for the first time in weeks
and notice all the leaves are gone, and there they are—
persimmons—fiery globes, hosannas and lauds,
and you can't help yourself, admit it, even sick
and miserable, mired in the dreck of winter,
you reach out your hand, take hold of the fruit,
oh yes, there's another world, there's a sun
within the sun, yes, kindness is real,
oh yes, blessings are everywhere.

DAVID SWANGER

David Swanger's most recent book of poems is *This Waking Unafraid*. He has been awarded a poetry fellowship by the NEA, and has authored two other books of poems, a chapbook, and a book about poetry. He currently teaches at the University of California, Santa Cruz.

"What works best for my poetry is some abrasion between place and me. It's hard simply to praise my surroundings; I'm

© Mark Wiley

more likely to write about them when they cause me unease or are scary—and California gives us plenty to celebrate as well as plenty to fear. The splendor is on shaky ground; verdure turns to tinder. Soon after arriving in the state in 1971, my wife and our two, then three, small children found ourselves precariously domiciled in the Santa Cruz Mountains, on a sandstone bluff accurately labeled 'Rattlesnake Hill.' You could see forever from our notch in the mountain; but you also had to watch where you put your feet. As if there wasn't enough worry, I acquired first a pony, then a series of horses—I who only knew about horses the fictions I had seen on television in New Jersey. I fell off a lot; sometimes the horse fell also. Fortunately, no one was seriously hurt; and we got to see the land in a very old-fashioned way. It's been an adventure, wandering horseback through the coastal microclimates, stepping from vertiginous, angled forests into hotfoot sand flats into sienna meadows less benign than they first appear. The territory is beautiful and intimate and volatile."

Knob Pines

Insufficient, like all apologies,
they are the arms of the starved
dead, stiff extrusions from shallow
graves. The loggers clear-cut first,
then planted these excuses and left.

We watch the knob pines wave; even
the fog moving inland is enough

to make them sway: their defeated
roots gnarl around too little clay,
and they fall, unhonored, into bone-

yards of themselves, making a low,
tangled sky, the last landscape
of snakes. Heavy with their resinous
cones, the knob pines hold each other
and conspire; their only wish is fire.

If fire were to rise from the crotch
of the hill; if fire were to suck life
out of air like a slow, red mouth; if
fire unsprung these cones into glowing
seed; the dead could rise after.

We make large, decisive noises
against the resurrection of these trees,
and listen, at noon, to their silence.

Natural Disaster

Overflow advances across strawberry
fields, insinuates streets and suddenly
everyone has a house on the water. And
such rich, redolent water, water carrying
land with it, effluents, aromas, stranded
cars, bodies in cars; water driving snakes
ahead of it, water augering through levees
and piling the fluid tonnage of itself against
bridges that break, great trees that swim
away from the bank and ride the roiling
surface until they are snagged by other
trees and slam sideways, trees logging up
into dams over which the river schusses.

The names of the creeks: Lompico, Bear,
Soquel, Zayante, Kings, Two Bar, Empire,
Aptos, Granite. And the rivers: Pajaro,
San Lorenzo. The names of the dead:
George, Leon, Sheila, Juan, Unknown and

Unknown. The names of the gods: Jaweh,
Father, Holy Spirit. The name of the lake
on whose bank grows a tree said to form
an image of the Virgin Mary in its bark:
Pinto. The name of the lucky one, not
home when his house slid over the edge:
Robert. The name of the thing that brings
the rivers up and the hills down: rain.

Wayne's College of Beauty, Santa Cruz

> I know what wages beauty gives.
> *Yeats*

We have dropped out of the other schools
to enroll here where no one fails; everything
is fixed, fluffed, teased into its temporary best
at cut-rate prices because we are all novices
in the art of making beauty, learning that beauty
is not so hard. Beauty is not so hard we learn,

because it is not chemicals or varieties of fashion.
Our scissors and combs, our libraries of lotions,
our bright mirrors assure the timorous or imperious
elderly they have come at last to the right place.
Wayne's is not the Heartbreak Hotel, and when they
leave beautiful, it is because they are briefly unlonely.

We have said, "How are you?", "How would you
like your hair?", and we have touched them not cruelly,
and with more than our hands. When it is over
we swivel their chairs so they can see themselves
carefully from several angles while we hover silent
just above their doubts, a calculation that provides
two faces in the mirror, ours smiling at both of us.

AMY UYEMATSU

Amy Uyematsu is a poet and teacher from Los Angeles. Her first book, *30 Miles from J-Town,* won the 1992 Nicholas Roerich Poetry Award. A second book, *Nights of Fire, Nights of Rain*, was published in 1998.

© Sandy Usui

"I'm a third-generation Angelino and Japanese-American. My grandparents immigrated to the United States in the early 1900s. My formative years were spent in Sierra Madre, a small town of 10,000 adjacent to Pasadena (famous for its annual Rose Parade). During that period (1950s through the mid-1960s), home never truly felt like home because of the underlying racism. When my parents built a house on family-owned land, our neighbors circulated a petition trying to prevent them from building it. The physical beauty of Sierra Madre—with its shady jacaranda and eucalyptus trees and showcase purple wisteria—contrasted with the cross that burned on the front lawn of the Jewish family who lived down the street.

"To really feel at home, we'd leave Sierra Madre for downtown Los Angeles, where there was still a bustling Little Tokyo, major concentrations of Japanese-Americans in the Crenshaw and Eastside sections of the city, even movie theaters which featured all-Japanese films. Based on the drive my family would make into Little Tokyo for special occasions, '30 Miles from J-Town' also reflects the gradual assimilation and resettlement of Nisei families into suburbs. As an adolescent, I attended a high school where interracial dating didn't occur, so I went outside Sierra Madre for a social life. Throughout the 1960s, hundreds of Japanese-American teens would gather at the Rodger Young and Parkview Auditoriums for Saturday-night dances. In 'To All Us Sansei Who Wanted to Be Westside,' I relive those years with great fondness—and the music we played (from Smokie Robinson to Little Willie G. & the Midnighters) still sounds as good now as it did then."

30 Miles from J-Town

1

dad was a nurseryman
but didn't know that sansei

offspring can't be ripped
from the soil
like juniper cuttings.

    2

we were fast learners
we spoke with no accent
we were the first to live
             among strangers
we were not taught to say
             ojichan, obachan
             to grandparents
we were given western
             middle names
we collected scholarships
             and diplomas
we had a one word japanese
             vocabulary:
             hakujin
             meaning: white
it became my dictionary.

    3

and in the summer when
        girlsmooth cheeks turn mexican brown
we were given the juice of a lemon
        an old country notion, its sting should return
        us to our intended feminine selves

    4

if you're hip in l.a. you eat
sashimi at least
once a month you know
the difference between
fresh and saltwater eel you cultivate
a special relationship with one
sushi chef you call
each other by first names-san.
as for me
I had sashimi on hot august nights
steaks grilled rare, 5 cups steamed gohan,

maguro never mushy sliced thick red,
and while the tongue burns sweet
from the mustard of wasabi,
mom brings in wedges
of moist chocolate cake
for cooling.

5

they didn't force the usual
customs on us.
no kimonoed dolls in glass cases
no pink and white sashes
for dancing the summer obon
we weren't taught the intricacies
of folding gold and maroon squares
into crisp winged cranes, but
we never forgot enryo
or the fine art of speaking
through silences.

6

every two or three years america goes asia exotic
          rising sun t-shirts and headbands
               rock stars discover geishas and chinagirls
and asian american women become more desirable
          in fashion
               almost a status symbol   in some circles
be careful it doesn't go to our heads
in videos blond hero always rescues us from yellow man.

7

quickchange sansei
we can talk cool whether we're from
southcentral lincoln heights or the flats
and even when we're not
we can say a few pidgeon phrases
a crude japanese english
offered to grandparents
before they die,
we can fool
sound just like an american

over the phone,
and in public places
we usually don't talk at all.

8

on important occasions
dad drove us into j-town
through the eastside barrio
past the evergreen cemetery
his sister and brother
never knew manzanar
kanji and english inscribed
on their gravestones
then over the first street bridge
into nihonmachi

this was the center
this was the lifeline

9

I go to japanese movies
whenever they come to town
  curious I see few and fewer like me
there are muscular young black men
and white men with indoor complexions
   some don't even need subtitles
   but they cannot know

I have to be here
I must spend these three hours
  with faces voices
  warriors farmers lovers
I would know
and to my soul
  these quivering notes
  of the shakuhachi
melodies I have heard long ago

10

grandma morita had no time
to learn how to drive the machine
but she took us by bus

to woolworth's
a dollar each to buy treats
for two girls who could never
talk to her about dreams.

The Ten Million Flames of Los Angeles

a New Year's poem, 1994

I've always been afraid of death by fire,
I am eight or nine when I see the remnants of a cross
burning on the Jacobs' front lawn,
seventeen when Watts explodes in '65,
forty-four when Watts blazes again in 1992.
For days the sky scatters soot and ash which cling to my skin,
the smell of burning metal everywhere. And I recall
James Baldwin's warning about the fire next time.

> *Fires keep burning in my city of the angels,*
> *from South Central to Hollywood,*
> *burn, baby, burn.*

In '93 LA's Santana winds incinerate Laguna and Malibu.
Once the firestorm begins, wind and heat regenerate
on their own, unleashing a fury so unforgiving
it must be a warning from the gods.

> *Fires keep burning in my city of the angels,*
> *how many does it take,*
> *burn, LA burn.*

Everybody says we're all going to hell.
No home safe
from any tagger, gangster, carjacker, neighbor.
LA gets meaner by the minute
as we turn our backs
on another generation of young men,
become too used to this condition
of children killing children.
I wonder who to fear more.

> *Fires keep burning in my city of angels,*
> *but I hear someone whisper,*

> *"Mi angelita, come closer."*

Though I ready myself for the next conflagration,
I feel myself giving in to something I can't name.
I smile more at strangers, leave big tips to waitresses,
laugh when I'm stuck on the freeway, content
just listening to B.B. King's "Why I Sing the Blues."

> *"Mi angelita, mi angelita."*

I'm starting to believe in a flame
which tries to breathe in each of us.
I see young Chicanos fasting one more day
in a hunger strike for education,
read about gang members preaching peace in the 'hood
hear Reginald Denny forgiving the men
who nearly beat him to death.
I look at people I know, as if for the first time,
sure that some are angels. I like the unlikeliness
of this unhandsome crew—the men losing their hair,
needing a shave, those with dark shining
eyes, and the grey-haired women, rage
and grace in each sturdy step.
What is this fire I feel, this fire which breathes freely
inside without burning them alive?

> *Fires keep burning in my city of angels,*
> *but someone calls to me,*
> *"Angelita, do not run from the flame."*

To All Us Sansei Who Wanted to Be Westside

It didn't matter where we lived
within a hundred miles of LA—
if you were Japanese growing up here
in the sixties, you weren't really buddhahead
unless you knew about the Westside,
Dorsey High School, dances at Rodger Young
followed by pork noodles at the allnight Holiday Bowl,
gangs called the Ministers, Baby Black Juans,

Buddha Bandits, and the boys who joined them
with the usual names, Kenny, Ronnie, and Shig.

By high school it was already too late for me.
I was from Pasadena and never got over
being forcefed a bleached blond culture
of cheerleaders, surfboards, red Corvettes,
lettermen's jackets I was never asked to wear.
Somebody had decreed the only places
you could stay Japanese and cool were the Westside,
Gardena, a few neighborhoods on the Eastside,
each with their own reputation—
hardly anyone from the outside ever got in.

This didn't stop me from hoping.
My sister and I made the long drive
into town on Saturday nights, thinking we'd get lucky,
get picked out of the crowded dance floor
by a pretty boy in a preacher jacket,
his hair in a 3-inch front,
so in profile everyone knew he was Westside
and could put on an almost black, Southcentral strut
whenever he wanted to.

I guess you could say even I had my chances.
At least before they heard me talk,
I was often mistaken for a girl who'd been around,
I had that mature look—
imitated sansei chicks with ratted hair,
glued on eyelashes, shiny adhesive slivers
taping eyelids round like blackeyed lacquer dolls.
But as soon as a Westside boy
asked my name, where I lived,
I sounded just like any other hakujin,
"No, I'm not related to Billy Uyematsu,"
whose dad ran a fish shop on Jefferson and 8th,
no sense in lying when my lack of dialect
revealed too many years in white classrooms.
But I really gave myself away when we slowdanced—
no one had ever taught me how

a genuinely rowdy sansei could slowdance
though she barely moved her legs.

I envied Linda Watanabe who had gone
to my Sunday school. She was mean enough
to hang out in the bathroom at Parkview Auditorium,
eager to fight, along with the toughest Westside girls
amusing themselves as we scurried by.
Then she started going out with blacks
and our parents told us to stay away.
When Linda got pregnant, her family said
she was going to visit her relatives in Japan.
It became a frequent inside joke,
another sansei daughter spending her summer
back in the old country.

I never got my Westside boyfriend
though I acquired a permanent taste for romance,
dark men, harmonizing to groups so smooth
only they could get away with calling themselves
the Stylistics, Flamingos, Delphonics,
Rosie and the Originals.
I went to concerts where *we* were the majority,
like the time Mike Sato from Gardena
took me to hear Smokey sing, "Ooh, baby, baby,"
long before it was a Ronstadt remake,
or I danced to "Are you angry with me, darling"
as the real Little Willie G. of the Midnighters
stood no more than ten feet away.
And now, over twenty years later,
when I meet other sansei, they'll say,
"Didn't you grow up on the Westside?"—
and a girl doesn't get asked that
unless they think she's got some degree of cool.

ROBERT VASQUEZ

Robert Vasquez was born in 1955 in Madera, California, and raised in nearby Fresno. While in high school, he became a full-time worker in less-than-ideal jobs and did so for over a decade. He was educated at California State University, Fresno; University of California, Irvine; and Stanford University (Wallace Stegner Fellow in Poetry, 1988–90). He has won three Academy of American Poets Prizes, three National Society of Arts and Letters Awards, a National Writers' Union Award, and the San Francisco Foundation's James D. Phelan Award for his collection of poetry, *At the Rainbow* (University of New Mexico Press, 1995), which was also a finalist in the Associated Writing Programs Award Series in Poetry. His poems have appeared in various periodicals, including *The Los Angeles Times Book Review, Missouri Review, New England Review, Parnassus: Poetry in Review, Ploughshares,* and *The Village Voice,* and in several anthologies, including *After Aztlan: Latino Poets of the Nineties* (David R. Godine), *Atomic Ghost: Poets Respond to the Nuclear Age* (Coffee House Press), and *Highway 99* (Heyday Books). In 1993 he was the King/Chavez/Parks Visiting Professor of English at Western Michigan University. He currently teaches at College of the Sequoias in Visalia, California.

"Whether it's the Sierra's granite stonescapes or Fresno's 'tagged' neighborhoods, the physical world calls to me in dialects always on the verge of translation. To a degree I'm a translator. However, I always keep in mind what the Chinese say: A translation is the reverse side of the brocade; we see the knots, the loose ends, the blurred shapes, but we don't see the handiwork of the finished side; rather, we experience the other side's hidden beauty.

"Like most writers, I live for moments of discovery when some spirit within a cloud-clogged vista or beyond a brick wall forces its way onto the written page and demands attention. Haunted and blind, I try to palm these universal presences that, like me, seem lost and wander the unlit avenues. If the scratched, polished instruments within us are in tune, even the darkest notes can sing us home."

At the Rainbow

for Linda, Theresa, and Phyllis

At fifteen, shaving by then, I passed
for eighteen and got in, in where alcoves
breathed with ill-matched lovers—
my sisters among them—who massed
and spun out their jagged, other selves.
I saw the rhythmic dark, year over

year, discharge their flare: they scored
my memory, adrift now in the drifting place.
Often I watched a slow song empty
the tabled sidelines; even the old poured
out, some dragged by wives, and traced
odd box shapes their feet repeated. *Plenty*

and *poor:* thoughts that rose as the crowd
rose—my sisters too—in the smoked air.
They rise on....They say saxophones
still start up Friday nights, the loud,
troubled notes wafting out from where
I learned to lean close and groaned

into girls I chose—no, took—and meant it.
In the Rainbow Ballroom in Fresno
I sulked, held hands, and wheeled among
the deep-bodied ones who reinvented
steps and turns turned fast or slow,
and this body sang, man to woman, song to song.

Early Morning Test Light Over Nevada, 1955

Your mother slept through it all,
her face turned away
like the dark side of the earth.

We'd heard between *rancheras*
on the radio
that the ladles
and the two bears

that lie among the stars
above Nevada
would fade at 3:15 as though seared
by a false sun.

The stove exhaled all night
a trinity of blue rings. You entered
your fourth month
of floating in the tropical,
star-crossed water
your mother carried under her heart
that opens and closes
like a butterfly.

When the sky flared,
our room lit up. Cobwebs
sparkled on the walls, and a spider
absorbed the light
like a chameleon and began
to inch toward the outer rings
as if a fly trembled.

Roosters crowed. The dog
scratched at the door. I went outside
hearing the hens and thought *weasel*
and found broken eggs, the chicks
spongy, their eyes
stunned and shrouded
by thin veils of skin.

"Don't open your eyes,"
I whispered to you when darkness
returned. I thought of your bones
still a white gel, I remembered the story
of blood smeared on doorways,
and I placed my hand on the balloon
you rode in—that would slowly sink
to your birth. I said
the Old German name your mother already picked
for you, *Robert*. It means *bright fame*.

for Jose Mercado Vasquez and Frances Roman Vasquez

...I like the idea that nothing
in decades has changed: the garage
still a bedroom; grapes
my father hung on nails
still drying in the toolshed;
the ceramic pink flamingoes
atop the TV, the matching
birds in the mirror about to drink
from the eyes of my mother,
who stares when alone, whose stare
I've inherited and carry
into years of rooms where I
will be alone; the dirt corner
beyond the bedroom window where
I can take aim at cactus and,
with BBs through green
flesh, leave my mark.

Pismo, 1959

The day ends with the blur
you wanted, full of watery hours,
the light weathered like aluminum,
gulls twining the air—summer's
floating script in the sky
refusing to pull together. The sun

breaks down each body
to silver, each bar of flesh
waist-deep in foam and brine.
The day flares out: wreckage
of orange on blue. Sea stars
wheel into place; like you,

they witness the tide, the whitecaps
tipped with distance, the distance
large with blown sails and spray.
And the whole beachway goes cold

while strands of ocean light
sink like heavy netting.

So this is the sun's passage
through dark doors of water....
So this is the scrolled shell
on fire, magnified. There is no one—
no lifeguard—to call out all
the bathers from calling water,

though you sense the dark
roll in, grain by toe-felt grain,
its curl slick and seamless
like a wing or a wave. Home's
still a hundred miles inland. You say
the globe is three-fifths blue

and rocks forever toward us, you say
we will never die, and I believe.
I'll sleep the whole drive back
beside you, leaning close and small
like a shadow reeled in, your face
precise with fine sand and shining.

JON VEINBERG

Jon Veinberg lives in Fresno, where he works as a mental health counselor. His books include *Nothing about the Dead* (1980), *An Owl's Landscape* (Vanderbilt University Press, 1987), *Stickball till Dawn* (winner of Soundpost Press Chapbooks Series, national competition, 1997), *Oarless Boots, Vacant Lots* (Orchises Press, 1998), and he was co-editor of *Piece Work: 19 Fresno Poets* (Silver Skates, 1987). He has been anthologized in *Piece Work: 19 Fresno Poets; Many Californians: Literature from the Golden State* (University of Nevada Press, 1992), *What Will Suffice* (Peregrine-Smith, 1995), *Full Court* (Breakaway Press, 1996), and *Highway 99* (Heyday Books, 1996). His awards include NEA grants in 1984 and 1995. He has been published in *Poetry, Missouri Review, Gettysburg Review, Pacific Review, South Florida Review,* and *Red Brick Review*.

"As a ten-year-old, I was certain my sister had psychic inclinations. When we were packed and ready to start the car to California from Pittsburgh, Pennsylvania, I noticed a glossy and blank look, interspersed with tears. I, on the other hand, could hardly contain my exuberance, but out of respect and deference to her I had my own vision to feed. I saw myself leaning against a palm tree just before making a wild splash into a wave that filmed my body with ancient and exotic salts. In front of a tunneled waterfall I shook hands with Mickey Mouse, and for hours I practiced staring into my windshield-reflected eyes as if they were Annette Funicello's. I was sure that on my walk home from school I would pass Marilyn Monroe watering her tulips who, because she took a keen interest in my scholastic achievements, would ask if I needed help in math. When we entered the San Joaquin Valley, specifically Fresno, I knew that my sister had had the correct vision in the extent of her mourning. She had foreseen what would not be available. For a long time I walked an unaffectionate landscape of ditchbanks, railroad tracks, vacant lots, dismantled motels, and assaultive suns. I saw my world as if I were peeking into an attic window: gloomy and dust-bitten, cheap and splintered, then easily forgotten. My lone marvel was both sad and curious at the hard risks my neighbors took to keep things moving on a daily basis through droughts and the tinkering with evaporative coolers, dry rot, skeletonizers, black widows, and the constant watering of brown-patched lawns. I remember our first landlord kicking his shovel into hardpan and always coming up lame, only to start again the next morning, and how he would drive through the chowdery fog for a bag of sunflower seeds.

"I don't know how or when or why the landscape even bothered, but one day it seemed to accept me just as words accepted me after the arduous process of learning how to read. Maybe it was the human characteristics I attached to it, or more likely the images it attributed to me. To paraphrase Neruda, everything I knew became new. Winos became the shade they fought for, vacant lots were galaxies, fog was the rain's white-washed cousin. Dogs with faithful limps took on voices equal to the sadnesses of buzzards, hummingbirds, and the taken-for-granted snakes. My most enduring California landscape is my backyard, where its images endear me to it by every now and then proclaiming me its king and allowing me to extoll on the ambition of wisteria, the persistence of oleander, the grittiness of privet, the wonder of where it will all go after my death."

An Owl's Landscape

to dream of wings
I've heard it said about this valley
that certain birds, on suspecting their death,
dream a landscape, then fly off to find it.
I knew a farmer whose throat was spliced shut
by cancer and at each new sprouting sore
his body reminded him of a vacant lot
overgrown in thistle and his spirit, he thought,
was a cluster of small black birds whose wings
became entangled in a network of weeds.

I once dreamt I'd been born
with a wound in my breast
the size of a small black moon.
They laid me on a quilt
under an apple tree where
my body became landscape for an owl
who later perched on my stomach.
Its shy face cast a morning shadow
across my eyes, peered inside the wound,
saw a garland of thorns growing inward,
dirt not yet plowed, a bullet
never to be used. It climbed inside
as if looking for laughter
or some firmament of light, saw
the gold needle that would one day
sew my eyes shut. Soon after

silence entered and closed up the wound,
hemmed in the owl who died inside.
I heard its echoes start up in me.
The apple tree was swaying in the breeze.
The stars outside gleamed like icons,
already they were starting to fade.

the ghost of the Kings

It used to be so quiet here
                    at the river,
black water spreading like spilt ink
below the mountain's ribbed cage.
I would close my eyes in fake prayer
and invent postcards of gold harvests
in old countries I'd like to walk through—
small fires blinked on the roadsides,
old men warmed their hands
and mothers traded rumors of fall.

On the opposite bank two men
speaking in broken English
are dragging the river, the gulls
circle their heads, a cluster
of moths dives into a plane of light,
dissolves into the unsure clouds,
into a horizon of silks. I am cold.

heat

The children run naked
and bogged in sweat.
She draws pictures of mountains.
The breadpans could be the Alps
and the empty tin cans
are as close to the stars
as she'll ever get.
And who could tell her
that her children aren't horses
galloping off into a scorched pasture?
Fletcher comes home early and drunk.
He wants to sit in his underwear
and laugh. The cat washes its paws

and squints its eyes into the hot sun.
The mountains are being filled in with snow.

hummingbird

For two days
I watched your mate
twirl its wings
in the lush leaves
of the persimmon
and for no reason
drop to the ground.
Hours after the body
had stilled
I could hear
the steady pounding of wings.

Once you stop moving
you're dead.
Honey falls lazily
onto the cat's tail
just beyond your grasp.
Wasps hover inside
the wounds of trees.
Tiny harbor of wind,
it must be tough sprinting
from shade to shade.
When I hear your heart thumping
I hear wings beating
inside the bodies of all my dead.

the ditch

When it grows dark I imagine the sky turning in on itself.
Green stars of wisteria sag and scratch at the screen.
Bells of blueweed lie open and still.
Spicebush and snail hide deep in the meadow.
I remember a girl fresh off the swing shift who disappeared.
They said she wandered the streets often and alone
in a pair of jeans embroidered with lemons.
We found her body in a ditch outside Orange Cove,
her eyes dazed to the glaring arc of lights
that shone through to her skull. What she wanted

was to dance all night in someone's arms.
The moon lay curled and sightless among the creased
rafters of oak.

the winos

It's hard to imagine them
as ever having mothers.

When I pass by
they shield their eyes.

Old newspapers fly wildly
across their legs

and the wind buzzes
inside their cuffs.

In the alleys
who could notice them

camouflaged against the scorched
brick, the gutted lumber
and the sun's assault?

Could this be as far south
as they'll ever get?

In New Orleans they're considered our future saints.
Here is where they must come to die.

thanksgiving dinner at the Eagle Cafe

If you eat the eggs you're drunk.
If you drink the coffee you're a ghost.
Someone reprimands an old man for spilling gravy
on the curled and fading photo of Carmen Basilio
and the jukebox hasn't worked in nine years.
Gomez tells me the ants have chewed up his radio,
his dog can't walk anymore
and tomorrow he'll go check out his cough.
To the blind woman at the counter
who sells me a handful of lucky charms
and tells me only the guilty wear sunglasses,
I am grotesquely rich.
I come here because it is safe.

a sparrow's testament

I'm at one with the mud and lime root,
my eyes set in a channel of salt,
in a scarred patch among the green seam of lawns.
My only hope is to set the whole habit of stars
to sputter and weep and shiver at my rusted
and unsplendid body. I know too much of beggars,
bullshit artists, and low-rise birds to go on.
Listen to how my one good wing still twitches
while I try gracefully and unably to rise.

Next to Tut

You know, Tut, they were wrong
about us ending up the same.
Even now I admire you, how your hands
lie luminous and crossed, steamed
into the gold of many histories
and how your eyes remain unfired and cloudlike
as if held under the weightless custody of stars.
Where I come from people turn red
at thoughts of being buried naked.
For seven years Mrs. Knight rehearsed her death
ironing the pink gown she would one day die in
and my father took with him
two sacks of misery, big as bird nests
under each eye and no shame.
He wasn't very pretty, Tut, and
even though I've never seen it
I still believe in frail and simple death.
They tell me your people fooled
with acupuncture, boiled exuberant herbs
for migraine and madness, and how
you could charm the servant girls
couched on your harsh and beaded world,
chewing manna grits out of mosaic bowls.
But what have you ever done
for my uncle's bad heart, Tut? Where I come from
heaven is flying off to a better swap meet

and laziness is just another case
of the stray dog blues.
It must be hot having your eyes gilded shut,
your body bound in silks where the only
cool thing that moves in you
is someone else's breath. Where I am
there is plenty of space for the wind
to fit and swirl and every now and then
the sun swindles its way in,
lots of room for my ashes to take on flesh.
My mother is still scraping leftovers
for the cat. I smell Mama Botta's pizza
and cheap tobacco spilling out of the pockets
of old men asleep on the porch,
and sometimes I wonder what mess
Johnny Mendez will be in when he gets here.
No, Tut, your bones were put together
someplace else. You will remain young and untarnished
because what we want to remember
is your bronzed and unripened face,
your blank and tender eyes. In the next
finger of wind we'll walk down my street
where I happen to be very important
because where I come from, Tut,
all the dead are vanished jewels.

To an Exeter City Cocktail Waitress

for Rocco

Broken down, somewhere near Bakersfield,
between Farmersville and Weed Patch,
where a bloated belly
would plead another beer.

I know what keeps you here.

It is the street
that boasts carnival posters
and reed mats,
where the mudhen's print

maps out the dirt sidewalk
leading here.

It is the ghost of your father
and your grandfather
who burned his name into flanks of steer
and sold, as ornaments,
the hollowed cow skulls and whittled ropes
hanging above your head.

Don't tell me different. You'll become
the used car dealer's wife,
wiping rust from the damaged parts,
hair turning white
as easily as the grasses turn.
Your lungs will fill with dust,
with grain
blown in from the cattle barns.

This Saturday night,
during the cake fair celebration,
between mumblings of jukebox and pinball,
wait for me.
Steal away from the men of your childhood,
in from the grasslands
who struggle like sparrows
flushed out by rain.

I'll come get you.

DIANE WAKOSKI

© Robert Turney

Diane Wakoski was born in Whittier, California, in 1937 and educated at the University of California, Berkeley. She has published twenty full-length collections of poems and many other slim volumes. Her most recent collections from Black Sparrow are *Emerald Ice: Selected Poems 1962–1987*, which won the Poetry Society of America's William Carlos Williams Award in 1988; *Medea the Sorceress* (1990); *Jason the Sailor* (1993); *The Emerald City of Las Vegas* (1995); and *Argonant Rose* (1998). She is currently Writer in Residence at Michigan State University.

"I was born in Whittier, California, where my mother had migrated, in the early thirties, from North Dakota and where she met my father, who was a sailor from Massachusetts, at a public dance hall on the Long Beach Pier. Both my parents were first generation Americans, one German, one Polish. Born in 1937, I grew up in Southern California when it was still orange groves and avocados, long stretches of bare brown hills and pumping oil and gas wells. When I was in fourth grade we moved to Orange County, to a little town of 1,900 people, La Habra, which had no high school of its own; so after eighth grade, I was bussed to the big, wealthy Fullerton Union High School. Fullerton High had 2,000 students, many of them college bound, many of them upper middle class, and this student population was in fact larger than the population of my hometown, La Habra.

"In these poems that Chris Buckley has chosen for this anthology, I recall in 'Night Blooming Jasmine,' the *beau monde* of Berkeley, California, and being a poor undergraduate there from 1956–60. It's where I learned about what kind of life I wanted, where books and music could lead me. In 'Bonjour Tristesse,' I offer the groundwork for my Medea myth, the events of my teenage life that set me on the course towards being a poet and which haunted my four years at Berkeley, following that time which so marked and defined me. 'Remembering the Pacific' also alludes to a time spent in Southern California. After I graduated from Berkeley, I moved to New York City. But in 1969 I returned to California for a summer at Solano Beach, and then in 1974 I returned for about a year to live at Laguna Beach. Growing up poor and very landlocked in Whittier and then La Habra and Fullerton, I spent my youth longing for the beaches of California, and when I did return for brief California sojourns, it was beach towns in which I chose to live. That same ambiance also floods my poem, 'Imagining Point Dume.' My mentor—

to whom 'Bonjour Tristesse' is addressed—David Smith, with his wonderful French wife, Annette, built a house on a cliff overlooking the Pacific Ocean at Point Dume. This house and its location represent the ultimate in beautiful living to me. David was my greatest mentor, and his wife now a longtime and important friend, the more so since his death.

"Though I have lived in Michigan for over twenty years now, I have never felt that I really belonged in its landscape. The place I might prefer to be is New York City, where I lived for the decade of the sixties. But the place that is in my fantasies, my imaginary life, and every gesture towards myth that I find in my world, is California, especially its coast, its palm trees, its golden poppies, its deserts, and the Pacific Ocean. In recent years, my imaginings have included the enchantment of Hollywood and movie life."

Imagining Point Dume

for the Motorcycle Betrayer

There are so many photographs of that curve of rocky beach
like a scallop shell itself, only reversed,
the green and blue striped ocean like the tray
of this calcified fan, the white coast,
my hand that holds Athena's shield,
this shell without its meat
of pinkish flesh

California motels, pink stucco,
with palm trees and the aura of World War II
populate movies and any flashes I have of my childhood,
but you were not there, you were glowering
at your father on Long Island,
you were wearing leather jackets and smoking cigarettes
and looking out of your hooded Clint Eastwood Hungarian
     eyes,
I only remember the big hand, cupped over a match
lighting your Lucky Strike.

And in those pink-tiled bathrooms constructed
in every housing development house
in the early fifties, we looked in steamy mirrors
that told us we weren't beautiful enough.
The mirror in the living room with pink flamingos painted
    at its

edges, also told us about our inadequacies.
But mirrors were unnecessary
because we had the ocean,
because we walked the dusty roads past the irrigation
        ditches,
filled with imported water,
because we washed our hair in water
filled with the minerals of the desert. Oh, the mirror

only added to the gleam of truth
that water represented in our lives.
Water which I imagine
as the Pacific Ocean
which is of course just
beyond the trees
of my backyard here in Michigan. I have carried it
with me
all my days
that mirror
reflecting the pinkish scallop shells,
                the pink flamingoes,
                the pink stucco
                of my childhood
like a pink Las Vegas dawn,
composed of neon light.

Night Blooming Jasmine:
The Myth of Rebirth in Berkeley, California

It wasn't on Crete, but in the hills of Berkeley
where the Daughter disappeared. And forget crocus. It
was the pink rhododendrons, like festival lanterns
or sunsets over the bay, which attracted her.
Their season is the season of that town.
The Maybeck houses
with their brown woody, thrushy sides
grow like hedgehog mushrooms, out of the slopes.
She lives there, hidden all winter in one of them,
and then like Garbo going out for groceries

in her shades, spring
    with tulip trees and hawthorn,
    with azalea, the pinks and whites, not even her colors,
    not the girl in the swing ruffled with the beauty
    men do not know how
    to touch—spring
brings her out, could that be?

No, she is going for *The New York Times,* she is slim
in her dark clothes, she has cheek bones and ankles
that the screen will notice. She is not made to protest
war or the loss of free speech, she is made for a dark espresso
bar, a grocery
smelling of fresh pasta and tins of tomato paste,
the coffee bean store with vials and philters, and alchemical
ways of extracting aromas,
her foot in its thin shoe, entering the bakery,
the boulangerie, where long sticks of bread or round
    pannikins
of whole grain are waiting.

This is the town where poets lurk, and books contain
musical notes often stamped with gold leaf. It is the
place where you can learn that everything has a skeleton, a
    structure
of bones that is more important than the flesh, so
changeable, which covers them.

Corn bread here is
a sculpture of meal and moisture. Polenta a cake
stirred until the spoon stands alone in the mixture, where
soft things gain stiffness, it is the place where wine can be
    truly
conceived of, if not made, and it is where everyone learns
    to be
an architect.

I envy those who dwell in this city, the
bones of the world, I call them. Am a different
kind of Daughter than the Mistress of Chez Panisse,
or the woman who taught me I could not be a pianist.
Not elegant-boned, more a carapace,

I walked through the streets, wearing my own shades,
    disguised
as one of the young, oh so sad, bums, an alcoholic cloud
of Night Blooming Jasmine wafting from my moonlit hair.
You'd never know it was the city of rebirth—
a concept incomplete without a sojourn underground
coming first. I know what happens when you look back/
I'm not doing that. Some part of me never left;
I belong to the place
    like the Maybeck houses,
        the Edward Teller of the Atomic Bomb,
            the Greta Garbo women cooking
                in the fragrance of night blooming jasmine.

Reading *Bonjour, Tristesse* at the Florence Crittenden Home for Unwed Mothers

for the late David Smith, my greatest mentor

I was empty as a new car, and
you brought me the novel, just published in English,
by the 17-year-old waif-like French girl. It was
1956. In 1957, the movie
was the first one to star the also very young
and waif-like Jean Seberg conniving
to drive her father's mistress, Deborah Kerr as the Parisian
Haute Couture, off a cliff near the Riviera.
I was lying in the hospital bed,
ready to face the sad cafes of exile
without cars
but not without love, and I
didn't read this book as if it were about selfishness,
willful children, speed or decadence,
though it is,
but as if it portrayed
    what?
men as betrayers, women
as poets, the singers. The sacrificers? I read it

as if it were about me, the girl with the extremely white
bare feet.
This isn't, I think
a very accurate perception,
but it prepared me to want to be
like Piaf,
to sing like Juliette Greco,
to live my life
as if only love, which to me WAS sex,
was the only whiteness, the only light, the only speed that
could articulate
beyond longing.

David, I walked in the dusty yard of The Home
memorizing Shakespeare's
"When in disgrace with fortune and men's eyes
I all alone beweep my outcast state."
I wanted
my Avocado-groves boyfriend to love me, I wanted him to
        wear
white bucks and have a crew cut like you, I wanted to look
        like Jean
Seberg and be rich
on the Côte D'Azur, I wanted
a David Niven playboy father to love me, but I was
one of those pale chunky girls from the orange groves,
disgraced and only reading books.
I read *Tess of the D'Urbervilles*
and *Jude the Obscure* while I was at that place,
books that have driven me through my life, whereas
I haven't once thought of Sagan's *Bonjour,*
Tristesse
since I flew off in my chariot drawn by dragons, not
off a cliff but into my Medea life.
Not once
until I watched the film on video this week
and found myself thinking
of you haunting your Point Dume house.
And of your beautiful French wife who defends me against
        her sister who thinks I am an unnatural woman,

one who gave up her children
because they were simply flesh, and that was not the
      part of sex that
I believed in.
And of the past.

Do I still believe it is sex that has the only power to
      transform?
Do I still understand its urgent message that only
one moment
counts:
the one at hand?
Do I still believe that orgasm is the only clue
we have
to death?
Bare white feet, lily moon face,
a diamond wheel-of-fortune spinning out of control,
my once long hair cut into a silver cap
around my head,
just like the late fifties French haircut
of the legendary Jean Seberg?
Bonjour, Tristesse, hello sadness, hello death,
what lady sings that song now?

Remembering the Pacific

I don't remember seeing it at night. It would look like
the groom at a wedding, in his black tuxedo
with only a crest of foaming shirtfront.
Of course when I
lived just a block away from the ocean
in Laguna Beach, or in Solano Beach, California
I must have seen it often
at night. But I have a hard time
pulling the image to my eyes, the way
when someone you love dies,
your husband, your father,
you suddenly realize you can't remember
his face.

It panics you, it frightens you, it
most of all
makes you sad, then angry;
what is the matter with your mind,
your mind that once was like a history book
filled with everything that had ever been recorded?
Night is when you stayed away, if you
were going to
stay away.
Night is when the oranges rolled out the door,
or the spoons rattled in the drawer. Night
is when the cup emptied itself, night is when
books broke their leather bindings, and toothbrushes
disappeared.

At night, the ocean swallowed everything
until the whole world was invisible. At night,
my father betrayed my mother, my husband slept with
        others,
and I could only look at the ocean and be fearful
that nothing in it was an orange, a rose,
a glove, a book, or
anything I could count on to take care
of me. Not even the white crests of groom's-shirt waves, so
        often
imagined in Classical literature as horses. No
white horse, or even a surfer on an old board, coming
out of those waves to carry me
to safety. No I can't
remember what the ocean looked like
at night, though I do think
of the ocean
all the time.

CHARLES HARPER WEBB

Charles Harper Webb uses three names because there are so many Charles Webbs in the world. He is a rock singer turned psychotherapist and Professor of English at California State University, Long Beach. His book *Reading the Water* (Northeastern University Press) won the 1997 Morse Poetry Prize and the 1998 Kate Tufts Discovery Award.

"When I was a kid in Houston, Texas, in the sixties, my friends and I dreamed of moving to California: land of surfers, hippies, psychedelic rock, the fabled 'Sunset Strip,' crawling with (what else?) naked girls. Now, incredibly, I find I've lived in L.A. for twenty years. I don't write a lot of purely landscape (or cityscape) poems, but the city and the state constantly creep into my work. Even more than the physical L.A., the metaphysical one pervades my poems as an attitude, a state of mind. It's a smart-assed, iconoclastic attitude, but tender and loving sometimes, and self-mocking too. It's the attitude of the audacious outsider, the long shot coming home to win—and, incidentally, the attitude of a lot of Stand Up poetry. I had that attitude in Houston, and later in Seattle, which is very likely why I wound up here.

"I dislike a lot of things in L.A.: crime, racial tension, over-regulation, the Hollywood mentality, where if you don't have a dozen big deals happening at once, you're a loser. But I like being on the cutting edge of American culture, however debased that culture may be. I like being where 'it,' whatever it is, is happening. I like the weather (when it's not smoggy and 100+, which it usually isn't, but is today). I like the colorful clothes, as opposed to New York black. I like the freeways, when they're not jammed (which they usually are), and the palm trees, which look like invading Martians. I like the restaurants and theaters and concerts and swimming pools and the proximity to ocean (though it's pretty much fished out, and too cold and polluted for me to want to swim in it). I like the mountains—the local ones, including the Verdugo Hills in which I live, and the Sierras, where I've had some great fly-fishing—though I don't like the crowds and the long drive to relatively untouched spots. I like the fact that beautiful women flock to L.A., or in the case of my wife, were born here. I like the energy, the vitality of Southern California. I don't think L.A. poetry gets the respect it deserves. But it's a good place for me and mine."

Arson

Fire's army overruns Topanga's hills.
Fire's breakers crash and roll down to the sea.
Fire's hounds track people running for their lives.
Fire's houses shine like jack-o-lanterns: orange within orange,
      flickering.

The orange beard of fire crackles in the wind.
The orange hair of fire is styled into spikes.
The orange eyes of fire flash, looking for food.
The orange teeth of fire chew and chew.

Every TV in the city features flames.
We sit around them like Boy Scouts,
Watching fire's architects build towers in the air,
Watching groves of fire spring from orange seeds,

Watching hills of fire shrug off walls of steam
As homeowners build water-fences to hold fire back,
And, failing, mill and cry and fill the streets like refugees,
Spines bent beneath the unfamiliar weight of loss.

At Summer's End

I rise at dawn, and stumble up steep, crumbling
Rock to sit on a downed tree and lock
This morning in my mind: this mountain grooved
And channeled by spring runoff, poppies dancing
Like tethered butterflies as wind brushes
The deep harps of the trees. As a boy,

I played in woods like these, stalking the green,
Trilling warblers and rosy grosbeaks
That flocked to Houston, fleeing Canadian snow.
I notched my bb gun for every one I dropped,
And hung their wings above my bed to hover
With my dreams. Where, today, high-rise

Condos block the sky, I netted monarchs
And red admirals; I tracked a fox
One whole Saturday, barely seeing the tall

Loblolly pines, they were so common, the stands
Of sweetgum and post oak where jays rasped
Just as they do here, while far away,

Bulldozers out-grumble the wind. Overnight,
I'm forty, near divorce, joints stiff
In morning chill, bald spot spreading like a meadow
In the trees. My bold resolves scatter
Like quail—so many so fast, I can't bring
Down even one. I zip my coat and stumble

Uphill over ground studded with stone,
Pitted with holes where chipmunks curl, still sleeping
In the earth's warm pouch. Decay surrounds me—
Ice-cracked rocks, sun-withered flowers,
Pineneedle peat, brown boulder-faces pondering
The mountain's end. Sage mist rises.

Snow-scoured tree stumps twist and bend: the seasons'
Swirl sculpted in wood. My house in town
Keeps seasons out. Nothing gets inside
To heal me. Nothing makes me proud to join
The mountains dance of change, their jagged, dwindling
Peaks vaulting across the sky. Here,

In a patch of dried asters, a butterfly
Blue as a chip of morning clings, waiting
For sun, which moves toward us—a slow avalanche
Of light—as I turn and, hand-in-hand
With gravity, start my long, stumbling
Dance downhill.

Invaders from South of the Border Imperil Native Population

—The Los Angeles Times

Squadrons swoop down, shrieking—
scarlets, yellows, greens vivid and loud
as Aztec murals, as Mayan serapes:
parrots, red and lilac-crowned, reinforced
by parakeets and conures screeching

and squawking in imported sycamore,
palm, eucalyptus trees. Escaped
from pet stores, freed when owners lose
interest, parrots don't wander like dogs,
bewildered, letting themselves be caught

by Animal Control and put to "sleep."
They fly up to the tops of trees
and scream "I'm here," then troop off
with their rescuers to rain runny
white bombs onto Blonde Heaven.

Their orange-ringed eyes scout for food.
Their sickle-beaks crack nuts, slice fruit,
shove aside whatever's in their way.
Oh, the public may protest the loss
of Robin Red-Breast, saucy Mister Jay.

But who will mourn the dusky junco,
the drab, secretive sage sparrow?
Who will miss the mourning dove's
sad ocarina welcoming another
sunny Southern California day?

You Missed the Earthquake, Bill

One instant I was asleep in bed; the next,
I was bucking and bouncing like a tuna
on the floor. Power-transformers flashed
like bombs; then black poured in. "Oh shit, oh shit,"
I prayed until the jolting stopped. Alive,

my house standing—as far as I could tell—
I groped for clothes, and stumbled into them
outside, where car-alarms whooped
and caterwauled in pre-dawn chill. The yellow
feelers of flashlights twitched up and down

the black trees, black sidewalk, black street.
Art Campo's radio reported freeways buckled,
buildings down, exploded gas lines,

spewing water mains. We tried to think
we were lucky as aftershocks rolled in

like bowling balls. When I think of you, Bill,
I usually think of some good thing you're missing:
redheads, pow-wows, barbecues, thunderstorms,
the Hubble telescope tuning in a cosmos clear
enough to see the souls in heaven. (I didn't

see you.) But the dead miss bad things too—
getting fired from a good job, which I just was,
or dumped by a woman you love,
which I was too, or trapped in your apartment's
rubble or your mini-van, screaming

as chunks of overpass crush it, then you.
I thought I heard your kids crying three blocks
away as darkness grabbed our homes and shook,
your wife—still hating you for Jane in Idaho—
screaming, "Goddamn it, Bill, why aren't you here?!"

A cop was motorcycling through silvery fog
when a freeway bridge dropped out
from under him. Dying, he missed a week
of sixteen-hour shifts, rescues, crushed bodies,
looters, gapers, gorgers on misfortune.

He might've liked those things, who knows?
We never know what we've enjoyed till we look back.
He was too startled, probably, to enjoy
his arcing flight, then too afraid. But what
a ride he must have had, Bill, what a ride.

M. L. WILLIAMS

M. L. Williams's work appears in *Verse and Universe: Poems about Mathematics and Science* (Milkweed), *What There Is: The Crossroads Anthology, Prose Poem, Solo, Quarterly West, Hubbub,* and elsewhere. He is currently editing *The Obsessive Refrain: French Forms in Contemporary American Verse* with co-editor Chryss Yost. He teaches at the University of California, Santa Barbara.

© *Chryss Yost*

"In the San Joaquin Valley, hands still matter more than machines, hands and talk. Doesn't matter what language. Shirts and skins at Quigley Park, March wind, family dominoes, all the chatter and movement. These sifting rhythms hold forth over the white noise of machinery and the haze of dust, July baking shade at 110 degrees while hot engines tick over oil and asphalt and white lines that can't keep anything straight. Winter tule fog erases chain link and every headlamp in front of you and the sound of your breath dissolves into the missing sky. Everything falls apart openly: old harvesters rust into primordial lace; beams twist over the settling ground, exposing all the failing infrastructures of pig iron and fir-stud. Easton Market sags visibly over aisles of shiny cans and bags and the squeaky wheels of a grocery cart and *no, not today, it's too much.*

"Poetry comes from silence, by the way it gives up to speech and the music always behind it—traffic and power mower, strident crickets, screen-door hinge and slam—silence and the road out to anywhere, sigh of tires, whistle of air through a window wing. Every trip is long, bothered by signs scrawled opposite the oleander, and traintracks and cotton greening the distance. The stone-blue August sky gives up to cumulus erupting its blood of light over all of this. Rows of vines still make a visual iambic I can't stop watching through the window of an old Dodge Dart, long gone, my breath timing the light against the chugging warp of a low tire or my own breath, too slow to keep up. Poetry's gift is its failure, its giving in to the weight of so many voices against the quietude it wants to explain. This is what growing up in the San Joaquin Valley taught me. I've tried to listen, find the silence behind it all, explain it. And I fail…add to the noise. *It's too much.*"

152 Into 5, *El Centro Palabra de Fe*

i. Driving

You might be sleeping next to me. Your head
bobs against the window, past the alfalfa,
past the corn which climbs to nothing and gives
up in pale ears. But you ignore
the whistle from the wing, the physical clatter
of car and road and friction, the rhythm
of white lines that settles out and falls
at the headlights' fading edge past the shoulder.

Our children can only stare quietly at the hulk
of distance risen up against the night,
corners of a picnic blanket when you
were young enough to see so far. Sleep on.
The moon rides with us, a gold knob over
the Sierras open to the glow
of their eyes shining back in the rearview mirror
and caught there, watching, riding the shatter
of lines pulling back into 152 toward home.

ii. Blowing

The wind curls out of the coastal range,
buffets the poisoned wetlands and sloughs,
and it stops—maybe it stops—at the Red Top Cafe
to have a quick cup and ignore the large-mouthed
bass collection mounted over the counter.
Maybe the wind holds its newspaper up
against the tepid counter light, or against
the pretty waitress wiping the formica too
often against her boredom. Maybe she sets
coffee out for a handsome Highway Patrolman
before he sits down at the same counter stool.
Maybe he knows her by name and says it—
Debbie or Claire—as he stirs the dark out
of his steaming coffee with half-and-half. But I don't stop.

If I stop, the wind might slow a bit and turn
and argue otherwise in its dusty voice,
and I might argue back until the waitress
stares and pours my coffee nervously

when she sees the seat I'm near is vacant,
that he left the local paper but no tip.
So I drive on, the wind shivering the aerial
into static, the sound too low to make out any song.

iii. Damage

We only wake up from ourselves when the dog turns
its eyes from the bitch he chases along the median
into the fender of my blue Ford, and the kids
scream, and you wake into your horrible silence.
I close my eyes into the darkness so I
won't see the red glow of my brake lights cast
on the jumble of legs and the snout in the mirror,
so I won't feel guilty about thinking
too soon about the cost of fixing the plastic
blue cowling I never wash the bugs from anyway,
so I won't think too long about the damn dog.

Buzzards never feel guilty about the blessing
of road jerky, or bother about the hover
of flies and cars three feet away from the lines.
They hunch into the prayer of body and beak,
gather in the sanctuary of the berm we made
to catch the spillage of water and oil and blood.

iv. California Spanish

I've learned to ignore the Spanish names
and Arabic numbers telling us how far.
But when I reach the city limits, I see
a weathered sign scattered by my lights
telling me in a language I understand
just well enough to know I'm lost in it

that I have reached *El Centro Palabra de Fe.*
I won't turn in. The candles there would flicker
like the lights that tremble on this fault-churned road,
my back sore against the hard pew,
and people I don't know nodding off
in the quiet dark, the low music,
the silhouette haloed and uncertain
above the clear horizon of the altar.

So I drive on, past this center of the word,
past faith and all the signs commanding me to stop;
it isn't faith, but doubt that keeps us going.
I drive too fast through the fading lights of town,
past this city's absent limit until
I'm far enough to forget this road I travel
from one nowhere to another, forget
the sound of air, forget my hands against
the wheel; I signal, and flash my brights to pass.

Astronomy

We used to look for satellites
falling through perfect arcs
over our lawn—Sputnik, Telstar—
I didn't care. Every orbit
is a kind of falling. We lay
on our backs and stared past the dark
until our eyes erased the light
from a dim star's lit core, or till
a flashing meteor would draw
a gasp, then someone's small complaint
of "only" across an autumn sky
still hung with smoke from burning piles
of sycamore leaves. A wink of red
would rise and curl toward the Pleiades,
join them for a moment, fade out.

My uncle pointed to a pin
of light in Gemini, near Pollux,
etching its pale line—thirty seconds
over this town's night, we figured,
and someone knew how high and fast
it flew, and measured it in sunrises
per day. Finished, we entered the house's
incandescence satisfied,
and ate together. They settled
back into their game of dominoes,
the click of wood, talk blending

with the TV's flickering blue.
The sky was theirs that night, and each
cold swallow of beer, each play of double
fives on the print cloth expanded
that constellation into what
would add to winning and losing, enough
to take us closer to the end
of night, when I would finally fall
asleep on the dusty couch and dream.

South

Down 99, south from Portland, then
the San Joaquin's long flat haze of bugs
and stars scatters across the windshield glass.
My wife sleeps, my daughter nods in the dark
against a book, and my son chatters on and on
about anything I stopped listening to
three miles back. "Go to sleep," I tell him.

Near Sacramento, the radio spits a talk show
through the static—a poet reading poems set to jazz.
I turn it up, try to listen to his wisdom
scattered through the haze of white noise,
listen to the fuzzy bass confused at the boundary
my car skirts between stations competing for the night.
My hearing drifts. My eyes gaze
into the finitude of white lines
racing mile after mile toward the glass.

My son goes on—about the stars which follow us,
about the moon rolling like a nickel
behind us over the flat landscape.
"Why?" he says. "Why?" I say "Yes," at first,
and offer explanations: the literal one
he doesn't want, then a clever lie to steal
his silence. "But why?" he keeps on, so I
finally shrug, offer only my silence,
and try to hide in the oblong shape my shadow
makes from the headlights into the back seat.

I listen to the poet, watch the bleached
lines come out of the dark, and play
with the radio knobs to clear the static.
The poems keep falling in and out of the sky.
Fragments batter against the pavement, the poet's broken
name sounding in the dissonance of road-hiss and jazz
like a message in a language I can't figure out,
like the sky I can't figure out to please my son.

My son is asking still, but not me, I notice.
Stars glint in the bent rectangle of glass,
in his eyes, in his dark mouth finding
its tongue a charm against the night,
against the hiss of stars and the muffled
animal sigh of wind squealing under the car.
"Sleep," I tell him and speed to pass a slow truck,
to lose the blank moon always in my mirror.

SHERLEY ANNE WILLIAMS

Sherley Anne Williams's books in-
clude *The Peacock Poems* (1976,
National Book Award Nominee);
Someone Sweet Angel Chile (poems);
the novel *Dessa Rose;* the children's
book, *Working Cotton* (1992, a
Caldecott Honor Book); and *Girls
Together* (1999). She lives in San
Diego and teaches literature and
fiction writing at the University of
California, San Diego.

© Thomas Victor

"I was born in California near the
end of World War II at a time
when most black people were still
in the South. As a child I was im-
pressed with California's size, the
economic richness I learned about in school, with the fact that California was
not the Old South country my parents had escaped from, and also, I was to-
tally alienated by the reality of California as I knew it: poverty and back-
breaking labor.

"I moved to Southern California in the early seventies at a time when one
could still see, even in its sprawling urbanopolises, vestiges of what its primal
landscape might have looked like. This was very liberating for me: I had been
so focused on cities—San Francisco, L.A.—and on the land as agri-business
made it in the Valley that I hadn't seen the landscapes around me. I imagined
the world as anthropomorphic with personalities pretty much like some black
people I know and created 'Myths for the 21st Century' (unpublished). I'm
also working on a novel set in 1969 in the Valley. The state today is run by
people who want to turn circumstances back to a time when white people
didn't think there were consequences—or thought somebody else would pay
them. In my mind the state is still the land of giants and elemental forces
where black people roam and make songs and are free."

california light

I have come in my own time
to the age at which she bore
me, rooted among memories
made phantom by my thoughts

say…She was a weaver, born
in an age of ready-made
cloth studying over threads
and colors while some machine
stamped her man's health, Nourishment
for the Kids, the dreams of her
youth, Two Bedrooms in the Project—
But these are symbols of
memory, not memories
themselves, the meat of vision
unfolding. The past does not
always come when you call it:

we are herded through hard clear
light, across a graveled lot;
I see the deep shadows of
cream-colored houses and white
men in brown suits as one is
jerked to the ground. That ball of
flesh and dress is mamma, her
roar precedes her; this is the
time the County declared her
'unfit,' called in the Sheriff.

Emblem of Project-County,
the face of the woman who
fought so is memoried in the
flesh of Miss Le'a's daughter.

The Green Eyed Monsters of the Valley Dusk

Sunset knocks the edge from the
day's heat, filling the Valley
with shadows: Time for coming
in getting on; lapping fields
lapping orchards like greyhounds
racing darkness to mountain
rims, land's last meeting with still
lighted sky.

This is a car
I watched in childhood, streaking
the straightaway through the dusk
I look for the ghost of that
girl in the mid-summer fields
whipping past but what ghosts lurk
in this silence are feelings
not spirit not sounds.

Bulbous
lights approach in the gloom
hovering briefly between
memory and fear, dissolve
into fog lamps mounted high
on the ungainly bodies
of reaping machines: Time
coming in. Time getting on.

from The Iconography of Childhood

i

A town less
than ten stories tall

Spring rains wash the wind
   light annihilates
       distance
snow flecked Sierras
  loom at land's end

  Land flat as hoecake
   Summers hot enough
to fry one Crops fanned

out in fields far as
        eyes can see
          every
Time we work a row
  another appears
        on the horizon

vi

Summer mornings we
rose early to go
and rob the trees
bringing home the
blossoms we were told
were like a white girl's
skin And we believed
this as though we'd
never seen a white
girl except in
movies and magazines.

We handled the
flowers roughly
sticking them in oily
braids or behind
dirty ears laughing
as we preened ourselves;
savoring the brown
of the magnolias
aging as though our color
had rubbed off
on the petals' creamy
flesh transforming some
white girl's face into
ornaments for our
rough unruly heads.

vii

The buildings of the
Projects were arrayed
like barracks in
uniform rows we
called regulation
ugly, the World in
less than one square block.
What dreams our people
had dreamed there seemed to
us just like the Valley
so much heat and dust.

Home training was
measured by the day's
light in scolds and
ironing cords; we
slipped away from chores
and errands from
orders to stay in
call to tarry in
the streets: gon learn what
downhome didn't teach.

And
Sundown didn't hold us
long. Yet even then
some grown-up sat still
and shadowed waiting
for us as the sky
above the Valley
            dimmed.

the wishon line

            i

The end of a line
is movement the
process of getting
on getting off, of
moving right along

The dank corridors
of the hospital
swallowed him up
(moving right along
now—from distant
sanatorium
to local health care
unit—the end of
that line is song:
T.B. is killing

me. We traveled some
to see Daddy on
that old Wishon route
but the dusty grave
swallowed him up.

ii

These are the buses of
the century running
through the old wealth of
the town, Huntington
Park Van Ness Extension
the way stops of
servants; rest after
miles of walking and
working: cotton, working
grapes, working hay. The
end of this line is
the County: County
Hospital, County
Welfare. County Home—
(moving right on—No
one died of T. B.
in the 50's; no one
rides that Line for free.

CHARLES WRIGHT

© Nancy Crampton

From the late sixties through the eighties, Charles Wright lived in Laguna Beach and taught at the University of California, Irvine. In 1983, *Country Music: Selected Early Poems,* won the National Book Award in Poetry. In 1993 he won the Ruth Lilly Poetry Prize, and he received the Lenore Marshall Poetry Prize from the Academy of American Poets in 1995 for *Chickamauga.* Most recently, *Black Zodiac* won the Pulitzer Prize for Poetry, the National Book Critics Circle Award, and the Los Angeles Times Book Award. *Appalachia,* the last book in his last trilogy, came out in 1998.

"What I remember most is the pepper tree, the huge pepper tree, that shadowed our front deck and bedroom windows in Laguna Beach. Each year we'd remove another slat in the deck as the tree reimagined itself after the winter rains. The rest of the landscape in that house—around that house—was stereotypically Southern California Coastal: scrub hills, scrub canyons, ill-advised housing sites, and there, just out of the left corner of the eye, like a giant sheet of Reynolds Wrap, the ocean, unrolled and slightly crumpled to the clear horizon. 1771 Thurston Drive.

"Before that, 599 Oak Street, again in Laguna, the backyard of *China Trace.* Originally arranged and planted by a landscape architect who had lived in the little board-and-batten house back in the 1930s—and who had tried to plant one of every exotic plant and tree he could find—the yard, by the time we arrived in 1972, had mostly shrunken back to little pockets of unusual vegetation (guava trees, cherimoya, and sapote trees and the like) among the more standard California limes and lemons and avocados. A palm tree, roses, a banana tree, enormous camellia bushes. Lushness was all. And always, at the bottom of the street about four blocks away, the ocean like a sleeping dog, its side rising and falling and twitching occasionally in the aftermath of some dream or other.

"My California. Two yards and the flat back of the ocean, another tri-color splinter forever broken off in my heart. Little imagistic irritant for seventeen years. I'd never pull it out, even if I could. Sweet hurt."

April

The plum tree breaks out in bees.
A gull is locked like a ghost in the blue attic of heaven.
The wind goes nattering on,
Gossipy, ill at ease, in the damp rooms it will air.
I count off the grace and stays
My life has come to, and know I want less—

Divested of everything,
A downfall of light in the pine woods, motes in the rush,
Gold leaf through the undergrowth, and come back
As another name, water
Pooled in the black leaves and holding me there, to be
Released as a glint, as a flash, as a spark...

Autumn

November the 1st. Gold leaves
Whisper their sentences through the blue chains of the wind.
I open a saint-john's-bread.

Green apples, a stained quilt,
The black clock of the heavens reset in the future tense.
Salvation's a simple thing.

California Twilight

Late evening, July, and no one at home.
In the green lungs of the willow, fly-worms and lightning bugs
Blood-spot the whips and wings. Blue

Asters become electric against the hedge.
What was it I had in mind?
The last whirr of a skateboard dwindles down Oak Street hill.

Slowly a leaf unlocks itself from a branch.
Slowly the furred hands of the dead flutter up from their caves.
A little pinkish flame is snuffed in my mouth.

Clear Night

Clear night, thumb-top of a moon, a back-lit sky.
Moon-fingers lay down their same routine
On the side deck and the threshold, the white keys and the black
   keys.
Bird hush and bird song. A cassia flower falls.

I want to be bruised by God.
I want to be strung up in a strong light and singled out.
I want to be stretched, like music wrung from a dropped seed.
I want to be entered and picked clean.

And the wind says "What?" to me.
And the castor beans, with their little earrings of death, say
   "What?" to me.
And the stars start out on their cold slide through the dark.
And the gears notch and the engines wheel.

Saturday 6 a.m.

The month gone and the day coming up like a bad cold
Insistent behind the eyes, a fine sweat on the mustard stalks.
There's something I want to say,

But not here, stepped out and at large on the blurred hillside.
Over my shoulder, the great pane of the sunlight tilts toward the sea.
I don't move. I let the wind speak.

Sitting at Night on the Front Porch

I'm here, on the dark porch, restyled in my mother's chair.
10:45 and no moon.
Below the house, car lights
Swing down, on the canyon floor, to the sea.

In this they resemble us,
Dropping like match flames through the great void
Under our feet.
In this they resemble her, burning and disappearing.

Everyone's gone
And I'm here, sizing the dark, saving my mother's seat.

Stone Canyon Nocturne

Ancient of Days, old friend, no one believes you'll come back.
No one believes in his own life anymore.

The moon, like a dead heart, cold and unstartable, hangs by a
    thread
At the earth's edge,
Unfaithful at last, splotching the ferns and the pink shrubs.

In the other world, children undo the knots in their tally strings.
They sing songs, and their fingers blear.

And here, where the swan hums in his socket, where bloodroot
And belladonna insist on our comforting,
Where the fox in the canyon wall empties our hands, ecstatic for
    more,

Like a bead of clear oil the Healer revolves through the night
    wind,
Part eye, part tear, unwilling to recognize us.

CHRYSS YOST

A third generation San Diegan, Chryss Yost lived there until age twenty-four, when she moved to Santa Barbara and attended the University of California. She is the co-editor, with Marty Williams, of *The Obsessive Refrain: French Forms in Contemporary American Verse.* Her work has been published in *Quarterly West, Crab Orchard Review,* and in a chapbook, *Escaping from Autopia.* She lives with her daughter in Santa Barbara, where she works as a graphic artist and writer.

"I've heard San Diego called a borderland. In fact, San Diego is *many* border-lands, a stacked intersection of on-ramps and off-ramps, a porcupine of pineapple on toothpicks, the trunk of an aluminum Christmas tree, holding shining, disparate branches together for an artificial moment; between the Pacific Ocean and the Anza Borrego, Hollywood and Tijuana, suburban sprawl and chaparral. We dangle within the tinsel of memory and desire, watch the lights sway in the Santa Ana winds. We carve communities into the canyons, sprinkle snow on our windows, and rewrite the world as if it had never been written before.

"As a writer, I pick up my crayon, place my stories on the surface of my home, and press colors into things that have always been: the feathers of the gulls, the sandstone, the scrub oak, and Torrey pines. In San Diego, the new stories are important, even if they only last a moment."

Descanso, California

The rich, black humus, airborne, glimmers gold,
gray granite boulders softly wrapped in moss
beneath the dusty light of oaks as old
as California. Creeks just right to cross
with one wide leap and lined with cottonwood,
river stone chimneys, an abandoned bridge
which finally lost its lumber in the flood.
Manzanitas bend beneath the ridge,
the muted clop of horses down the street
melts the whispered rasp of raking leaves
filtered slowly through the mountain heat

beneath the stellar blue of make-believes:
    I rest within Descanso's summer spell,
    wrapped in a heritage of chaparral.

Escaping from Autopia

but even leaving, longing to be back,
to do again what I did yesterday—
I, Miss Highway, I couldn't drive off track

or crash. I joined the candy-coated pack
to follow yellow lines and concrete, gray
but even. Leaving. Longing to be back

beyond those lines, in other lines. Like smack
these flashback rides, E-ticket crack: You pay
you have to stay. I couldn't drive off track,

or spin to face my enemies' attack.
The road signs told me "NOW LEAVING L.A."
but even leaving, longing to be back

to go again. I knew I had a knack
for getting there and going. Child's play,
And anyway, I couldn't drive off track,

once safety-strapped onto that strip of black.
I couldn't lose or get lost on the way,
but even leaving, longing to be back
and be okay. I couldn't drive off track.

From San Diego

Even this far, with two paper cups and miles of taut string, I could de-
scribe a ghost of myself. I watched little girls run through a kitchen and
into a yard where I played. They hid behind camellias and calla lilies,
tangerine fish and a shell-white castle. *Marco.* They took turns stroking
the black cat until he closed his eyes, then came back with the
Christmas smell of crushed mint. The clip of parakeets echoes over bare
tile. Tonight, there are no stars, no way to run a line from this empty,
empty house. The empty sky. The stars have fallen through the day un-

noticed, blossoms from a jacaranda against the lavender blue. They've dropped into the loose, rolling folds of California like shining children giggling on an unmade bed. Let's grab the corners of the sheet and pull so that the snap of distance between us shoots them back like laughing rockets into the air. Then we can fold our empty sheet, our map, back carefully in half, then fold again, in half, again, until our hands are touching. Until the distance between us fits in a cabinet. Tie a piece of yarn around my wrist. *Marco.* Play jump rope with me. *Marco.* Braid my hair. Come swimming. Don't let go. *Marco. Polo.*

California Poem

His arm grew heavy on me as he slept, the oaks'
grey branches scratching the roof of the Chevy.
How close to my home we drove, east on 8,
not stopping 'till we curved into the mountains.
The morning was still cool and wet,
my wrists bound tight, my throat grown tight.
I pretended to sleep in California
where poison oak was red already,
the river stretched out thin across its bed.

The miners grab the river with both hands,
up and downstream, where my stiff arms point.
Hush, hush, hush the gravel circles shallow pans,
and we search, sift, sink deep in California.
The live oaks leaves with dusty thorns anoint
my broken skin. *Be quiet, flesh to sand, reborn,*
so he loved his first-loved girl to stone.

At swimming holes, I used to pull my shoes
off and let the water take my feet beneath
the glittered silt and wet my ankles, calves, wet
the parts of me that you called yours on my last night.
I'd swim until the river wove itself into my hair,
then lay out in the sun, half asleep, half awake,
lay my body down within the mountains.
I felt my pulse carve through the sandstone wash.

Now I hear the ocean through these hills.
the river in my mouth, this taste of gold.

AL YOUNG

Born in Ocean Spring, Mississippi, in 1939, Al Young was raised in the South and in Detroit. He attended the University of Michigan, then emigrated to Califonia, where he graduated from the University of California, Berkeley with a degree in Spanish. For his whole adult life, he has lived in the San Francisco Bay Area. Al Young's twenty books include the novels *Seduction by Light, Sitting Pretty,* and *Who Is Angelina?; Heaven* (Collected Poems 1956–1990); *Conjugal Visits; Mingus Mingus: Two Memoirs* (with Janet Coleman); *Drowning in the Sea of Love* (Musical Memoirs); and *African American Literature: A Brief Introduction and Anthology.* He has taught creative writing and literature at Stanford, the University of Michigan, the University of Washington, U.C. Berkeley, U.C. Santa Cruz, and the University of Arkansas. His honors include the Wallace Stegner, Guggenheim, NEA, and Fulbright fellowships; the PEN-Library of Congress Award for short fiction; and the PEN-USA Award for non-fiction. He has written scripts for Bill Cosby and Richard Pryor. He also travels internationally and extensively, reading, lecturing, and often performing his work—translated into more than a dozen languages—to music. He is presently at work on a novel, and co-editing (with Jack Hicks, James D. Houston, and Maxine Hong Kingston) a two-volume anthology of California literature.

"With me, poetry happens. Like any artist who works and plays with the almighty moment—an improvising musician, or on-stage actor or actress—I've got to stay ready for it, I've got to stay in shape, keep my chops up. I've got to know my instrument language by heart. Plus, as Victor Hernández Cruz once put it, 'You've got to keep your tips on fire.'

"When the flat, literal distances of my Mississippi and Michigan childhoods gave way to California now-you-see-it-now-you-don't landscapes and other vistas, I knew the UFOs had come home to roost, and I had mutated. So had my vision. Could poetry be far behind? In Michigan, Southern Michigan anyway, you could look off at the horizon and get the idea that, if push came clean down to shove, you might—with a Baby Ruth and a Coke, and little bit of spunk—you might even walk all the way from Ypsilanti to Kalamazoo, the same way Ernest Tubb meant when he wrote and sang 'Waltz Across Texas.'

"'But,' I can hear some drowsy oldtimer setting me straight, 'you sure as hell ain't walking from no Sackamenna to Truckee. You could, I guess. But I just can't see it.'

"The point of course is that in most of the country, what is out of sight is grandly out of mind. In California out of sight brings questions to mind. What lies around that mountain? What rests beneath the mist? How will the sun feel and look when the fog burns off? What's on the other side of that ocean? If I put a poem in this bottle, it might float all the way to China or Japan, and, for all I know, someone might be sailing a note or thought to me right now. After all, this ocean of eternity connects us.

"That's the kind of thinking that decades of residing in California induced in me. The proof, of course, is in the poetry I write, which inevitably reaches for the oceans and mountains of mystery that hibernate behind the plainest, simplest-looking insight, or thought, or re-consideration.

"Don't tell the poet pundits I said so, but language all by itself is like a whisper without a listener. When artists, especially poets, start slinging around their intentions and projections, look out! Things get risky and dicey, and profoundly analytical and speculative, and, you know, shaky.

"California has breathed her life into my language. How can my poems not mirror and match all that I've experienced and soaked up in this beautiful, heartbreaking country? I'm talking (and singing) feelings, observations, people, jobs, ups and downs, and places, geography, landscapes, the lay and look of lands and fields, hillsides, orange groves, footpaths, turkey farms, wineries, riverbanks and river raft trails, forests, and blocks, vacant lots, downtowns, lakefronts, the desert, beaches and beach towns, the mothers and sons of all traffic jams, canneries, whole whopping districts, neighborhoods, coastlines, alleyways, silicon rushes, toxic dumps, eco-racism, valleys, parks and national parks, campsites, Mission stops, suburbs, slurbs, barrios, ghettos, and erogenous zones of love."

California Peninsula: El Camino Real

In 15 minutes
the whole scene'll change
as bloated housewives
hems of their skirts greased
with love mouths wide open
come running out of shops
dragging their young
moon in their eyes
the fear upon them

Any minute now
the gas-blue sky over El Camino Real

is going to droop for good
shut with a squish &
close them all in like
a giant irritated eye

They'll scramble for cars
the nearest road out
clutching their steering wheels
like stalwart monkeys

It couldve happened yesterday
It couldve happened while they
were sighing in Macy's Walgreen's 31 Flavors
Copenhagen Movies or visiting the Colonel
Like that earthquake night
that shattered L.A.

Whatll they will their children then?
Whatll they leave for them to detest?
What tree, what lip print, what Jack in
what Box, what ugly hot order to go?

Already I can smell the darkness
creeping in like the familiar shadow
of some beloved fake monster
in a science fiction flick

In 15 minutes
48 hours days weeks months
years from now all of thisll be
a drowsy memory barely tellable
in a land whose novelty was speech

The Mountains of California: Part 1

These demonstrations of the one God,
green in the springtime in wintertime too
& all that time Jonn Muir was out here
                    living with them,
breaking himself in on them,
I just ride amongst them inside a car,
flip the radio off out of respect

& out of the feeling that there are
more important waves
floating in & out of us, mostly thru us

The mountains of California,
do I have to say anything?
I love all this evidence
set up to surround me this way,
mountain, ocean, you just name it

The Mountains of California: Part 2

Slow-rolling beauty
without end or beginning
assures our immortality.
The way an orchid chorusing
her fragrance in waves
says no goodbye is possible
in this joyous voyage.
Nowhere do we feel the fall
more fully than in spring,
for summer is the mirror
winter warrants. Transfigured,
life masks and mocks itself,
pretending to be dead asleep,
as if it cannot help
but leaf and flower from itself.
As enchantment keeps
reaching us in looks and take,
so the firm and melting faces
of the irreducible are always
losing their life in its love.

One West Coast

for Gordon Lapides

Green is the color of everything
that isnt brown, the tones ranging
like mountains, the colors changing.

You look up toward the hills & fog—
the familiarity of it after so many years
a resident tourist.

   A young man walks
toward you in vague streetcrossing denims
& pronounced boots From the pallor of
 his gait, the orange splotch twin gobs of
 sunset in his shades, from the way he vibrates
his surrounding air, you can tell, you can tell
  he's friendly, circulating,

  he's a Californian: comes to visit,
 stays for years, marries, moves a wife in,
kids, wears out TV sets, gets stranded on
    loneliness,
  afternoon pharmaceutica,
so that the sky's got moon in it by
  3 o'clock, is blooo, is blown—

   The girls: theyre all
 winners reared by grandmothers & CBS.
Luckier ones get in a few dances with
 mom, a few hours, before dad goes back
in the slam, before "G'bye I'm off
 to be a singer!" & another runaway
 Miss American future drifts
  over the mountain &
  into the clouds.

  Still
 there's a beautifulness about California.
It's based on the way each eyeblink toward
the plams & into the orange grove leads backstage
  into the onionfields.

Unreachable, winter happens inside you.

Your unshaded eyes dilate at the spectacle.

You take trips to contain the mystery.

GARY YOUNG

Gary Young is a poet and artist whose books include *Hands, The Dream of a Moral Life,* and *Days.* His newest book, *Braver Deeds,* won the Peregrine Smith Poetry Prize. He has received fellowships from the NEA and the National Endowment for the Humanities, and his print work is represented in many collections, including the Museum of Modern Art and the Getty Center for the Arts. He edits the Greenhouse Review Press from Santa Cruz, California.

© Peggy Young

"I was born in Southern California at mid-century, the descendant of families that had migrated west from the farmlands of Texas, the fresh water oyster beds of the upper Mississippi, and the coal mines of West Virginia. My parents, grandparents, and great-grandparents recalled their home states so vividly, persistently, and with such obvious affection while I was growing up, it was clear their identity as immigrants described and situated them in a state each had adopted and adored without reservation. They believed—and I was taught—that California was a true promised land, a gift from God, a distillation and refinement of the best the continent had to offer. I grew up believing that California is as close to paradise as any place we will ever find on this earth, and I have lived here all my life.

"I repeated my family's migration in miniature by moving from the congested southern part of the state northward to the central coast. For thirty years I have lived at the edge of the Monterey Bay, first in Santa Cruz, and for nearly two decades in the Santa Cruz mountains. I still feel a childish nostalgia for the orange groves and horse pastures where I played as a child, and for the bean fields and the orchards that have long since given way to freeways and urban development. The California of my childhood is gone. The salmon that once spawned in the stream below our cabin have all but disappeared; the farmland of the San Joaquin is becoming a vast suburban sprawl; the delta is disintegrating and the southland is an abysmal gridlock. Be that as it may, if they were still alive my family would say California was meant to change, and we were destined to change it and change with it. My kin belong to this state now; they are all buried here. When I die, I will be buried here, too."

Eating Wild Mushrooms

After the rain, when the earth releases
a little wheezing breath and loosens
its brittle hold on the surface of things,

wild mushrooms appear under the trees,
against logs and along the rotting
boards behind the barn. I see them lift

the ground under the quince and spread
the scallions apart and rise, and open.
I have been shown by those who know

the slick-skinned Blewit, the Prince
like a man's head, and Satyr's Beard
with its yellow mange. But for the rest

I cultivate an ignorance and pick
puffballs a particular shade of beige,
toadstools with the prettiest caps

or purple, spongy stem. What I don't know
can't hurt me. What I do know
is that mushrooms rise from the dead

to die again, to enter the death
of whatever enters the earth. When I
pick an unfamiliar mushroom and eat it

the ground gives up for once and is cheated.
It is like kissing a stranger on the mouth.
It is knowing what you are and being forgiven.

from Days

I don't know where the owls go when they leave this place, or if they
never leave, but simply leave off calling sometimes in their hollow voices.
But tonight they are here: one in a redwood beyond the creek, one high
in the fir tree above the house. Rappelled through their voices, those three
long vowels the darkness speaks in, I forget my own worthlessness which
has troubled me all day.

•

Our son was born under a full moon. That night I walked through the orchard, and the orchard was changed as I was. There were blossoms on the fruit trees, more white blossoms on the dogwood, and the tiny clenched fists of bracken shimmered silver. My shadow fell beside the shadow of the trees like a luster on the grass, and wherever I looked there was light.

•

The stream echoed through the canyon, and it seemed the current no longer flowed, but hovered, and was held as we were, in the insulating mist where time circled itself, uncertain of direction, until a peacock screamed, a tractor coughed, and the thousand wheels began to spin again.

•

On the third day of the gale I climbed over the barrier and onto the pier. Salt spray spun from the pilings and met the rain in fierce, broad planes. A slit in the horizon released a sliver of muddy light. Gulls drew themselves in and sat, heads to the wind. The waves crested above, and broke over the pier. The wind stuttered and howled, the timbers squealed, and I was walking on the storm.

•

Queen Anne's Lace crowds the air; cicadas call from beyond the stream. Monkey flowers rouge the hill below a pasture where six horses crop sage; and beside the road, between riprap at the river mouth, down gullies and the wasted ravines, thistles are showing us their hearts again.

•

Where deer tracks enter the stream, the water's erased them. Bay leaves and oak leaves drift along. It's autumn, and everything seems to be falling away. Even that old bitterness has left me. The crayfish have lost their shells. They walk backward through the shallows, their new skin so vulnerable, translucent, and blue.

from If He Had

Fog descends over the tidal surge and the shallow lagoons. The marsh grass and the alders at the water's edge fade, then vanish in the mist. The tan oaks and the redwoods are only shadows that waver for a moment then disappear. The world is beyond us. It is held now in a vaporous light, the smoke from a fire burning somewhere in heaven.

from **Braver Deeds**

It's Sunday, October ninth, and the earth here is barren after harvest. A cottonwood and a stand of poplars are all that disturb the horizon. A dust devil skips across the stubbled field, and a hawk drifts in and out of the twisting wind. There isn't a single cloud over the valley. The sun is at my back. A crescent moon slips through haze at the lip of the coastal range. I could die today with only two regrets.

from **If He Had**

An owl drifts slowly through the canyon where three flickers worry a pitted oak for grubs. Jays make a racket in the redwoods. Mourning doves sit motionless in the orchard. Robins gorge themselves on the pyracantha, and a hummingbird hovers just out of reach. Ravens, wrens, thrushes, hawks. I have tried so hard to be content doing nothing. I thought I'd done nothing all day, and then I remembered the birds.

Our Life in California

Near San Ardo the grasses tremble
and oak trees bend to the south against a constant wind.
Here our faith is tested
by the air that passes us ceaselessly
and takes each lost breath as we stumble through the hills.
The monotony of breathing, like our heartbeat,
is not the reassuring monotony
of the hills stacked row upon row
beyond our bearing and our ken.
The sun moves with the wind and will be gone,
but there is another light
coming from below, casting trees from the shadows.
There is a shadow beneath me
which moves as I move,
and the tracks I leave in the fragile grass
know more than I know of my duty here,
my worth and my chance.

PERMISSIONS

KIM ADDONIZIO: "Conversation in Woodside" and "China Camp, California" copyright © 1994 by Kim Addonizio. Reprinted from *The Philosopher's Club* with permission of BOA Editions, Ltd., 260 East Ave., Rochester, NY 14604. "At Moss Beach" first appeared in *Willow Springs,* and is used by permission of the author.

FRANCISCO X. ALARCÓN: "Blues del SIDA / AIDS Blues," "Viernes Santo / Good Friday," "Los árboles son poetas / Trees Are Poets," "Las calles lloran / Streets Are Crying," and "Frontera / Border" from *From the Other Side of Night/Del otro lado de la luna,* published by the Third Binational Border Poetry Contest, copyright © 1999 by Francisco X. Alarcón, and used by permission of the author.

ABIGAIL ALBRECHT: "Passing Piedras Blancas," "Below White Cliffs," "Elkhorn Slough," and "Anacapa" copyright © 1998 by Abigail Albrecht, and used by permission of the author.

B. H. BOSTON: "Apiary," was published in the *Western Humanities Review,* "By All Lights: 1959," in the *Marlboro Review,* and "The Savage, Our Fathers" in *Down at the Santa Fe Depot.* All copyright © by B. H. Boston, and used by permission of the author.

CHRISTOPHER BUCKLEY: "Father, 1952" and "Sycamore Canyon Nocturne" from *Camino Cielo,* Orchises Press, copyright © 1997 by Christopher Buckley; "20 Years of Grant Applications & State College Jobs" and "Concerning Paradise" from *Fall from Grace,* Bk Mk Press/University of Missouri-Kansas City, copyright © 1998 by Christopher Buckley, and used by permission of the author.

MARILYN CHIN: "The Years Pass in My Morning Teacup" from *Dwarf Bamboo,* Greenfield Review Press, copyright © Marilyn Chin. "How I Got That Name" and "Leaving San Francisco" were published in *The Phoenix Gone, the Terrace Empty,* Milkweed Editions, 1994. Copyright © 1994 by Marilyn Chin. Reprinted with permission from Milkweed Editions, Minneapolis, MN, (800) 520-6455, www.milkweed.org, and with permission of the author.

KILLARNEY CLARY: "Restless before the canary..." and "Mr. Dooms would meet us..." appeared in *By Common Salt,* Oberlin College Press, copyright © by Oberlin College Press and reprinted by permission. "Another hot afternoon..." and "When my heart asked for a way free..." from *By Me, by Any, Can and Can't Be Done,*

ABOUT THE EDITORS

CHRISTOPHER BUCKLEY is Chair of the Creative Writing Department at the University of California, Riverside, and is the author of nine full-length collections of poetry and a dozen poetry chapbooks. His biography and poems are featured on page 18.

GARY YOUNG is a poet and visual artist, and has been the editor and publisher of the Greenhouse Review Press since 1975. His biography and poems are featured on page 433; he also created the image on the title page.